Advance

Transforming Wounds into ...

This is the gem we have all been waiting for! *Transforming Wounds into Wisdom: Change Your Attitudes and Save Your Life* is a straightforward, down-to-earth, and practical book about our lives and relationships. But do not let Davidson's refreshingly easy-to-understand ideas fool you. This volume is a sophisticated and profoundly important road map that is firmly rooted in over a century of depth psychology.

Far from raising simple questions and giving pat answers, Davidson delves into the very heart of what it is that creates our problems to begin with. On the one hand, sometimes our parents give *Too Much*; on the other hand, sometimes our parents give *Too Little*. But we need not spend our lives stuck, compulsively ruminating on, and re-enacting, what they did or did not do back then. Our job is to look realistically at the ways we carry the adverse effects of a lifetime of patterned relational experiences into our daily lives with our loved ones, our friends, and our colleagues. And then it is for us to do the work that is necessary to free ourselves from the infantile ties that bind us to the rigid attitudes and relational patterns that are interfering with our movement forward in life.

A significant and impactful insight from depth psychology and attachment theory is the realization that our internal world consists of learned patterns of expectation that govern how we look at the world and how we interact with others. Integrating this concept with current knowledge about how the brain develops, Davidson skillfully takes us through the varieties of childhood experiences with caregiving others that have formed the very foundations of our being, experiences that set the stage—for better *and* for worse—for later emotional and relational development.

Davidson demonstrates the ways in which derailment in early life can ultimately prevent us from realizing our fullest creative potential. Indeed, perhaps the most moving parts of this beautiful and heart-felt book are the poignant vignettes of clients who, over the decades, have sought out her wise counsel and expert guidance for help with understanding and refashioning the complicated dimensions of their internal worlds.

But—far more than enabling us to appreciate how injurious experiences during our formative years have left us with psychic wounds and scars—

Davidson goes on to speak to how we can re-organize our current lives and relationships in order to heal those wounds and reduce those scars through healthy relating in the present. She motivates us to engage in taking the steps necessary to transform our self-sabotaging patterns into healthier, more-evolved ways of being—steps that enable us to acquire ever-greater wisdom.

Having been a mentor, colleague, and friend to Jolyn for more than 30 years, I have followed with great interest her intense efforts to take complex theoretical concepts from her study of the trauma, attachment, and psychodynamic literature and make them accessible to her clients. It has been a delight to watch her integrate these ideas with a broad range of psychological approaches, creating growth strategies that people can use to make positive changes in their lives.

Davidson keeps a white board in her office and often finds herself jumping up to draw working models filled with circles and squares, lines and arrows, sketches and cartoons—passionate in her desire to help people visualize the dynamics of the conflicts they are struggling with in their personal and relational lives.

In our professional peer case conferences, Jolyn is always the person in the group who is able to describe in plain simple English what the client is wrestling with and how we, as therapists, need to position ourselves in order best to facilitate that client's growth. Her breadth and depth of emotional responsiveness, tender compassion, and complex understanding have contributed substantially to my own professional and personal growth over the years. I was extremely pleased that she permitted me to publish in my books, *Terrifying Transferences: Aftershocks of Childhood Trauma* and *Working the Organizing Experience,* some of her very powerful and evocative work with clients.

I highly recommend this magnificent book to anyone interested in how people grow and how they can then transform the survival mechanisms that they developed early in life into more adaptive, more flexible ways of feeling, thinking, and acting.

—LAWRENCE E. HEDGES, PhD, PsyD, ABPP, is a psychologist-psychoanalyst in private practice in Orange, California, specializing in the training of psychotherapists and psychoanalysts. He is Director of the Listening Perspectives Study Center and the Founding Director of the Newport Psychoanalytic Institute in Tustin, California, where he is a supervising and training analyst. Hedges has been awarded the prestigious distinction of honorary membership in the American Psychoanalytic Association.

Transforming Wounds into Wisdom

Change Your Attitudes
and Save Your Life

Transforming Wounds into Wisdom

Change Your Attitudes and Save Your Life

Jolyn Davidson, RN, LCSW, DCSW

Foreword by
Martha Stark, MD

New Perspectives Press

To all those on their heroic journeys of
"transforming wounds into wisdom"

and

To my mom,
who taught me to persevere
with fortitude ...

Contents

PART II
Common Core Attitudes
That Develop in Early Relationships

PART III
Attitudes Impact How You Live in the World

Acknowledgments

Throughout my life, I have been blessed with many treasured mentors, friends, colleagues, and family members who have helped shape my life. I am *forever* grateful for each one! Their wisdom and knowledge are woven throughout this book. I would like to acknowledge several of them who have been exceptionally influential in making *Transforming Wounds into Wisdom* possible.

This book would not exist had it not been for the foundational contributions of **Lawrence Hedges**. Through my many years of training at the *Listening Perspectives Study Center*, Larry has discussed with us countless innovative writings, which have contributed immensely to my perspectives in this book. He has also continually challenged and supported me in my development as a person, a clinician, and a writer with unfaltering openness, immeasurable insight, and extensive knowledge and wisdom.

John Carter's influence on what I have written here cannot be overstated. He has faithfully traveled alongside me through the years on my journey to transform many of my life lessons into book form—from the first brainstorming glimmers—through years of wrestling *and* playing with the material—and through writing's challenges. John has been a consistent, reliable, wise, and safe haven in which I have been able to develop, integrate, and expand a multitude of thoughts and experiences.

Years ago, **Althea Horner** graciously agreed to talk with me about my dream to share the wealth of what I had been learning in an accessible book. Althea's advice to me was "Write until you can't think of anything else to write," and "Don't listen to the nay-sayers." Taking Althea's advice seriously, I spent the next three years writing until my brain had had enough—675 pages later, to be exact! At that point, I encountered some of life's roadblocks, which, at the time, I could not circumvent. So I reluctantly relegated the manuscript to a box on my office floor where it languished for several years.

Enter, **Martha Stark**. In true healing physician fashion, Martha, with her indomitable spirit, filled with unflagging energy, enthusiasm, and tenacity, has helped revive my long-neglected original manuscript and me. Through her brilliance, masterful guidance, and profound ability to see and attend to the "forest, trees, seedlings, and seeds" of the manuscript development, Martha has been a creative force, refining fire—and major lifeline.

Words cannot adequately express my gratitude for my stalwart friends and colleagues: **Sally Bowers, Audrey Seaton-Bacon,** and **Barbara Brewer.** These amazing women have steadfastly supported me throughout all the years of bringing this book to life. They have spent countless hours reading and giving me judicious feedback on the constantly changing manuscript, as well as my writing process. Through their staunch, patient labors of love, they have not only helped me expand, clarify, and refine my thoughts and writing, but they have also mobilized me to continue moving forward when my spirits were flagging.

On this journey filled with a multitude of twists, turns, and sometimes, unexpected blind alleys, **David** and **Renée Sanford's** enthusiasm for, and belief in, this project have been indomitable. They have been extraordinarily generous with both their personal support and their knowledge, expertise, and resources acquired during many years in the publishing industry. Their guidance and efforts in getting this book to readers has been exceptional.

I will never cease to be indebted to **Tom** and **Rosemary Thompson** who have been instrumental in making this book possible. Through their belief in the mission of this book and in me, and through their unbelievably generous spirits, they have been never-failing beacons of hope and confirmation on this journey.

In putting this book together, I am greatly appreciative of **Amanda Bird, Cara Johnson,** and **Garrett Trott** for their expert assistance in the editing of the manuscript. I am also profoundly grateful to the creative graphic design artists involved in this project: **Anneli Anderson** for designing the amazing artwork and cover for the book; **Katie Blaine** for her refining eye and skills; and **Raquelle Andazola** for visualizing beyond the mundane to create the artwork for the *Davidson's Attitude Model.* The collaborative efforts of these talented editors and graphic designers have been invaluable.

I am also grateful to **Mark Bacon, Linda Barnhurst, Ben and Melanie Davidson, Rod Davidson, Stephanie Jefferson, Laurie Lucas, Louris Matthews, Pamela Matthews, Alida Luch, Margaret Mitchell, Asher Nelson, Pattie Pratt, Karen Trahern, Anita Troop, Dorothy Davidson,** and **Steve Turnidge** for their respective support during the book's gestation.

And last, but definitely not least, I want to express my immense gratitude for **all of my clients**, past and present, who have bravely allowed me to join with them on their healing journeys. They have taught me what truly is involved in *Transforming Wounds into Wisdom.*

Jolyn E. Davidson

Foreword

This exquisitely honed masterpiece contains the distilled wisdom of Jolyn Davidson, a seasoned clinician whose passion, over the course of her 35-year career as an independent practitioner, has always been to help her clients get better. Equally compelling for Davidson has been her intense desire to understand—and to put into words—the actual process whereby her clients' "wounds" (resulting from the cumulative impact of early-on traumatogenic experiences that, for whatever complex mix of reasons, could not be adequately processed and integrated at the time) can be transformed into "wisdom."

Over the course of her decades of deep immersion in her clinical practice and intensive study of psychodynamic psychology literature, Davidson has received invitations to contribute chapters to scholarly volumes edited by others, which she has readily accepted with pleasure and delight. But Davidson's long-cherished dream has been to pen her own book—a book that would capture the essence of what she has come to believe is at the heart of the healing process.

What shines through on every page of this uplifting volume is Davidson's firm conviction that wisdom is acquired not in spite of the wounds we have sustained in our time but by way of working through, and rising above, the damage caused by those wounds—sadder perhaps, but wiser too and stronger for having survived. No pain, no gain. I am here reminded of Ernest Hemingway's observation: "The world breaks every one and afterward many are strong at the broken places" (*A Farewell to Arms*, 1929).

Also relevant here is Steve Goodier's evocative quote: "My scars remind me that I did indeed survive my deepest wounds. That in itself is an accomplishment. And they bring to mind something else, too. They remind me that the damage life has inflicted on me has, in many places, left me stronger and more resilient. What hurt me in the past has actually made me better equipped to face the present" (*Lessons of the Turtle*, 2002).

In truth, most of us have been psychologically wounded at some point or another along our journeys. But only some are fortunate enough to have found themselves in the company of someone—be it a counselor, spiritual leader, therapist, family member, mentor, colleague, or friend—who, with compassion and without judgment, was able to guide them as they have struggled to understand, and work through, the roadblocks limiting their capacity to live meaningful lives. For those less fortunate, however, Davidson has lovingly and painstakingly crafted this deeply thoughtful book about how people can extricate themselves from ties that bind them to inflexible, outmoded, defensive ways of acting, reacting, and interacting so that they can adopt healthier, more adaptive, and more evolved ways of being and doing.

Davidson's *Transforming Wounds into Wisdom* is a refreshingly accessible and eminently readable road map that can be used both by those seeking guidance and by those helping professionals seeking to fine-tune their ability to offer such guidance. Although solidly grounded in time-honored psychodynamic psychology principles, Davidson manages to bring these concepts alive as she deftly and convincingly translates complex theoretical constructs into simple but profound truths about the therapeutic process.

Ever refusing to use off-putting jargon, Davidson, writes with clarity, precision, and humility about how important it is that people become, on the one hand, ever more aware of the price they pay are paying for their self-indulgent/self-destructive thoughts, feelings, and behaviors and, on the other hand, ever more respectful of their investment—even so—in maintaining their attachment to these dysfunctional attitudes/patterns. As people come to recognize that the price they are paying far outweighs whatever unconscious benefit they might have been deriving, they will find themselves gradually relinquishing their compulsive and unwitting repetitions in favor of more conscious, unfettered living.

The therapist's office has always been a sacred space that affords client and therapist the opportunity to find each other and, over time, to develop mutually satisfying ways of working, loving, and playing together. But ordinarily the magic that takes place there is a very private matter and not for public viewing. Davidson, however, courageously and vulnerably dares to give us a glimpse of what goes on in her office, which not only makes everything so much more real for us but also enables us to experience directly her humanity, her bountiful capacity, and her extraordinary giftedness as a healer.

At the end of the day, by offering us both a conceptual framework and numerous extended clinical vignettes that speak to the direct application of theory to practice, Davidson is able to go a long way towards demystifying the otherwise bewilderingly obscure process by which therapists are able—gently and tenderly—to guide their clients towards a deeper, richer, and more nuanced understanding of the changes they must be willing to make if they are truly to be able to save their lives and become master of their own destinies.

Transforming Wounds into Wisdom is an important book that is at once both inspired and inspiring.

Martha Stark, MD
Faculty, Harvard Medical School
Co-Director, Center for Psychoanalytic Studies, William James College
Bestselling Author of Psychoanalytic Books on Theory and Practice

Transforming Wounds into Wisdom

A Bird's-Eye View

As you look back over your life experiences, have you ever asked yourself:

- *Why can't I get my needs met in a relationship—no matter how hard I try?*
- *Why do I keep getting into situations that leave me frustrated and wounded?*
- *Why can't I find satisfaction in my work life?*
- *How can I create a life that is meaningful, vibrant, and fulfilling?*

One day as I sat curled up in my favorite chair with a cup of tea, memories of clients who had asked me these questions drifted through my mind. At first, my memories tumbled around like pieces of colored glass in a revolving kaleidoscope. Then, gradually, the recollections settled into patterns. Each instance, although unique, also contained elements that reflected common ways young children adapt to their environment.

As the chips of the kaleidoscope fell into place, the designs occasionally brought to mind my clients who had formed healthy, sustaining connections with others early in life. These bright arrangements also evoked the delight I had shared with those who, despite their difficult childhood experiences, had developed strength and resilience through our joint efforts to help them create a new life.

Gradually, my kaleidoscopic memories reconfigured themselves, falling into fractals composed of the life-long patterns that had propelled my clients to seek my help in the first place. At times, the jumbled shards settled into configurations reminiscent of a war zone, in which angry people had battled with one another, and with their internal demons, over conflicting expectations and demands.

Although these distressed warriors had frequently directed their anger at others, they had also aimed their frustration at themselves. Exhausted, yet stuck in their resentment and defiant rage, they had been unable to find a way to end the costly war.

Now and then, the tumbling bits of my memories formed into lackluster patterns evocative of barren landscapes. These constellations reminded me of clients who had spent their lives searching endlessly for someone who would quench their thirst for maternal nurturing. Clinging desperately to their relentless hopes and beliefs that they could find an oasis in the desert, they had returned to the same mirages—over and over. Inevitably, instead of obtaining the relief they longed for, their frequent disillusionment had left them feeling emotionally parched.

When my memories shifted one last time that morning, I found myself peering into dark caverns where people were huddled, eyes wide with terror or downcast with shame, too afraid to come out. Occasionally a few of these cave dwellers had ventured out briefly into the world. But when their internal voices had begun telling them that they could only be safe inside their dens, their fears had pulled them back into hiding once again. Although their retreat had provided them with the illusion of safety, it had also left them longing for freedom from their confinement. Others— those who were very entrenched in their isolation—were unable to find the will even to attempt to wend their way out of their self-imposed plight.

As my memories of clients gradually retreated, I was left with the acute awareness that the answers to many of their questions lay in the unique constellations of emotional, cognitive, and behavioral tendencies that had formed during their childhoods. Some of these configurations— those resulting from positive, early life experiences—were helping them live in the world in satisfying ways. Unfortunately, the traits that had emerged from their painful early experiences were making it difficult for them to live a full and enriching life—a life whereby they could realize their potential and dreams.

In *Transforming Wounds into Wisdom: Change Your Attitudes and Save Your Life*, you will discover how the people whose images arose in my musings began answering their questions about the roadblocks that had been impeding their ability to establish a fulfilling life. As you read their stories, you may find yourself revisiting some of your experiences.

If you explore these glimpses into your life further, you will have the opportunity to find your own answers to the questions *you* may have about why you feel, think, and act in certain ways. In your exploration, you will discover paths you can follow that will help you bring about the transformative changes needed to resolve your dilemmas.

In childhood tales, heroes undertake epic journeys to overcome dark forces. On your epic journey to make your life and relationships more rewarding, you too must face many challenges and overcome dark forces.

I have designed this book to be a road map that can help you on your odyssey as you navigate these challenges and learn to manage these forces. As a map, it both reveals and guides, directing you through the emotional and interpersonal terrain you will encounter on your journey. For, without guidance, you could wander around in that landscape for years, feeling bewildered, helpless, and frustrated.

As you peruse this map, you will discover key markers that will direct you to critical pathways, which, when traveled, will move you forward on your journey to be in the world in life-enhancing ways. On these pathways, you will be developing your ability to:

- *Identify and understand your attitudes and their associated relationship patterns.* As you grow and develop in early life, the interplay amongst your emotions, thoughts, and behaviors coalesces into attitudes. Because attitudes become part of the way your mind is configured, throughout your life they play a critical role in how you tend to relate to yourself, others, and the world. Identifying your attitudes and understanding how they function will help you work with your mind-body system to change the attitudes that are not serving you well.

    This book presents five common styles of parenting and the attitudes that frequently evolve in children as they strive to cope creatively with their experiences in order to survive psychologically. One of these styles is healthy; four are not. When parents are consistently emotionally available, their children will acquire healthy attitudes that enable them to manage their lives effectively.

    However, when parents utilize unhealthy styles of parenting, such as emotionally enmeshed, over-controlling, absent, or inconsistent, their children will encounter barriers to healthy development. These parenting styles force children to adopt ways of relating that might work for them in the short term but are often problematic in the long term.

- *Actively focus on how the attitudes you acquired early on are affecting your life now.* The attitude (and relationship) systems that formed early in your life operate automatically, often without your awareness of them. This lack of consciousness, as well as the resistance to change that is inherent in any system, can undermine your ability to cultivate a deeply satisfying life.

    In order to save your life from self-defeating attitudes, you must learn to be mindful of how the unhelpful attitudes you acquired during childhood are negatively affecting you in the present. As you become aware of how your attitudes and relationship patterns are undermining you, you can engage in the process of making the changes necessary for your well-being. It is also vital that you actively attend to your internal experience without judgment but with tender compassion. As you cultivate a healthy curiosity about how your attitudes affect your life, you are opening a door to possibilities for changing your problematic attitudes and thus transforming your life.

Awareness of your attitudes and their effect on your life is crucial. In the absence of mindfulness, it is difficult to make the necessary changes that will enhance your life and relationships. Instead, you may find yourself endlessly searching for someone who will provide for your unmet childhood emotional needs.

When others do not provide for these needs, you may feel helpless, be quickly flooded with frustration and anger, and find yourself engaged in relentless battles. Eventually you may stop searching and fighting altogether, and give up in a resigned retreat. You may also find yourself caught up in other repetitious "self-protective" strategies, particularly those that develop in response to traumatic experiences that were never fully processed, integrated, and resolved.

- ***Relinquish your attachment to harmful attitudes and relationship patterns and develop life-enhancing ones.*** Ultimately, on your quest for a fulfilling life, you must free yourself from your ineffective childhood approaches to dealing with life, which I will refer to as your *childhood survival system*. Although these ways of feeling, thinking, and behaving may have been necessary for your psychological protection when you were little, aspects of this early survival system may have long outlived their usefulness.

Unfortunately, even though these early survival methods may no longer be helpful, it is not easy to develop new, more adaptive ways to manage your life. The process of transforming old ways of being into new ones is neither quick nor painless. It takes time, effort, and commitment to free yourself from the grip of unhealthy patterns and to develop new attitudes and relationship constellations in the mind.

Nevertheless, it is possible to do the work necessary to bring about the attitude changes that will enable you to develop a more rewarding life—a life that will include mutually satisfying relationships.

As you increase your capacity to be aware of how your early attitudes and modes of relating are affecting your life in the present, you can begin to reinforce the attitudes that are serving you well. You can also begin to invest your energy in establishing new attitude patterns that will help you navigate your life more successfully than the ones that are currently impinging on your efforts.

A major aspect of this investment in establishing new attitudes will involve grieving your early losses and disappointments. As you grieve these heartbreaks and release your attachment to the childhood survival system that has maintained your harmful attitudes, you will develop new psychological structures that are more robust and resilient. This more flexible and adaptive attitude system will make it possible for you to regulate your emotions more effectively, think in more reality-based ways, and act in ways that enhance your life.

In this new life you are creating, old attitudes—flooded by emotional storms, strewn with conflicting beliefs, and undermined by unhealthy behaviors that erode parts of your self—will be transformed.

The road map I am sharing with you here is an integrative approach to psychological, interpersonal, and spiritual growth, which I refer to as *transformational living*. I have forged this approach from the wealth of knowledge, insight, and wisdom that I have garnered from brilliant mentors and inspired writers over the years. This approach also arises from the crucible of experiences I have encountered on my life journey and in the work I do with my precious clients.

I hope that you, as the hero of your life story, can use this treasure trove to help you on your epic journey to *Change Your Attitudes and Save Your Life*—your journey of *Transforming Wounds into Wisdom*.

*****

Important to Note

- The names and identifying specifics of people who are mentioned in this book have been altered in order to protect the privacy of those who have worked so courageously to change their lives.

- The parenting styles and attitudes presented here are commonplace. Because every person and every relationship is unique, however, these relationship styles and attitudes will undoubtedly not reflect your exact experience. Even so, I hope they will serve as examples that will help you understand your attitudes, observe how they function in your life, and nurture new attitudes that will serve you well.

- Research has made it clear that the attachment pattern you develop with your primary caregiver in early life forms the foundation for how you operate in relationships all through your life. For most people throughout the world, the primary caregiver of infants and young children is still the mother. Therefore, I will use the word *she* in reference to the primary caregiver, regardless of gender. I will also use the terms *mother, primary caregiver,* and *parent* interchangeably to refer to early primary caregivers.

Part I

What Attitudes Are
and
Where They Come From

CHAPTER 1

What Are Attitudes, Anyway?

*Your living is determined not so much by what life brings to you
as by the attitude you bring to life; not so much by what happens
to you as by the way your mind looks at what happens.*
—John Homer Miller, *Take a Second Look at Yourself*

Attitudes. How would you describe your attitudes? Would you say you generally have a cooperative, impatient, energetic, selfish, laid-back, angry, or happy attitude? Do you tend to think of your attitudes as usually "good" or as "bad?"

Ask any person on the street about attitudes, and, in all likelihood, the person will tell you that a "positive" attitude will make you successful, and a "negative" attitude will undermine your success in life. People use the word "attitude" in so many ways that it can be confusing. Sometimes they use the word to refer to emotions. Other times, they use the word to describe behaviors. All sorts of theorists in the fields of social psychology, psychology, business, and religion (to name a few) have studied attitudes to try to determine what attitudes are and how to change them. Even so, many people still ask the crucial age-old question: What are attitudes, anyway?

Attitudes, from my perspective, are part of what many researchers call your *internal operating system*. They determine how you perceive, make sense of, and correspondingly react or respond to your life experiences. In effect, attitudes are part of the programming of your mental and nervous system, which develops as your senses are busily gathering information from your experience and inputting it into your mind-body system. Whether the information comes from inside or outside your body, you record and organize it into interconnected mindsets (databases, so to speak) so that you can access the information.

Attitudes are multidimensional and evolving. They can be obvious or elusive. They can be positive overall but still have negative aspects.

9

Regardless of how they manifest themselves, they are always present and ready to provide you with a response to your experience.

The importance of attitudes cannot be overstated. Your attitudes pervade your life. They affect you, your family, your friendships, your workplace, and, more generally, the world around you. Attitudes determine how you view and treat yourself and others, and they influence how others treat you. They can make your life vibrant in some aspects and mundane in others. Attitudes can also undermine—and even destroy—your life.

When you strip your life down to the barest of essentials, what remain are your attitudes. Strip your life down even further and what is left is your power to choose—it is your birthright. What you choose to do with your attitudes is up to you, whether or not you recognize it at the moment.

Every day you choose, consciously or unconsciously, how you perceive your experience, the meaning you make of your experience, and how you respond to your experience. Whether you know it or believe it yet, you have the power to change the attitudes that are not serving you well and to develop ones that enrich your life and the lives of others.

Viktor Frankl, a distinguished Viennese neurologist, psychiatrist, and Holocaust survivor, speaks to the importance of attitudes: "*Everything can be taken from a man but one thing: the last of the human freedoms—to choose one's attitude in any given set of circumstances, to choose one's own way*" (Frankl, 1963, p. 104, emphasis added).

What I offer you is a way to think about what attitudes are, how they develop, and how they affect your life today. I also present a path that, when followed, will help you transform your attitudes in ways that make your life meaningful and fulfilling.

So, to begin, let me share a story with you.

Laura's Story

Laura was a 29-year-old woman who came to see me several years ago because of the difficulties she was experiencing in her relationships. This was our first session.

> "You need to change your attitude, young lady!" Laura said with a parental voice tone as she lifted her head and looked at me with eyes mixed with pain and anger. "My parents used to tell me that all the time. I *hate* that word! Attitude. What does that really mean, anyway? I've never quite figured that out, much less how I was supposed to *change* it. All I know is that I think my attitudes must have caused me problems my whole life."

As I listened to Laura, I could feel the tension of the battle raging inside her. It was a battle filled with frustration and helplessness.

I reflected, "It's very painful when someone berates you, especially when you are confused about what you're supposedly doing wrong and don't know how to make things any different."

Laura became still for a moment. Her pain and sadness were palpable. "You know, I wish I could have a close relationship with someone, but my relationships never work out. I guess I don't really know how to have a relationship. But I do know that it hurts too much to try to get close to someone and have things fall apart. It's just not worth it." She paused briefly, then her affect switched. "You need to know right up front that I feel very torn inside about trusting people. I struggle with letting my guard down because the minute you start trusting someone, then you have to worry that the person might turn on you. I get that you can't make or keep friends when you're always ready to push people away at the drop of a hat. But I just can't seem to stop getting a little prickly when I try to relate to others. It's just too scary."

I gently responded, "Sometimes it's hard to feel safe when you don't know for sure what or who you can count on."

So began Laura's and my journey together. It was clear that Laura was struggling not only with some areas of her self that had not developed adequately but also with unhealed psychological wounds. So we worked together to identify Laura's goals.

Our goals were multi-faceted. In order to make the changes she desired it was important that Laura develop her ability to be aware of, identify, and observe her attitudes. In addition, it was imperative that she develop the ability to evaluate her feelings, thoughts, and actions and to understand how both her healthy and unhealthy attitudes functioned in her life.

Laura also needed to identify what she has missed emotionally and how she had been wounded as a child and let herself grieve her losses. Doing so would make it possible for her to move forward in the work of changing the attitudes that were causing difficulties in her life and creating ones that served her better. Our ultimate goal through this process was to transform Laura's wounds into wisdom so she could create a fulfilling life.

As Laura and I were working to help her become more aware of her attitudes, we focused initially on her struggle with ambivalence. Laura longed to be in a close relationship where she could feel loved and valued. Her longing, combined with her hope and belief that it was possible to find someone to care for her, had drawn her into trying to find someone she could count on. Unfortunately, her fear of the pain of disappointment and rejection, her beliefs that everyone would eventually hurt her in some unbearable way, and her difficulty controlling her reactive behaviors, were all interfering with her ability to establish a stable relationship. Her longing and fear were in fierce combat with each other.

Over time, we came to understand that Laura's ambivalence was one of her *core attitudes*. Core attitudes are attitudes that play a primary role in determining how you relate to others, the world, and yourself. They are comprised of your basic assumptions about how life works.

Your core attitudes function in ways similar to how your body's core muscles operate (the muscles in the center of your body). Just as your physical mobility is highly dependent on your core muscles, your psychological and interpersonal functioning is highly dependent on your core attitudes. If your physical core is weak or injured, it will be difficult to keep your balance, move easily, or resist forces on your body. Similarly, if your core attitudes are "weak," or if overwhelming experiences "injure" them in some way, it will be difficult to keep your balance emotionally, think in flexible, reality-based ways, and resist your impulses so you can control your behavioral reactions.

Laura and I continued working toward her goal of changing her attitudes that were interfering with her ability to care for her needs. Keeping in mind her core attitude of ambivalence, we also came to identify and understand other attitudes associated with her ambivalence (e.g., mistrust and inadequacy) and the way those elements affected each other and her life.

Let us now consider, as Laura and I did, the components of attitudes and the relationship between the components.

The Three Parts of Your Attitudes

Attitudes, as I will be using the term, are comprised of three components: your *emotions* (affects), *cognitions* (thoughts and beliefs), and *behaviors* (actions). Simply put,

- *the emotional component* of your attitudes consists of all of your emotions, emotional processes, feelings, and tendencies to feel a certain way;
- *the cognitive component* includes all of your thoughts and beliefs, thought processes, and tendencies to think a certain way;
- *the behavioral component* involves all of your behavior and your tendencies to act in certain ways.

Davidson's Attitude Model

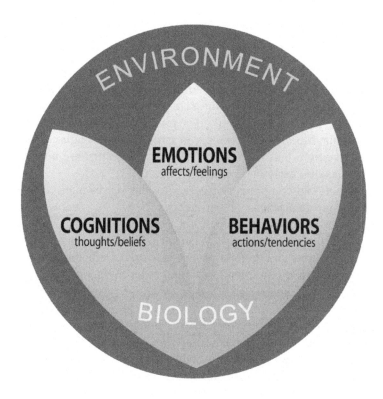

Figure 1. The three inter-related attitude components that are part of our internal operating system are affected by the environment and our personal biology. *Copyright © 2015 Jolyn E. Davidson. All rights reserved.*

Your mind-body system links these attitude components together, which allows them to communicate with each other. Your attitudes, both your core and more peripheral attitudes, become part of the internal operating system of your body's neural network.[1] As you go about your daily life, these three components of your attitudes (which are pre-programmed and ready for someone or something to activate them) are constantly affecting each other. They affect everything about you: how you feel, what you think, and how you act and react.

---

[1] From my perspective, the concept of mind is the psychological correlate of the body's entire nervous system, which includes the brain. Therefore, I will be using the terms "mind," "brain," and "mind-body system" interchangeably.

Let us look at these components more closely for a moment. Even though we will be exploring the components individually, remember that, in actuality, they function together.

Your Emotions

Your emotions are part of your attitudes. Some are innately part of you from birth (e.g., joy, fear, anger, and anticipation). Other emotions (e.g., love, guilt, shame, and helplessness) develop during infancy and early childhood as you interact with your primary caregiver and other key people in your life. The emotions you experience throughout the rest of your life arise from the combination of your affects that are innate and the affects you acquire early on in life.

The emotional component of your attitudes serves many functions. In its role as an *interpreter*, it influences how you perceive emotion, including how you read and interpret nonverbal signals, such as body language and facial expressions. When it is functioning as a *manager*, it helps your emotions and thought processes work together as a team. It also determines what you pay attention to and react to and what you consider important. It even helps you *think about your feelings while you are feeling them!*

Emotions are necessary for creative thinking, flexible planning, and motivation. In addition, your emotional processes operate in the role of *evaluator*, helping you assess and create meaning from new information. In this capacity, your emotions determine whether you experience something as "good" or as "bad" or as some variation of the two (Siegel, 1999, p. 139).

One of the most important functions of the emotional component of your attitudes is to regulate your emotions. This role as a *regulator* is critical to your ability to function effectively in life. Although you might feel like avoiding, minimizing, or suppressing your emotions, sometimes you need to experience your feelings (and their associated body sensations) for a time in order to process and release them. Even so, it is also important to be able to tone your emotions down when they become too intense and are disrupting your ability to think or to manage your behaviors.

A variety of triggers, both positive and negative, can activate your emotional system. For example, on the positive side, if you think about or visualize someone who was supportive of you in the past, those thoughts and images will tend to trigger positive feelings. This occurs because your internal operating system had stored your supportive experience with the person in mindsets connected with positive emotional memories.

Your affective system can also be protective, such as when you are apprehensive around someone who has proven to be emotionally unsafe in the past. In this situation, your emotional response signals that you need to be on the alert around the person or keep away from the person altogether.

Triggers that affect your emotional system negatively usually generate problems. For example, imagine that you grew up in a home where your parent was constantly berating you and others. In this scenario, you may find yourself as an adult *feeling* criticized by others when they, in fact, are *not* criticizing you. This misperception is occurring because the attitudes that developed during your childhood experiences with your critical parent are *interpreting* the current experience as "critical."

When the emotional component of your attitudes interacts with the cognitive component in a way that distorts your experience, it can cause you to feel unpleasant emotions (e.g., hurt, embarrassment, shame, or rage). Misperceptions such as these can result in your unwittingly re-creating the painful experiences from the past in the present.

As Laura and I explored her life experiences over the next two months, we began to see more clearly how the emotional component of her attitudes that she developed as a child affected her daily life. In one session, Laura described her experience with her parents and its impact.

"When I was a kid, my parents said they loved me, but it sure didn't feel like it. Even though my mom was fun and helpful at times, she was also very critical and demanding. She would praise me once in a while, but she was truly a perfectionist. I always felt like I had to walk on eggshells around her because I never knew when she would snap at me. I didn't feel safe around her, and I never felt like I could measure up to her expectations. To top that off, the more she criticized me, the more I would get nervous and scared, and that made me mess up even more.

"My dad didn't help the situation out at all. Even though we got along better than my mom and I did, I didn't see him very often. He and my mom were divorced, and he spent most of his time at work or hanging out with his girlfriend. When we were together, sometimes we'd have fun, but a lot of times it was just boring because we just sat around watching TV. I tried to talk with him about my frustration with my mom a couple of times, but he'd just say, 'That's why I left her, honey. You'll be okay.' I gave up trying to talk to him about anything important. I felt pretty helpless and trapped. I figured my situation was hopeless."

Laura paused, and then, with a touch of resignation, commented sadly, "Even though I haven't lived at home since I was 18 years old, most of the time I still feel hopeless about ever feeling good about myself or my life. It's really sad. My feelings are really messing up my ability to do my job at work, and they sure make it difficult for me to have any friends. At work,

I'm constantly worried about whether or not I'm doing the right thing or if what I do is good enough. If my co-workers tell me I'm doing something wrong, I get really defensive, even though I rarely say anything. I can tell they don't like me. I'm terrified that my boss will get upset with me and write me up, even though she's told me several times I'm doing fine. I just can't seem to relax and feel good about what I do. I've talked to my friends about how I feel, and they try to reassure me that I'm okay and that they love and appreciate me. The problem is—I just don't *feel* loved or valued."

I replied, "It's hard to feel hopeful when your childhood experience of being unloved and inadequate is still in charge of how you feel. It's the only thing you've ever known, so it *feels* very real, even though you're getting very clear messages from others that let you know that the old emotional system is not accurate."

Laura had not developed an internal affective core sense of security and confidence as a child. This lack of security made it difficult for her to deflect negative input from others. In addition, she did not have an "I'm lovable" or "I'm valuable" attitude that could process the positive feedback she was receiving from others and integrate it into a sense of self-worth. Her attitudes were filtering out the love and appreciation expressed by her friends and the affirmation from her boss.

Because Laura's mind could not retain a sense of others' caring, she was unable to use it to help meet her needs for love, self-worth, and identity. And every time Laura was unable to take in and retain the positive messages, the current experience reinforced her negative childhood attitudes that were already in place.

Fortunately, Laura continued working through her feelings of hurt and anger about her parents' difficulty being emotionally available to her and the impact this had had on her and her life. She became more aware of how and when interactions with others triggered her conflicted emotions. We continued to focus on developing her ability to identify and observe her emotional and physical responses as they were occurring and to create new attitudes so that she could protect herself in healthier, more effective ways.

Your Cognitions

The cognitive component of your attitudes also plays an important role in how you experience and deal with your life—it makes it possible for you to solve problems and make decisions. The parts of the brain that operate your thoughts and beliefs begin developing when you are an infant. However, the rate of their development increases when you are about 18 months old and continues into adulthood. That is why you are a better able to solve problems at 10 years old than you were as a toddler.

Just as the emotional component of your attitudes does many things at once, so too, your cognitive system is busy multi-tasking as it processes the information that you receive through your senses. The cognitive component of your attitudes helps you pay attention to external and internal stimuli and, functioning as a *gatekeeper*, determines what information you take in and what information you discard.

Because of its role as a gatekeeper, your cognitive system is actively involved in creating and managing your memories. As a *memory-maker*, it affects what you remember of your experience and how well you remember it. It also helps you retrieve and use the information stored in memory.

The cognitive component also plays an important role in helping you make sense out of your experience. It makes it possible for you to assess, interpret, and assign meaning to the information your senses acquire. Because the cognitive component functions as a *meaning-maker*, it affects what you think, what you believe, and what you value. It even makes it possible for you to develop the ability to *think about what you are thinking, as you are thinking it!* This ability allows you to evaluate what you are feeling, thinking, and doing. Moreover, it helps you determine what is motivating you and how your attitudes are affecting your life.

Finally, as a *cataloger*, your cognitive processes are busy taking in information from your experience, making sense out of the data, and storing it in your memory in categories. As the brain links the different kinds of information, the information forms into patterns (which we will be looking at in more depth later). These categories and constellations help you to think in cause-effect ways, to anticipate what to expect, and to access stored information more efficiently.

As Laura and I observed and discussed her experience, we were able to identify several cognitive patterns that she had developed as she had taken in and stored information in her memory during childhood. We explored these beliefs and thought patterns and the meanings she had made of her experience as a child, and the ways these early patterns were continuing to reinforce her childhood attitudes in adulthood.

About 19 months into therapy, Laura talked about how some of her thoughts and beliefs were interfering with her developing relationships.

"It seemed like I was constantly doing something wrong as a kid. I remember thinking that my parents didn't love me or want me around because I was a burden and a nuisance. They always said they loved me, and they probably did, but I've never totally believed what they said. How could I? On one hand, my mom would get mad at me and would punish me—out of the blue, for no good reason, as far as I could tell. I guess I just wasn't measuring up to her expectations. After a while, I started believing I was stupid and a failure."

As Laura described her experience, her jaw tightened, and her body became tense. "My dad, on the other hand, didn't make much effort to hang out with me. The trouble is, I never could figure out what I could do to make my mom happy or to get my dad to pay more attention to me. But I sure knew that neither one of them could be counted on to be there when I needed someone."

I commented, "Those are pretty painful beliefs to be carrying around with you all these years. It must be very hard to believe positive things about yourself and others when you experience such a barrage of negative messages coming at you."

Laura's tension lessened slightly, but she was still scowling as she responded, "It's awful!" Then her affect eased even more as she observed, "I blame my parents for a lot of my problems, but I'm definitely not helping my case. It's hard for me to talk to people, much less develop friendships with them, because I'm constantly second guessing myself. I tell myself that I don't have anything to offer anyone, so no one would even want to spend time with me. If I do talk myself into going out with other people, I feel stupid the whole time and act standoffish. I keep thinking, 'You're dead weight. No one will ever invite you out again. Don't even think about trying to meet a guy because no one can love you anyway.'"

Laura leaned forward in her seat toward me as she said, "Part of me believes I'm a failure at relationships. But another part of me is starting to believe I can do things differently." She paused, sat back in her seat, and grinned as she said, "I guess it's all up to you and me now."

Laura was beginning to take ownership of her attitudes. As she was becoming more aware and observant of her emotional and cognitive patterns, she could see more clearly how she undermined herself in her relationships. She was also beginning to realize that she could do something to change her attitudes and her future and that she did not have to do the work alone.

Your Behaviors

Your behaviors, including both how you act (what you say and do) and how you are prepared to act, are an integral component of your attitudes. As you are growing up, you act in ways that aim to help you adapt to both your internal experience and your experience of the outside world. These behavioral modes of adapting—some healthy and some unhealthy—become part of your attitude system as you cope with positive and negative experiences. Over time, your familiar behaviors become automatic and habitual because the tendencies to act in certain ways are primed and ready for something to activate them. (We will be examining this process in more depth in the next chapter.)

Because stressors (anything that produces stress) can have a major impact on how your attitudes develop, let us examine for a moment how stressors can affect the behavioral component of your attitudes (as well as the affective and cognitive components).

Both internal stressors (e.g., distressing emotions, thoughts, or biological states) and external stressors (e.g., environmental situations) can activate the behavioral component of your attitudes. Sometimes this process is useful, such as when manageable stress motivates you to be more productive or to care for yourself in healthy ways. Other times the activation of these behavioral responses may not be helpful to you. For example, when your attitudes filter stressors as threatening when you are not truly in danger, you may find yourself consciously or unconsciously acting to defend yourself unnecessarily.

Whether a stressor presents a realistic threat, or you perceive it as a threat when it is not, your mind-body system activates what researchers refer to as the *Fight-Flight-Freeze* response (FFF). When this occurs, your body releases stress hormones, which cause you to react by fighting against or avoiding the stressor in some way. Your mind-body system may even shut down as a way to preserve itself.

Peter Levine, a medical biophysicist, psychologist, and expert in the fields of stress and trauma, expands on the FFF concept in his writings. He describes the five biological responses that usually occur in response to the sense of danger as "'the A, and four Fs': *Arrest (increased vigilance, scanning), Flight (try first to escape), Fight (if the animal or person is prevented from escaping), Freeze (fright—scared stiff) and Fold (collapse into helplessness)*" (Levine, 2010, p. 48, emphasis in original).

Consider the following example of the *Arrest-Flight-Fight-Fold-Freeze* response (AFFFF). Imagine that someone makes a comment to you, and your biological system (which includes the emotional and cognitive components of your attitudes) perceives the comment as a threat to you. When this occurs, your body releases stress hormones, mobilizing you to take action and protect yourself. A rush of these hormones causes body sensations such as increased muscle tension and hyper-alertness (Arrest).

In addition, you are likely to experience the body sensations related to the emotions of anxiety or fear, and you may respond behaviorally by moving away from the person (Flight). You may also experience the feeling of anger and react to the person by becoming verbally or physically aggressive in an attempt to protect yourself (Fight). If you feel intense fear and feel trapped and helpless, you might react to these sensations by instantly freezing up (Freeze), which makes it difficult for you to say or do anything. If the sense of fear and helplessness evoked by the stressor overwhelms your capacity to manage it, you are likely to collapse emotionally into helplessness (Fold). When this occurs, you can experience numbness to the point that you cannot take any action.

Although the intensity of the emotions and the ability to respond in these situations may vary, feelings of intense fear, helplessness, and incapacity are associated with both the Freeze and the Fold response. Whether you freeze in paralysis or collapse in helplessness, the overwhelming nature of these feelings usually cause people to experience both the Freeze and the Fold responses as traumatic (Levine, 2010, p. 48). When this occurs, your mind develops emotional, cognitive, and behavioral connections that become associated with these traumatic experiences.

When your mind associates a current stressor with your past traumatic experiences, it usually activates your body's AFFFF response system. When this occurs, you tend to *experience the present as if it were the threatening past*, and you may automatically respond to the stressor by taking action to protect yourself. Sometimes this is helpful, such as when you are in danger. But when your mind misreads a stressful situation as dangerous when, in fact, it is not, your behavioral responses (as well as affective and cognitive) tend to be problematic.

As Laura and I continued working together over the next two years to help her make the changes she wanted, she experienced many situations that activated her Fight-Flight response. One episode occurred after she had begun dating a man in her computer class at the adult education school. Her plan had been to apply what she had been learning in therapy to the new relationship. One day, Laura told me about an experience that had occurred several days after our last session that had challenged her emerging abilities to change her attitudes.

"It's happened again! Part of me feels like a fool—another part feels good about myself. You know I've been taking a big risk by trying to develop a friendship with Gary. I've been taking things slowly, so I don't get too scared and start acting defensive about everything. I've also been trying to watch out for my negative thoughts and not let them run the show. And things have seemed to be going okay. But the last month or so, Gary has been driving me crazy!

"Sometimes he acts as if I'm the most important person in his life, but then I don't hear from him for days. He doesn't even return my phone calls or texts! When that happens, I start worrying that I did something wrong and my anxiety skyrockets to the point where I feel frantic. Sometimes I feel like driving around trying to find him or like running away (which is what I usually do)."

Laura paused and unconsciously began rubbing her forehead as she continued, "He did it again two weeks ago. This time I got so mad that I felt like chasing him down and yelling at him. That did it! I went outside, sat on the rocking chair on the front porch, and started paying attention to what I was feeling in my body, just like we've been talking about me doing. I noticed that my chest had tightened and that my jaw had clenched so hard that it was hurting. I was definitely ready to start fighting!"

As Laura described her experience, I noticed that her body was beginning to respond to her *recollections* as if she was in danger again. She had started leaning forward in her seat, her body had been tightening up, and she had begun talking a little faster. I asked her to focus for a minute on her current body sensations, observe them, and find a way to discharge her tension. Laura became still for a moment, and then she briefly shook her arms and legs.

"That's funny," Laura chuckled. Then she continued, "When I was sitting on the porch, I remembered us talking about how I need to discharge the energy from my upsetting emotions to help me not feel so threatened. So I went for a brisk walk. Later on, I did my deep breathing exercises and stretched for a while, really focusing on relaxing my muscles. I reminded myself that my relationship with Gary may or may not work out, but either way I would be okay. It really helped me calm down and get centered.

"When Gary called me a few days later, I told him that I get anxious and worry when he doesn't return my calls sooner. And I asked him if he could be more considerate of my feelings. At first, he just brushed me off. Then he started criticizing me for something he didn't like that I had done. We started arguing, and I started yelling at him. But I caught myself and stopped. I took a slow, deep breath, and then told him, 'I just wanted you to know what I have been experiencing, and that I'd appreciate your help.' He ended up saying that he'd do better, and for a few days, he did. But that didn't last long; he just went back to his old habits. I thought about saying something to him again, but I figured there was no point because he is who he is. I have to face the reality that he's not an emotionally safe person for me. In fact, he's just like my parents. Last night I broke up with him."

I responded, "It has taken a lot of courage for you to reach out and to try to connect again. I know that part of you is thinking you are a fool because the situation has been stirring up all the old hurt and scary feelings again. But you have taken care of yourself in new ways this time. I wonder if this situation feels any different to you than the other times you've tried to connect with people."

Laura looked at me for a moment with a puzzled but thoughtful expression, as her body began to release additional tension. Then she replied, "Well, I was able to hang in there and talk to him about what I was feeling rather than immediately running away or attacking him."

She started smiling and continued, "Usually I don't tell people what I feel because I get scared. But this time I thought, 'What the heck! I won't die if I tell him what I think.' It felt really good to tell Gary that I didn't like him not returning my calls and texts. And even though I lost it that one night and started yelling at him, I haven't been beating myself up with guilt or feeling as devastated as I would normally feel. In fact, even though part of me is sad, I feel proud of myself—*especially* for how I calmed myself down!" Laura was clearly looking pleased with herself.

I shared my observations. "You did a great job! Even though the relationship didn't turn out how you'd hoped, and the old attitude patterns were stirred up, you managed them much better than you have in the past. You didn't panic and run away or shut down. It's true that the angry fight response popped up to protect you, but you didn't let it take over and run the show. And you're not falling into the old thought patterns as much. Most importantly, however, you can see that you didn't get destroyed."

Laura grinned and commented, "Well, I took a gamble, and I didn't win the prize I wanted. But now that I think about it, I think I got something better. I can see that I am getting stronger and more confident, even though I know I still have a lot more work to do."

Laura's attitudes were beginning to change. In this situation, Laura was able to tolerate the tension of her ambivalence enough to risk trying to establish a relationship again. As a result, Laura was able to manage her fears, anxiety, frustration, and anger more effectively, and her thoughts and beliefs about herself were shifting. In addition, she was better able to act in ways that addressed her needs and protected her.

Laura also was learning how attitudes can serve you, and how they can hinder your ability to function effectively. Let us think about these two aspects of how attitudes operate for a moment.

How Attitudes Serve You

Your attitudes are your familiar companions; they have been part of you since early childhood, constantly serving you by filtering, organizing, and giving meaning to your experience. Because of these critical functions, you have a substantial investment in your attitudes *as they are*. After all, they have been making it possible for you to make sense of and manage your life for a long time.

Earlier in the chapter we identified how the components of your attitudes affect the way you function. Now let us examine in more depth how your attitudes serve you.

They Filter Your Experience

Attitudes function like filter systems. They determine what information the mind takes in and what they keep out. This filtering system is helpful in many aspects. Because your brain, like your computer, has limits to its processing speed and how much information it can handle, the filtering process protects the system from "data" overload. When your brain filters information, it is supporting your internal operating system's ability to function effectively.

In addition, your attitudes determine what you see and experience in life. You unconsciously pay attention to and take in the information that easily fits into your preconceived ideas—that is, your current system of emotional and cognitive perceiving. When new information does not fit in with your current ways of feeling and thinking, you tend to ignore it or discount it because there is no preset category in which to file the new experience.

Although this can have a downside (which we will consider later), it tends to keep the information in your system congruent, which can make your life less conflicted in some respects.

They Give Meaning to Your Experience

Part of being human involves making meaning out of your experience. Your attitudes play a critical role in this process because the way you emotionally and cognitively perceive and assess the information coming in through your senses determines your understanding of your experience. In turn, how you interpret your experience influences your perceptions, appraisals, and expectations. Because this process continues throughout your lifetime, naturally the attitudes you have at any point in your development affect the way you make sense of your experience.

Some of the meanings you create fit in with your pre-programmed modes of feeling, thinking, and behaving. Other explanations develop as your mind takes in new information and alters or replaces the old, automatic, reflexive attitudes. The ability to respond to experiences in a flexible manner (*response flexibility*), as well as to reflect on the interpretations that are currently part of your attitudes, is crucial for you to be able to change your attitudes.

When Laura was a child, she had made sense out of her mother's critical and demanding perfectionism by internalizing the meanings her mother had operated with (e.g., "Laura is inadequate."). In addition, Laura had attached her own explanations (e.g., "I'm unlovable, a nuisance, incompetent, and stupid.").

It would have been helpful if Laura had had the ability as a child to understand that she did not cause her mother's negative, critical attitudes or her father's detached, emotionally unavailable attitudes. Unfortunately, as a small child, Laura was not capable of discerning that her parents' attitudes were revealing her parents' psychological processes.

Fortunately, the mind is flexible and has the ability to create new meanings. This made it possible for Laura to work on changing her old attitudes that had misconstrued her experience and undermined her life and to create more reality-based attitudes.

They Organize Your Experience

There is so much information coming into your mind and body from inside and outside that you need an organized system to help you store and access information. Remember, as your senses take in all the information from your experience, your body and mind record, organize, and store it in linked mindsets along with the meanings you make of your experience.

These mindsets operate automatically and usually function outside your conscious awareness. They also interface with each other as they run your internal operating system. However, even with the extensive organization, you may not be able to access some of the stored information easily, or perhaps at all, because your mind stores it in inaccessible areas.

Two aspects of this organizational process that I would like to highlight here are *dualistic* thinking and *patterns of expectation*.

Dualistic thinking. People often refer to dualistic thinking as *either-or* or *all-or-nothing* thinking. When you are thinking in a dualistic way, in a sense, your mind has less work to do. It only has to route the information from your experience into one of the two categories. For example, I am good or bad, loveable or unlovable. Others are desirable or undesirable, safe or unsafe. When you think in a dualistic way, you do not have to think through the many dimensions of your experience or consider how the dimensions affect each other.

Although dualistic thinking simplifies how the information coming into your mind-body system is organized, and no major difficulties may result from this process, unfortunately, your system can oversimplify the information you receive. Because oversimplification leaves out a great deal of information, it tends to misconstrue the information, which can easily create problems. We will be discussing this in more detail shortly.

Patterns of expectation. As your mind is developing, you come to know the sequence, or pattern, of your interactions with others. These patterns of expectation make it possible for you to anticipate, or predict, emotional, cognitive, and behavioral responses, both your own and others'.

This ability can have an upside and a downside. For example, if your boss has been sarcastic when you have not completed your work on time, you can anticipate that he will be sarcastic in the future if your work is late. The ability to predict could be helpful in this situation if it motivates you to complete your work before the deadline.

Unfortunately, patterns of expectation are not helpful when you come to expect things that are not true in the present and act on your expectations. For example, if you expect your boss to be sarcastic and, in anticipation, you become defensive when he is not upset, your patterns of expectations can interfere with your relationship and with your functioning at your job.

It is important to remember that others are not, and cannot be, "perfectly" consistent, even though they may have generally predictable patterns of relating, so you can be mindful of your expectations.

How Attitudes Hinder You

Although the attitudes you developed early in life serve you in many ways, you can also pay a price for having and holding onto some of them. When you rely on attitudes that are not serving you well for guidance and protection, they undermine your ability to function effectively.

Troublesome attitudes can hinder you in many ways, but three common hindrances are that they can limit you, they can distort your experience, and they can cause conflict.

They Can Limit You

Long-term familiarity with your attitudes (emotions, cognitions, and action tendencies) can lead to the assumption that life is the way you perceive it. When you go through life on automatic pilot you enact patterns that you may not even see, much less understand. If you *are* aware of them, you may not know how to change them—and you may not want to because they are the tried-and-true patterns, and you have an investment in them. Familiarity provides a sense of comfort and security, even if it is sometimes false.

An example of this is dualistic thinking, which was mentioned earlier. Although it is normal to think dualistically as a small child, it often creates difficulties for you as you get older. It is very difficult to problem-solve creatively if you can only think of two possible solutions to your dilemmas since solving problems effectively often relies on possibility thinking.

In addition, dualistic thinking also prevents you from experiencing the many facets of yourself and others. This limitation can cause a mental struggle (*internal conflict*), which makes it difficult to deal with relationships. For example, it is difficult to form relationships if you tell yourself you only have two options—get close to others or keep a distance from them. It is also hard to sustain relationships if you think you have to either hate or love your parents (or others) when they do not act as you want or think that you need them to act.

Fortunately, as you grow older, you usually acquire a greater ability to make sense of yourself, others, and the world from multiple perspectives. For example, imagine that as a young child you learn from your parents that it is wrong to ask for help. As you get older and encounter people outside your family, you begin to see that it is common for people to ask for help. In fact, people are often encouraged and even commended for asking for help (e.g., "Ask the teacher when you have questions."). You become aware that people ask for help whether they "need" help or just "want" help, and many people do not consider them bad or lazy (although some people might). You may eventually come to believe that asking for help when you need it is acceptable.

Unfortunately, even with this ability to process your experience from several points of view, your attitudes can still become fixed and rigid. The downside of inflexibility is that it interferes with your mind's ability to process information emotionally. It also impairs your ability to think and act in new and more effective ways.

Continuing the previous example, although you may now believe intellectually that it is acceptable to ask for help, the early childhood "rule" still may be set firmly in your core attitudes. This inflexibility may make it difficult for you, as an adult, to ask for help. Or if you are able to ask for help, you may feel a sense of shame, guilt, or fear about doing so.

It is difficult to operate outside the box when your conscious or unconscious motto is "This is the way I have always done it." Being able to process information from different perspectives and to respond flexibly to new information helps make it possible to create a fulfilling life.

Another drawback to rigid attitudes is that inflexible things snap and break more easily than flexible things. For example, imagine that a friend does not treat you the way you believe that she should and you feel hurt and angry about her failure to meet your expectations. A rigid belief that "people who care about me will never do anything that upsets me" will undoubtedly affect your relationship negatively.

A more flexible belief that "people who care about me will usually treat me well, although they may occasionally do things I don't like," will provide more latitude for working through the conflict. Flexibility in your responses is critical to how your attitudes affect your ability to function in life and relationships. Inflexible attitudes can make you and your relationships more vulnerable to damage because they limit your ability to manage your emotions, thought processes, and actions.

They Can Misconstrue Your Experience

The affective and cognitive components of your attitudes assess the significance of your experience. As we have previously discussed, many aspects of this process are helpful. However, this evaluation process is not helpful when your mind does not accurately perceive, appraise, or interpret your experience.

The mind misconstrues what is real and true in two common ways:

- It can distort your experience by creating false negative meanings or making your experience out of proportion to what is real.
- It can create illusions by assigning truth or reality to something that is not true or by failing to see the truth for what it is.

When your attitudes cause your mind to misperceive your experience by creating false negative meanings, they are creating a *distortion*. Distortions are more likely to occur when you read into your experience things that are not there. For example, if you think that others are trying to hurt you when they are not and you are in no danger, it is a distortion. It is also a distortion if the interpretation produced by your perceptions and assessments is out of proportion with reality, either augmenting or diminishing the reality of the situation.

This process can occur when you operate with all-or-nothing thinking because dualistic thoughts are commonly out of proportion to reality. For example, if you determined that a family member no longer loved you when she was simply frustrated that you did not fix dinner, it would be a distortion. Your interpretation would be out of proportion to what was occurring. Or if you were to experience a friend as being in love with you when the person was just being friendly—it would also be a distortion.

In contrast, when your attitudes cause your mind to misperceive your experience by assigning truth or reality to something that is not true, your attitudes are creating an *illusion*. Illusions inaccurately attribute positive meanings to a person or situation. For example, you would be operating under an illusion if you thought you had the power to make others thoughtful and responsible, especially if that was not their nature.

Illusions are more likely to occur in situations in which you have partial information. For example, if you perceived and acted as if a person was trustworthy without sufficient information to verify the person's honesty or reliability, it would also be an illusion.

When your attitudes misconstrue your experience in a way that creates distortions or illusions they may continue to produce misconstrued perceptions and assessments, coloring your new experiences. It is hard to make reality-based decisions, or to protect yourself, when you lack valid information.

They Can Cause Conflict

When what you feel, expect, or believe differs from what you say and do, internal conflict usually results. This leads to a mental struggle between the different components of your attitudes or between conflicting attitudes. For example, you can find yourself not doing what you want to do or doing what you do not want to do. You may have unwanted feelings or thoughts or experience difficulty feeling and thinking the way you desire.

When you have mixed feelings, values, or priorities, it is usually difficult to make decisions and to act in ways that move your life in the direction you want and need. Internal conflicts are frequently exhausting, and they can cause conflicts in your interactions with others.

When you are trying to change your attitudes, it is common to experience internal conflict because the new information coming in to your mind-body system may not fit easily into your firmly entrenched attitudes. When you have experiences that are different from those that are familiar to you, such as a new way of thinking, you have to decide what to do with the new information. You may feel torn between different methods of processing the information. You can discount and discard the new experience, develop meanings out of the new information in a way that fits your current attitude system, or create a new attitude.

Although the internal conflict created by this situation can be difficult, the disruption to the status quo makes it possible for you to change old, ineffective attitudes and create ones that serve you better.

Summary: Attitudes Are Foundational

Many people are fond of saying, "Time heals all wounds." Time, however, does not heal emotional wounds. Time also does not change what you think and believe, nor does it enable you to change how you act. Time also does not rewrite the lines of your life story that you have already written.

Instead, *attitudes hold your past, present, and future in their arms.* They determine how you remember your past and the meaning you attribute to your experience. They affect how you feel, think, and act in the present. They create the frame on which you build your life in the future.

Some attitudes serve you well. Others, such as those based on illusions and distortions, may undermine your life. Attitudes filled with illusions hold out the promise of protecting you and enriching your life but in actuality leave you vulnerable to harm and emotional impoverishment.

Attitudes based on distortions can twist your perceptions and interfere with your ability to make accurate and healthy meanings out of your experience. Such problematic mindsets negatively affect your emotional life, your ways of thinking and believing, and your ability to act and interact with others. Therefore, it is important to ground yourself in what is real and true—even though the old system may cling tightly to its familiar ways of operating.

Fortunately, the brain's ability to change nerve pathways and connections makes it possible for you to change the attitudes that are not serving you well. It requires time and work. It also requires a relationship in which you can re-work the attitudes that hinder you while you also develop and reinforce others that will serve you well.

Through this process, you create new emotional, cognitive, and behavioral patterns that will transform your life.

To create a life that is meaningful and fulfilling, you must be willing to let go of the ways of dealing with the emotions, beliefs, and actions that are not serving you well.

But being willing to let go of the old, but familiar, ways of relating to yourself and the world is not enough to change your undermining attitudes and save your life. It is also important to understand how they developed in the first place.

So to continue on the journey of transforming wounds into wisdom, let us look further at how you have come to feel, think, and act the way you do.

CHAPTER 2

How Do Attitudes Develop?

The struggle to understand the parent-child bond touches us deeply because we intuitively sense that our first relationships hold many clues to how we've become who we are. —Robert Karen, *Becoming Attached*

From the moment of your conception to the end of your life, your attitudes are continually forming and re-forming as your mind interacts with others and your environment and processes these interactions. Your core attitudes develop during early infancy and childhood as you internalize various aspects of your primary caregiver's ways of feeling, thinking, and acting, as well as assimilate the ways you and she relate to each other.

Although other attitudes develop from later life experiences, it is your core attitudes and relationship patterns that have the predominant impact on how you experience and relate to yourself, others, and the world throughout your life.

Before we begin to look in more depth at different aspects of how attitudes and relationship patterns develop, let me share the story of Nathan, a 15-year-old adolescent with whom I worked for about two years.

Nathan's Story

Nathan's parents brought Nathan in to see me because they were concerned about his "I can't do it," "I don't care" attitudes that were becoming more pronounced as the school year was progressing. During the first session (which was only with Nathan's parents), they elaborated on their concerns about Nathan.

Nathan's father initiated the discussion by saying, "We're really worried about Nathan. We thought that he might have a *little* trouble adjusting to a new school this year since we just moved here and he didn't have time to make any new friends before school started. We hoped that he'd be okay because he's always been such a good student and is very outgoing, but he's failing several of his classes. If he has a hard time with an assignment or runs into problems on anything he's supposed to do, he might try to do it a few times, but then he gives up. I can't believe *my son* has become a quitter! Failing at academics is bad enough, but Nathan is flaking out in other areas. He refuses to get involved in school activities or even hang out with other kids his age. He's even withdrawn at home! All he does anymore is stay in his room and play computer games for hours on end. When he does happen to come out of his room, he makes snide remarks to whoever is around as he walks by."

Suddenly, Nathan's mother burst out in frustration and helplessness, interrupting her husband, "We don't know what to do! We've tried everything! Rewards. Punishments. It doesn't matter. No matter what we do, nothing works. Nathan still will not do what he is supposed to do. He still has a bad attitude."

After discussing their concerns further, Nathan's parents and I agreed that I would meet with Nathan in individual sessions and have family sessions periodically as warranted.

For the first few months of therapy, Nathan was quite defensive and sullen. He spent most of the sessions complaining about all the things he did not like about his parents. Nathan clearly felt safer focusing on his parents' attitudes than on his own. As the treatment progressed, however, Nathan became more open about how he felt about himself, his life, and his relationship with his parents.

Nathan frequently talked about how frustrated and hurt he was by many of the things his parents did and how painful it felt when they failed to give him the emotional support and security he needed. As he was talking about these experiences with his parents, he would fluctuate between spouting off his anger and falling silent and becoming unresponsive. It was clear that Nathan was struggling internally with the frustration he felt about his parents and his unmet emotional needs.

One day, about five months in to treatment, Nathan, who had propped himself up with pillows in a corner of the couch, admitted the following.

"I hate my life. My parents tell me I should have a better attitude. They're probably right. I know I should be doing my homework, chores, and hanging out with other kids, but most of the time I think, 'Why bother? It doesn't matter what I do or don't do, my life won't ever get any better.'" Nathan's body slumped slightly.

After a moment, Nathan continued, "I've given up on asking my parents for help because when I do, they *might* try to help me—at first. But if what they do doesn't work right away, they get frustrated, give up trying to help, and walk away. Or they get mad and start yelling at me and blaming me for whatever's happening. Then, as if that's not bad enough, they start lecturing me. My dad says things like, 'It's a dog-eat-dog world so you'd better be prepared to be the eater if you want to survive.' My mom acts all helpless, and says things like, 'There's no point in saying anything; nothing you can say or do will make things any better anyhow.' Like how's what they are saying and doing supposed to help me figure out my problems or make me feel better? What am I supposed to do now?"

As Nathan and I talked, we both could feel how Nathan's emotional wounds were causing him great pain. It was also clear that although Nathan was feeling helpless, sad, and defeated, he was beginning to recognize that maybe he needed to do something different to make his life better.

The following week, Nathan asked to have a family session because he had "something important to talk about."

Nathan curled up on the loveseat, tucked his chin down into his collar, and with eyes looking down, he mumbled, "I'm scared. Some of the seniors at school keep cornering me after school and shoving me around while I'm waiting for the bus."

A tear trickled down his cheek, and I heard a barely perceptible sigh escape his chest. "I told the guys to stop it, but it doesn't do any good; they keep doing it anyway. I've tried to walk away and ignore them, but they won't let me. I talked to one of my teachers about it, just like my parents told me to do, but she told me to go stand by some other kids. My parents tried talking to the principal, but he didn't do anything either. I don't know what else to do so I guess I'll just have to put up with it." Another sigh.

As Nathan talked, I was aware of slight changes occurring in his parents' body language. They were shifting in their seats and looks of resignation were settling on their faces. Nathan's father spoke up. "We tried to get it to stop, but what can you do? We had people hurt us when we were kids. We survived, so he'll just have to find a way to handle it, too."

As we discussed the problem, memories of previous meetings with Nathan and his parents came to mind. The father's primary way of dealing with his helpless feelings was to yell, criticize, and over-control his wife and Nathan. Nathan's mother, in contrast, cowered and put up with her husband's behavior. She bounced between making excuses for her husband and complaining about how frustrated and hurt she felt. Wrapped up in their own painful issues, both parents had abandoned Nathan emotionally by not protecting him from physical abuse or teaching him how to protect himself in healthy and effective ways. All three of them—

father, mother, and Nathan—were in obvious pain over what was happening, both at school and in the family.

As the afternoon progressed, my concern for Nathan's emotional and physical well-being and about the harm that the situation was causing the family as a whole continued to intensify. So I called the sheriff's department anonymously to see what they could do to help.

The sheriff on duty listened to my description of what was happening at school and expressed some concern, but stated, "We can't do anything because it's happening at school." Even law enforcement was relating to the problem with a powerless attitude!

Still thinking about the whole situation later that evening, I was determined to come up with a strategy that would protect this child. I did *not* want him to keep getting hurt. I did *not* want him to grow up believing that he was helpless and powerless to protect himself or his future children. I also did not want him learning that the only way he could protect himself was to become a bully.

I kept thinking, "There *has* to be a way to keep Nathan safe. There *has* to be a way to show Nathan and his parents that there is a different, more effective way to handle this situation. Their helpless and hopeless attitudes are hurting each of them and their relationships with each other."

My mind continued to run through various possible strategies until it finally came upon one that I was sure would work.

The next morning, I called the sheriff back.

"I have a *Suspected Child Abuse Report* to make," I informed the officer. I knew that she was now responsible, by law, to see to it that something was done to protect Nathan; I hoped the sheriff would recognize that fact, as well. As I went on to describe to her the particulars about what was happening to Nathan on school grounds, it was apparent that the officer remembered my call the day before.

Even though the sheriff knew I was making a mandated child abuse report, she still balked. "But that's not child abuse; it's kids hurting a kid."

Not to be deterred, I responded, "Where in the law does it specify that child abuse is *only* when adults hurt a minor?"

In a grudging tone of voice, the officer conceded, "Okay, it's abusive. But law enforcement calls it 'assault and battery.'"

I countered. "That may be, but a child is being hurt, and it's got to stop. So, I'm hereby making a formal *Suspected Child Abuse Report* to you, and you are now responsible, by law, to make sure something is done to protect this child."

And the officer did.

The following week Nathan practically sprinted down the hall to my office for our session. The minute we sat down, he grinned broadly and began to tell me what had happened to the bullies at school that week.

> "I don't know what you did, but a sheriff showed up at school and told the guys who have been bullying me that if they didn't stop 'assaulting' me she would arrest them, tell their parents, and put them in juvenile hall. Guess what? They're finally leaving me alone! ... Thank God!"

> Nathan sighed deeply and then became quiet and subdued as he relaxed into the couch. Then his eyes began to tear up as he looked at me with deep gratitude and said, "And ... thank *you*! No one has ever done *anything* like that for me before. I'm *so* glad you did something to protect me!"

After the school incident, in which I had intervened effectively on his behalf in a way that his parents had never done, Nathan began actively to engage with me and with the work we were doing together. It was clear that because of this experience, Nathan was beginning to feel a little more empowered himself. Although he still felt helpless and defeated at times, Nathan was now willing to look at and consider the ways he was making his life more difficult as well as things he could do to help heal his wounds and make his life better.

In an ongoing effort to help Nathan develop a stronger and more positive sense of himself and his ability to act effectively on his own behalf, we continued focusing on Nathan's attitudes. Nathan and I decided to use the experience with the school bullies (as well other situations in his life) to discover more about his emotional patterns, ways of thinking, and tendencies to act certain ways.

As we continued to mine his experiences, Nathan gradually began to see how his ways of behaving revealed his emotions and cognitive processes. For example, Nathan began noticing and paying attention to how frustrated and hurt he felt when his parents failed to respond to his emotional needs. He became aware of how his mind would flood with negative thoughts when he was distressed (e.g., "My parents don't care about me"; "Nothing will make things better"). He also began to realize he would make sarcastic comments to his parents or avoid talking to them in hopes they would pay attention to him and take care of his needs.

Over the next six months, Nathan became more and more alert to how often he fell back into negative modes of trying to get attention. He became aware of how desperately he wanted someone to help him because he felt so fundamentally unprotected. All he wanted was someone to be in his corner.

About a year into working together, Nathan shared his most recent observations with me.

"You know, I've been noticing that both of my parents make a big deal out of saying we need to solve our problems, but a lot of times they just create more problems. When my dad feels frustrated, he's mean. He starts yelling and trying to control everyone and everything. When my mom's upset, she just whines and complains about whoever or whatever is bothering her. After they spout off for a while, they end up doing something else. They are both a pain."

Nathan paused, and then sheepishly acknowledged, "I hate to admit it, but sometimes I act like both of them. I get snippy with others when I'm frustrated, even when what I'm bugged about isn't their fault. And sometimes I whine so much; I even irritate myself! What makes me feel even worse, though, is when I feel hopeless and give up trying to solve my problems. It really sucks."

For several minutes, Nathan sat quietly and sadly as he processed what he had been saying. Then he asked, "How did I get to be so much like my parents? I *hate* how they are! I don't *want* to be like them! I don't *want* these attitudes."

As I paused before answering Nathan, my mind raced through a list of the many factors that influence how attitudes develop. Internally, your biological makeup, temperament, hormones, and neurobiology influence how your attitudes develop. Externally, factors such as the relationships in your family and the larger socio-cultural environment you grow up in also affect attitude formation.

However, what I wanted to focus on with Nathan, and will examine here, is your experience with your primary attachment figure early in life. Therefore, let us begin to explore the answer to the question that was at the heart of Nathan's dilemma: "How do attitudes develop?"

Attitudes Develop in the Context of Relationship

Attitudes do not develop in isolation, but in the context of relationship, especially your relationship with your early primary caregiver during infancy and early childhood. As you are interacting with your parent, your senses are continually taking in the information from these interactions, as well as from the rest of your environment. As your mind assimilates this input, it organizes the information into categories, and records both the categories and the relationships between them in ways that enable you to make sense of your experience.

Over time, psychological and neurological structures consolidate from the stored experience and become part of your internal operating system. Both your core attitudes and peripheral attitudes that you use to manage your daily life are part of this mind-body system.

The most significant influence on how your attitudes form is your relationship with your primary caregiver during infancy and early childhood.

When Nathan asked me why he was so much like his parents, the image of the role of an understudy in the theater came to mind. In the theater, an understudy is a backup actor who learns the parts of one or more regular actors in a play so he can fill in if the regular actor is unable to perform. This multidimensional learning process involves more than simply memorizing the actor's script.

When learning the part of a regular actor, the understudy has to "get into the role." To do this, the understudy must experience and express the character's emotions. He must learn to think like the character, taking on the character's beliefs and ways of making sense of things. The understudy must act in a way that is consistent with the role of the character. He also has to learn the choreography of the part: where, when, and how to relate to the other actors and objects on stage.

It is important to note that when an understudy takes over for an actor, he does not play out the part exactly as the original actor would do it. Instead, the understudy interprets the part through his own personality, based on how he understands it.

In a sense, you function like an understudy to the primary caregiver in your life as you develop through infancy and early childhood. Her part is the one you learn best, because she is the lead actor in your life's play, early on, the one with whom you have the closest emotional connection.

As you interact with your mother, you are busy incorporating all the elements of your relationship with her:

- your own experience;
- your experience of her feelings, thoughts, and actions, especially toward you;
- your experience of how you and she relate to each other.

Then, at any given moment, when the situation seems to warrant it, you start operating unconsciously or at will, with the attitudes that have formed from your experience with the lead actor in your life. *Voila!*

The attitudes and relationship patterns you develop from your experiences with your primary caregiver will not look or operate the same in you as in your parent. Your biological makeup is unique to you, so your emotional, cognitive, and behavioral tendencies will be based on how you process the environment. Like an understudy, the attitudes are revealed through your temperament, based on how you experienced your primary caregiver, the other major actors in your life, and the world around you.

Let us look at this understudy process in more depth.

How You Develop as an Understudy

Although you record all of your experiences as an infant, the focus here will be on those involving your primary caregiver, because she has the most profound impact on your early development. In infancy, your interactions with your primary caregiver affect your developing mind and, therefore, the way your emotions, cognitive processes, and action tendencies develop.

The Way You Feel

Have you ever really paid attention to how you feel or thoughtfully answered the question, "Why do I feel like this?"

What your mind-body system registers of your early interactions with your primary caregiver influences how you will experience and relate to emotions for the rest of your life. Because your emotions shape your earliest experience, your emotional experiences are particularly critical during the first 18 months of your life, when the emotional part of your brain is developing most rapidly. Although you cannot fully understand emotions cognitively during this time because the cognitive parts of the brain are not yet adequately developed, you do experience, express, and perceive them.

Over time, through repeated interactions with others, particularly your primary caregiver, ideally, you will begin to recognize, label, manage, and communicate your emotions in realistic and helpful ways. However, any limitations or difficulties your primary caregiver may have with emotions—hers or yours—will make it difficult for her to help you develop healthy ways of relating to emotions.

When you and your primary caregiver are engaging each other in a way that keeps you emotionally regulated (i.e., not too excited and not too subdued), you will experience a sense of balance and stability. If you become overly stimulated too often or for too long, however, it is taxing on your brain and body. Your developing mind may experience a lack of regulation as traumatic.

This type of trauma does not just occur in infants. Being overwhelmed emotionally or physically for too long at any time in your life can be harmful. Traumatic experiences can make it difficult to manage the way you feel, think, and act throughout your lifespan if you do not care for yourself adequately in their aftermath.

In the episode of Nathan and the school bullies, although Nathan had started out trying to protect himself and to get others to protect him, when his efforts failed, he began to feel helpless—and hopeless. Because the ways he had learned to process and manage his emotions were similar to the ineffective strategies his parents had used to deal with emotions, Nathan's ability to handle the abusive situation was limited.

Eventually, when neither he nor his parents had been able to intervene in a way that relieved his distress, Nathan became overwhelmed and shut down emotionally. He believed that he was powerless to protect himself. He, like his parents, had given up in hopeless resignation. Nathan's "I don't care," "I can't do anything" attitudes reflected his traumatic experience of having been overwhelmed by his emotions (i.e., anxiety, anger, and depression).

By the time his parents brought him to see me, much of Nathan's energy was going into preserving himself. His negativity, angry sniping, avoidance of homework, and tendency to hibernate in his room with computer games, were all ways Nathan was trying to protect himself from his overwhelming emotional distress.

The Way You Think

In addition to recording the emotional aspects of your primary caregiver and the emotional patterns in your relationship, as an understudy your mind also records the cognitive aspects of her attitudes and your interactions.

To remind you, the word "cognitive," as I will be using it, refers to the way your mind processes information, or how you think. It includes your memory and your ability to concentrate, solve problems, and make decisions. Your interactions with others, particularly those closest to you, strongly affect how these thought processes develop and what you come to believe.

This impact occurs whether their ways of thinking are helpful or problematic. If your primary caregiver is able to process information in helpful, reality-based ways, you will be better able to think in ways that help you function. For example, if your primary caregiver can identify, think through, and solve problems with you, you will be more likely to develop the internal structures needed to solve problems effectively. If she is able to help you learn to think about what you feel and put your feelings into words, you will be better able to use your thought processes to help you manage your emotions.

When your primary caregiver's cognitive processes are impaired in certain ways, however, she will tend to have difficulty helping you develop these same areas in your mind. If your caregiver has distortions in her sense of herself, others, and the world, you will tend to internalize her distorted ways of perceiving and thinking. Her distortions will, in some way or to some degree, become your distortions because you have internalized them. After all, you are her understudy.

In Nathan's bully experience at school, Nathan's parents had tried to solve the violence problem to the best of their ability. When the common ways to handle school problems did not work, however, his parents had difficulty coming up with other alternative solutions. Their feelings of helplessness, their beliefs that they were powerless, and their difficulty thinking through the problem from different perspectives had influenced and limited their response to the painful situation.

Nathan was not able to experience his parents' thinking through (*processing*) the problem in a way that led to a positive solution. Instead, he internalized their classic "victim" scripts in which he *felt* powerless and *believed* that he was helpless and alone: "There's nothing I can do; it doesn't do any good to ask for help; no one else will help you."

By failing to resolve the bully problem, Nathan's parents, teacher, and principal had left Nathan alone, struggling with his overwhelming distress. The experience increased the risk that similar situations would trigger Nathan's internal victim scripts in the future.

The Way You Act

Because you are an understudy to the main actors in your life, what you internally record from your experiences with your primary caregiver affects your tendencies to act in certain ways. For example, if your parent becomes angry easily and yells frequently, you may internalize these experiences as "failure to regulate angry emotions." This situation will probably make it difficult for you to develop your own ability to tolerate frustration, control your impulses, and develop empathy.

In contrast, if your caregiver is able to calm herself and take care of herself and the situation that is bothering her, you will tend to internalize the sense that "life is manageable." Your primary caregiver's strengths and limitations will influence the scripts you develop to manage your emotions, make meaning of your experiences, and relate to yourself, others, and the world.

The ways you tend to act are also predictable. In Nathan's family, we could predict with a high degree of certainty that his mother would be passive in conflict situations. We could also anticipate that she would be indirect in expressing anger. We could expect that Nathan, as her understudy, would probably begin to respond the same way. Although he had internalized his father's ways of being also, Nathan usually played out his internal mother scripts in conflict situations. His feelings of helplessness, his thought processes and "I can't do anything" beliefs, and his tendency to act and react in passive ways reinforced his helpless, powerless attitude.

The importance of your early relationship with your primary caregivers cannot be overstated. These early experiences affect the way you feel, the way you think, and the way you act.

How Attitudes Influence Relationship Patterns

As previously mentioned, as a young understudy to your parent, you not only integrate her attitudes into your identity or sense of self, but you also internally record the pattern of your caregiver-child relationship. You incorporate both the child and the parent part of the relationship and the way you relate as a pair. These are your first experiences of "mine, yours, and ours." These interactional patterns are part of your attitudes, and they become part of the psychological and biological structures in your mind-body system.

For example, one common parent-child pattern of relating is a *victim-victimizer* pattern. The essence of this relationship pattern is that at any point in time, one person or entity is in the role of the victim while the other person or entity is in the role of victimizer.

To the degree you internally record the victim-victimizer relationship pattern, at times you will tend to experience yourself in your relationships as being mistreated in some way—a victim. At other times, you will find yourself consciously or unconsciously acting in ways that are hurtful to someone else—a victimizer. You can also switch back and forth between the victim and victimizer roles in a nanosecond.

The victim role is commonly a replay of your child experience. When you operate in this role you perceive the other person or entity as the all-powerful one (the parent) who is doing something hurtful *to* you. You feel and believe you are powerless, just as you once felt as a child, and you tend to act based on those perceptions, feelings, and beliefs.

The victimizer role is usually a replay of the hurtful aspects of your parent's attitudes and your experiences of the ways your parent treated you during childhood. In the victimizer role, you use your power in a negative way toward others, just as your parent (intentionally or unintentionally) once used her power against you.

The interplay between parent and child roles is the *pair dynamic*, or the way the roles operate together. As an understudy, if you experience victim-victimizer interactions with your parent, you will record all three parts of the pattern: victim, victimizer, and pair dynamic. The parts function as a unit.

Because the victim-victimizer dynamic is your known and familiar relationship pattern, you will tend to gravitate toward experiences with others that keep both parts of the pattern active. You may also unconsciously create victim-victimizer interactions with others.

It is clear that Nathan's father had operated with a victim-victimizer attitude as he tried to cope with his son's mistreatment at school. When his efforts to protect his son failed, he experienced the school as being in the role of victimizer—the powerful entity. He felt helpless and powerless—the role of victim.

To stop his distressing feelings of anxiety and helplessness, he unconsciously switched into the position of victimizer, in which he exercised power, as he berated and criticized his wife and son. He was also unconsciously replaying the victim-victimizer pair dynamic from his own childhood experience. Nathan's father had internalized both roles and how they functioned together.

This victim-victimizer relationship pattern had not helped Nathan's father solve the school bully problem. Nor had it helped him improve his ability to solve problems or manage his emotional distress. In addition, instead of strengthening his relationships with his wife and son, his victim-victimizer patterns had wounded them as well as him.

Those wounds, unfortunately, had resulted in breaks in the emotional connections between family members, making it harder for them to relate in ways that were mutually rewarding and fulfilling. Fortunately, as Nathan and his parents worked to change their attitudes and repair their wounds, their relationships began to heal and become stronger.

The attitudes and relationship patterns you internalize, record, and develop in your mind and body as a child are intricately tied to how you experience and live your life as an adult. Because these attitudes and relationship patterns are so important, we will look at several common relationship patterns in more detail in Part III.[2]

---

[2] The relationship patterns that I present in the next three chapters and use throughout the rest of the book are the result of my synthesis and adaptation of the research on attachment by John Bowlby, Mary Ainsworth, Mary Main, and many subsequent researchers on attachment.

Summary: An Understudy's Scripts

Attitudes begin to develop in the context of your first relationship—your relationship with your primary caregiver. From your earliest moments of life, you, as an understudy to your primary caregiver, begin to record your experiences with her in your mind and body.

As this is occurring, your mind is busy taking in and recording aspects of the ways your parent feels, thinks, and acts in a complex process, known as *internalization*. In addition, your mind-body system is incorporating the dynamics, or patterns, of the way you and your parent relate to each other.

These internal recordings become part of your attitudes. Over time, your mind, as an organizer, links related attitudes, creating mindsets and psychic structures that become part of your internal operating system. This system directs how you function in your life.

Whether your mind encodes the emotional, cognitive, and behavioral tendencies that developed from your experiences as core or peripheral attitudes, this internal repertoire will play a major role in how you create your future. Because it serves as the filter system through which you make meaning of your experience, it influences your expectations for how the world should be and affects how you choose to be in the world.

This repertoire of attitudes and relationship patterns will also affect whether you will perceive your experiences as positive or negative. In essence, the mindsets that you developed early on as an understudy to your parent become the life scripts that determine how you will experience and live your life.

To the extent that your early parent-child interactions are positive, such as when your parent tunes in to you and helps you stay emotionally regulated, you have the opportunity to develop healthy attitudes. These beneficial mindsets lay the groundwork for you to develop secure emotional attachments, which open the door to a rewarding, fulfilling life.

To the degree that the interactions with your parent are negative or traumatizing, they set the stage for you to develop dysfunctional attitudes, such as when your parent fails to connect with or intrudes upon you emotionally. These problematic mindsets, such as those anchored in fear, anger, and disconnection, result in insecure or chaotic attachments patterns that become part of your childhood survival system.

Although these scripts may be necessary for you to survive as a child, they make it difficult for you to establish healthy relationships and ways of managing your life later on. Instead, these deleterious attitudes and relationship patterns lead to further dysfunction and increase the risk that others will wound you again, interfering further with your ability to thrive as an adult.

As you develop the capacity to step back mentally and observe the patterned ways you feel, think, and act that developed as you were growing up, you will be in a better position to transform your wounds into wisdom.

Along your hero's journey of self-discovery and transformation, you will have the opportunity to gain a deeper appreciation for how your helpful and hurtful relational experiences have affected you. You will become more cognizant of your strengths, which you can then use to help you repair your wounds. You can also use the knowledge that you will have gleaned in the process to make healthier, more informed choices about how you will function in life.

Over time, as you work to change your negative attitudes and save your life from the destructive power of your dysfunctional childhood survival system, old undermining attitudes and relationship patterns will be less compelling and will have less and less influence over you.

Moreover, your mind will gradually begin to use your new experiences of healthy, mutually satisfying interactions to reorganize and restructure your old mindsets, thereby creating healthier, more flexible scripts.

With these newly fashioned, more adaptable scripts, you will be able to use the wisdom you have gained to reclaim your life.

To help you as you consider your internal repertoire of attitudes and relationship patterns, let us now explore several common childhood survival systems that develop when a child grows up with a parent who provides *Too Much, Too Little,* or *Just Right.*

Part II

Common Core Attitudes That Develop in Early Relationships

CHAPTER 3

Attitudes that Develop
When a Parent Provides *Too Much*

*Too much of anything could destroy you. ... Too much darkness could kill,
but too much light could blind.* —Cassandra Clare, *City of Lost Souls*

Some parents provide *Too Much*. Too much "love." Too much closeness. Too much control. Too much support. Too much correction. Too much of what could be a good thing, but when overdone, creates a problem.

A parent who provides Too Much consistently intrudes into and over-controls your life. Unfortunately, if your parent provides Too Much, she inadvertently places your developing self in a stranglehold. Usually, her intent is not to harm you in any way. Her conscious motivation may be, "I'm doing this for your own good." Unconsciously, however, she may be trying to meet her own unconscious emotional needs or even enacting her unresolved anger, power, and control issues.

Regardless of her motivation, when a parent is emotionally intrusive and over-controlling, there is often little to no regard for who you are, what you feel, or what you really need. When this occurs, you experience an impingement on your sense of self, and you may become overwhelmed by the experience.

Although a Too Much style of parenting can be overwhelming, it is important to remember that parental control is not all bad. When you are a child, it is the parent's responsibility to function as a regulatory agent, helping you develop your ability to regulate yourself.

In order to do this, your parent needs to provide structure so you can learn self-control and acceptable social behavior. She needs to challenge and support you in ways that correlate with your development stage and that facilitate your emerging personality.

As a child, you are not necessarily thrilled with this agenda. Nevertheless, this structure, if handled well, will help you develop the ability to function effectively in the world—a world full of limits.

Sometimes, however, a parent may go too far and over-regulate. When a parent provides Too Much, she is no longer guiding and shaping you in ways that match your developmental needs. Instead, she has crossed over into the realm of intrusion and over-control, a realm that can make it difficult for you to develop your self and healthy *autonomy*. (Autonomy is the ability to exist independently and to have control over yourself, instead of needing an outside authority to direct and control you.)

In addition, as you (an understudy to your parent) are internalizing aspects of your parent's attitudes, you are also recording the dynamic interplay of the control-impingement process occurring between you and your parent. This imprinting of her attitudes that underlie the over-control and the dynamics of your relationship with her can hinder your ability to live your life confidently and effectively.

To understand these parent-child dynamics better, let us consider two styles of parenting that provide Too Much—*emotionally enmeshed parenting* and *emotionally dominating parenting*. Then we will explore how they can affect you and the core attitudes you can develop.

When a Parent Is Emotionally Enmeshed

Maria's Story

Maria, a 36-year-old woman, came to see me several years ago. She was feeling overwhelmed and did not know how to handle her family members, who she said were "driving me crazy."

I had been working with her for about a month when the following occurred.

> One day Maria could barely contain herself as she entered my office. Before she even sat down on the couch, she burst out with frustration saying, "I am *so* upset! My mother called me up over the weekend and complained—one more time—that I hadn't been over to see her for a week. Can you believe that? I already call her every night because she expects me to, but no, that isn't *enough* for her. I don't know why I keep trying to meet her expectations. I resent the hell out of her. I just wish she'd just get it into that pea brain of hers that I'm a working mom with three children and a husband and have things I have to do!"

> Maria stopped for a moment, trying unsuccessfully to calm herself down, but then indignantly burst out, "You know, I'm sick of it! What I *really* want to do is scream at her, '*Leave—me—alone!*' I feel guilty about feeling that way, because I know I shouldn't … but I do!"

Maria began pacing around the room. Hardly taking a breath, she continued her tirade, "I'm entitled to be angry with her. She's a taker! She expects my brother, Evan, and me to be at her beck and call and take care of her. We're supposed to give her whatever she thinks she needs—whenever she thinks she needs it! Good grief! *Enough* already! I try *really* hard to help her out as much as I can, but no matter what I do, it is never enough for her. It infuriates me that she acts helpless when she is perfectly capable of taking care of herself. It's ridiculous! She's only 63 years old. She needs to stop wrapping her life around us and get a life! She's draining me dry!" Maria dropped onto the couch, clearly exhausted.

Aware of her internal struggle, I replied, "It's frustrating to care about your mother but not be able to make her happy. You love her. But you're in a bind. Even though part of you knows her expectations and demands are unreasonable, still another part of you believes that it *is* your job to provide for all her needs and keep her happy."

Maria responded, "I tell myself constantly that it's not my job to take care of my mother. But when she gets an idea into her head about something she wants, she keeps up the pressure until I cave in. If, by some miracle, I do happen to hold out, she acts like a martyr. She gets all huffy and won't talk to me for days.

"But that's not the worst. If I don't do what she wants, she complains about me to whoever will listen to her—even my grandmother, aunts, and cousins! The trouble is, no one wants to hear her complaints any more than I do, so they start pressuring me to do what she wants, telling me I'm an 'ungrateful and inconsiderate daughter.' I can't stand it! At that point, I usually give in just to get everyone off my back.

"What gets on my nerves even more, though, is that when my mother is upset with Evan, he just argues, or ignores her. Sometimes, he even purposely does things to annoy her. It's frustrating, because that upsets her more and leaves me stranded with the burden of dealing with her. It's just not fair!"

Clearly, Maria was struggling with intense feelings about her mother's overwhelming and demanding parenting style. Even as an adult, Maria was trying to find a way to manage her mother's intrusiveness in ways that could meet both her mother's needs and her own. Caring for her mother's needs, often at the expense of her own, was part of her childhood survival system.

Because an enmeshed relationship between a primary caregiver and child can have a profound impact on you and your attitudes throughout your life, let us examine the dynamics in such a relationship more closely.

The Parent's Style of Relating: *A Tangled Ball of String*

Most parents relate to their children in ways that blur the boundaries between themselves and their children now and then. It is inevitable. Parents are, after all, human. They have dreams, expectations, unmet needs, and unresolved internal conflicts that relationships with their children can activate.

Sometimes, however, these issues interfere with a parent's ability to experience you as a separate, distinct individual rather than as an extension of herself. This makes it difficult for her to support you in your developmental task—to separate from her psychologically and to become your own person.

When a parent has these limitations, she sets the stage for the two of you to become emotionally entangled—A Tangled Ball of String. Unfortunately, this psychological entanglement (often called *enmeshment*) interferes with your ability to develop autonomy. This can leave you, like Maria, experiencing a great deal of internal conflict about how to be yourself, act on your own behalf, make your own decisions, and still be in relationship.

A lack of psychological separateness and autonomy can also make it hard for you to set boundaries in relationships. Boundary setting involves differentiating your and others' areas of accountability. This makes it possible for you to care about others without taking responsibility for their emotions or problems, which belong to them.

When your boundaries are poorly developed and maintained, however, you, like Maria, may have trouble setting limits on others' intrusions. Conversely, like Maria's mother, you may become over involved in others' affairs.

When you are involved in an enmeshed relationship, you may experience direct or indirect messages that reveal underlying expectations, such as:

- "You should feel like I feel and want what I want."
- "You should think like I think and believe what I believe."
- "You should to do things *my* way."
- "You should provide for my needs and wants."
- "You should stay with me forever."

Expectations like these can easily become confused with love, but *enmeshment is not love*. When love is operating, both parties take into consideration and honor the other's need for autonomy. In contrast, the "love" of enmeshment is really more like A Tangled Ball of String. Some of the strings are love. Some are power, control, and dependency. Often, the strings twist together so tightly that it is hard to tell the difference between them or to separate them from each other.

Entangled strings can become the ties that bind you—
the ties that hold you hostage and leave you psychologically
helpless, powerless, and perhaps even choking to death in some way.

In psychological enmeshment, power and control issues (which are inherent in all relationships) may take different forms. When a parent's style of relating is A Tangled Ball of String, she is apt to develop an "agenda" for your life in her own mind, consciously or unconsciously.

She may spend her life grooming you to fit into the role she visualizes for you. Often this role is an idealized image she creates in an unconscious attempt to make up for her unmet emotional needs. It may also be a conscious attempt to realize her unfulfilled dreams.

When this occurs, your parent may have difficulty discerning what you want and need. Her own needs and fears can interfere with her ability to support you in ways that fulfill you as a unique, separate individual. She may convince herself, and even you, that her agenda is what you want. At the extreme, you may even get to the point where you no longer know what you want or even have desires.

Another way entanglement can appear is as a *role reversal* between you and your parent. When a parent has poor boundaries, especially if she is overly needy and dependent, you may experience pressure from her to take on the parental role as the family caretaker. Your parent may lean on you to be the family peacemaker and problem solver and her confidante. Sadly, the more you take on the parental role, the more your self tends to disappear, even to the point of becoming lost.

Maria and Evan encountered both forms of enmeshment with their mother. Their mother's conscious agenda was that they should stay with her forever and take care of her. Her unconscious expectation was that, in essence, Maria and Evan would function as *her* good mother, taking care of her physical and emotional needs. Her emotional manipulations, ways of thinking, and behaviors had entangled her children psychologically in her emotional web.

As a child, Maria had responded by becoming compliant towards her mother, while Evan had become defiant. Both of these responses resulted in a lack of autonomy. As a result, both Maria and Evan had difficulty developing healthy relationships as adults. Their true selves had disappeared into the enmeshed tangle.

Since compliance and defiance are common ways of dealing with enmeshment, let us consider these attitudes and relationship patterns in more depth.

The Core Attitude You Develop: *Compliant–Defiant*

As stated earlier, if your primary caretaker in childhood has an enmeshed style of parenting, you, as her understudy, internally record the experience of the enmeshment. As this occurs, both your parent's and your way of being in the relationship becomes part of your core attitudes.

Unfortunately, this internalized enmeshed relationship pattern interferes with your ability to develop a secure emotional attachment to your parent. It also can result in internal conflicts between your healthy developmental needs for emotional connection, psychological separation, and autonomy.

Children tend to cope with these conflicts by developing two common core attitudes: one based on compliance or one based on defiance.

Coping by developing a compliant attitude. If your parent's relational style is A Tangled Ball of String, you may employ a core attitude grounded in compliance to manage your relationships (and your life as a whole), in order to feel safe and secure in the world—and to survive.

As previously mentioned, when your parent has an enmeshed style of parenting, she relates to you as an extension of herself. She is likely to experience any attempts to separate from her psychologically or to develop autonomy as a threat to her own existence, since, in her mind, you are a part of her. To protect herself from this perceived—and felt—emotional danger, your parent may directly or indirectly threaten you with physical or emotional abandonment in order to keep you enmeshed.

Because your well-being, even your very survival, as a child depends on your parent's providing for your physical and psychological needs, the threat—or even thought—of abandonment is terrifying. You might try to prevent rejection and emotional desertion by complying with your parent's spoken or unspoken expectations.

Over the course of the next six months, Maria began to understand more clearly how her compliant attitude had developed during her interactions with her mother as she was growing up. She described her experience this way.

> "When I was a little kid, I remember feeling sorry for my mom because she was always so stressed out about everything. She worked very hard to make sure everything was done 'just so.' The problem was, if something didn't go according to her plans or the way she thought it should, she'd have a

meltdown. She would stomp around the house all agitated, or she'd cry and complain about whatever she thought was wrong. It was awful! I remember watching her reactions and feeling nervous, afraid, and all jangly inside. I also remember thinking, 'Just calm her down ... help her feel better ... figure out what she needs and take care of it ... *then* she'll be okay.'"

Maria paused and readjusted her sitting position. Her face and body then began tensing up as she continued, "The worst thing, though, was when my mom was upset with me. Usually she would try to pressure me into going along with what she wanted by acting all hurt and disappointed if I didn't do it. But lots of times she would make fun of me, or she would say something sarcastic or just plain mean to get me to do what she wanted. I couldn't stand it!

"I remember one time when I was in first grade, we were going to my grandparents' house, and Mom told me to get ready. So I put on my favorite green pants and purple ruffled shirt and fixed my hair up with lots of colorful bows. I thought I looked *beautiful*! But when my mom saw me, she wrinkled up her nose and sneered at me, saying, 'You look stupid. What do think you are, a Christmas tree? Get upstairs and put on something appropriate.' I was crushed!" Maria's eyes brimmed with tears.

After a moment, Maria reflected, "You know, after that happened, I figured that as long as I did what my mom wanted and acted how she wanted me to act, she'd be okay ... and I'd be okay. In some ways, I think going along with her did make my life easier as a kid. The trouble was, I felt tied up in knots most of the time because it was so stressful being around her. I would even wake up several nights a week complaining of stomachaches.

"What made the situation worse, though, was that I thought that if my mother were upset with me, it was my fault. I believed that something must be wrong with me—I just never could figure out what it was." Maria's eyes began to tear up again, as she said, "Even though I *knew* on some level that it wasn't fair that my mom blamed me that she was upset, I still felt bad. I didn't know what else to think—after all, it wasn't *acceptable* for me to be frustrated and angry with *her*."

Then with anguish in her voice, Maria burst out, "All I ever wanted was for my mom to be happy, to be proud of me, and to love me."

Gently, I reflected, "It hurts so bad to be longing to be simply recognized and appreciated for who you are. And then to be faced with the reality that someone you love so much is unable to provide the acceptance you need is just devastating."

Staring down at her hands in her lap, Maria was quiet for a moment. Then she looked up at me and said sadly, "I've tried so hard to make her happy and proud of me—but I have never been able to." Maria paused again, and then continued, "I just want her to love me for who I am ... but she won't ... or maybe she can't." Tears began coursing down her cheeks, as she cried softly.

Maria and I sat in silence, letting her awareness of, and sadness about, her mother's limitations sink in. Then I responded quietly, "Even though some part of you knows that you are not the cause of your mom's difficulties, it's still heart breaking for you not to be able to get the love from her you so desperately want and need."

Still subdued, but with tension and frustration re-emerging, Maria commented: "You know, even though it's not always my mom now, I'm still trying to get *someone* to appreciate me. I still think that it's my job to take care of others and to make them happy. The thought never crosses my mind about what *I* want and need. I'm scared to have my own opinions or to make decisions, because they might be wrong or because someone won't like them.

"Usually I try to figure out what other people think I should do and then go along with whatever I *think* they think. I know in my head that I probably shouldn't be second guessing others, but I still feel guilty and get mad at myself if I don't at least try to give others what I think they want to make them happy. You know, I'm a really insecure person ... and I *hate* that!"

I responded, "Although you know it's not your responsibility to measure up to everyone's expectations and make them happy, you still find yourself feeling afraid and sometimes re-acting in the old familiar ways—even when it makes you feel bad about yourself."

When you grow up, as Maria did, complying with your parent's expectations to psychologically merge and conform to her image of you, your sense of your self becomes impaired. Your identity (who you are) and individuality (who you are as a separate person) fail to develop adequately because being separate can be threatening to both you and your parent. There is also little to no space in this situation for you to develop autonomy, which empowers you to operate independently and make your own decisions.

In addition, in an enmeshed-compliant relationship, it is difficult to determine your true worth, since you tend to base your sense of self-worth not on who you truly are, but on how well you comply with and conform to your parent's expectations. Because your attitudes form as you internalize your experience of your mother and her experience of you, you may feel anxious, fearful, and guilty if you do not feel, think, or act the way she wants you to. You may also believe that you are bad, inadequate, or a failure if you do not to measure up to her expectations.

During our work together, Maria continued to develop insight into what her attitudes were, how they developed, and the effect they had on her current life. She continued working on changing her attitudes so her relationships could be healthy.

Coping by developing a defiant attitude. As Maria delved ever more deeply into how she had coped as a child and how the attitudes she had developed early in life were affecting her currently, she also began to understand her brother better. She began to realize that instead of developing a compliant attitude to cope with their enmeshed mother, as she had done, Evan had developed a defiant attitude. She came to appreciate that, although these two attitudes were different in some ways, both were attempts to protect the self from a parent's intrusiveness and over-control.

In a session about seven months into treatment, Maria made the following observation.

> "Evan is really different than I am. Even though he and I were both upset with how our mother acted when we were kids, instead of trying to make her happy like I did, Evan seemed determined to defy her every chance he got. He was always arguing with her about something. If he wasn't arguing, he was ignoring her or going on his merry way. He did everything she told him not to do, sometimes even when he didn't even *want* to do it! Evan only did what our mother wanted if it suited his purposes, and that drove our mother crazy. It still does."

> Maria paused, then smiled and said, "We always told him he was so good at arguing that he'd be a great lawyer. Guess what ... now he's a big-wig attorney in downtown Los Angeles!"

Although psychological entanglement with a parent may be comforting in some ways, the enmeshment is psychologically threatening. It jeopardizes your sense of self and is a threat to your needs for identity and autonomy.

In the face of your parent's intrusiveness and over-control, you may develop a defiant attitude in an attempt to survive emotionally. The frustration and anger that are part of defiance can be part of the biological fight response that tries to protect you from perceived danger. Your defiant attitude may also be an effort to have your worth based on who you are, rather than on conformity to your parent's expectations and demands. Moreover, going against what your parent wants or thinks may also be an unconscious strategy to become a separate person in your own right.

Unfortunately, when you defy your parent in an attempt to have a self, as Evan did, your apparent independence and freedom from parental control is an illusion. You, like Evan, are actually creating a negative identity because *you are defining yourself, not by who you are, but by who you are not!*

Although your defiant attitude is understandable, it distorts not only your self-perception but also your sense of who others are. Despite your attempts to be separate from your parent, the reality is that defiance still leaves you psychologically entangled with your parent.

> ***When you define yourself solely in relation to your parent—***
> ***whether by compliance or by defiance—***
> ***you do not base your identity on your true self,***
> ***but by the enmeshment with your parent.***

Consider compliance and defiance with this image in mind: When the earth orbits the sun, part of it faces the light (think "compliance"). Another part of the earth faces away from the sun's rays (think "defiance"). Whether the earth faces the sun or turns away from it, the earth is still orbiting the sun. The sun is still the earth's point of reference, so to speak. And the gravitational pull of the sun still controls the earth.

In a similar way, when you are growing up, your primary caregiver is the center of your universe, the point of reference for your life. As an understudy, you internally record her intrusiveness and over-control and your response to her. Then, like the earth orbiting the sun, whether you are turning toward your parent in compliance or away from her in defiance, you are defining yourself by this parent-child way of relating. The enmeshment locks you in its grip with its powerful pull.

Maria and Evan's relationship with their mother shows how a parent can continue to be your point of orientation far longer than you need it developmentally. In order for Maria and Evan to save their psychological and relational lives, they needed to change the attitudes and relationship patterns they developed with their mother. They needed to change their orientation to themselves, others, and the world.

In a sense, they needed to create a new orbit, a new point of reference, in order to transform their lives.

Maria and Evan's challenge was to observe the ways they were dealing with their emotions, thought processes, and behaviors so they could begin transforming their attitudes of compliance and defiance that were impinging on their lives and relationships. Others struggle with different attitudes developed in relationship with a parent who provided Too Much.

Let us consider Daniel's story.

When a Parent Is Emotionally Domineering

Daniel's Story

Daniel was an incredibly bright 10-year-old boy who was brought in for therapy some years ago by his aunt (Gina) because he was "having difficulty coping with the changes in his life." Daniel's father had died in a helicopter accident when Daniel was three years old, and his mother was currently fighting a long battle with leukemia.

When Daniel's mother became too ill to care for Daniel, Gina and her husband (Mike) agreed to take care of her and Daniel since no one else in the family lived in the area.

Daniel and I had been working together for about three months when the following episode occurred.

> Daniel was lying on the rug in my office with a large pad of paper in front of him. Silently and studiously, he was drawing elaborate and detailed space ships and tiny people battling against invading alien creatures. I sat near Daniel (as he had instructed me to do), watching as the people and creatures waged war.
>
> At one point Daniel lifted his head, his eyes looking intently into mine, and began explaining the parts of his drawing. "These giant aliens are attacking the fleet of space ships." Daniel paused and then pointed at several space ships that the aliens had blown up, scattering fragments of the people all over the page. "These people have already been attacked and killed!"
>
> Then he pointed at a tiny figure in the remaining space ship, which had holes in it but was still intact. "The aliens keep attacking this space ship. The pilot is all alone on his ship. He's setting up firewalls and force fields as fast as he can to protect himself from the aliens' blasts. He has to figure out new strategies to out-maneuver the aliens all the time so they don't blow him into tiny bits.
>
> "So far he's been able to survive the aliens' attacks, but there's no one to help or rescue him. He's afraid that no matter what he does, he'll get blown up with the ship anyway." Daniel pointed again at the shattered people whom the aliens had killed and then said, "Just like they were."

My heart went out to Daniel. He had brilliantly communicated his experience of his real life-and-death battle. "Alien" forces truly were destroying the world that Daniel knew and were endangering his personal survival. Not only was Daniel struggling to deal with the impending death of his mother from leukemia (without the support of a father), but he was also desperately trying to find a way to survive his aunt and uncle's domineering and often hostile style of parenting.

Although Gina and Mike were excellent at providing for Daniel's physical needs, psychologically they were providing Too Much. Their intrusive and over-controlling attitudes were interfering with their ability to be aware of and provide what Daniel truly needed emotionally. They had little ability to empathize with how alone, helpless, unloved, frightened, and even angry Daniel felt, and no insight into how his losses and their attitudes were overwhelming him. Daniel was very alone in his battle to survive the traumatic losses permeating his young life.

If you grew up with a parent whose parenting style was emotionally domineering, you too may have difficulty dealing with power and control issues. In order to deal with these attitudes, let us explore some of the patterns you may have developed as you interacted with your parent.

The Parent's Style of Relating: *In Your Face*

In Your Face parenting, like A Tangled Ball of String parenting, is intrusive and over-controlling, but it is much more structured and domineering. When a primary caregiver has anxieties and doubts deep within herself that prevent her from feeling emotionally safe, she has to find a way to cope with her distress.

To cope with these emotional vulnerabilities, and to obtain a sense of emotional safety and worth, your parent may develop a set of dogmas and codified rules internally. These rigid and highly structured internal rules usually govern her thoughts and beliefs about how people and life "should" be.

Not only do these harsh, punitive "shoulds" control your parent, but she usually demands that others comply with them as well. She has little insight into how her style of relating harms both you and herself. She is determined, and perhaps even compelled, to operate under these rules, regardless of your needs, wishes, or rights—or even her own.

Unfortunately, the expectations that your primary caregiver creates are often unrealistic, and they are certainly not protective, even though she may believe they are. The rigid thought processes make it very difficult for her to be flexible enough to take in and process new information. Instead, her current attitudes may filter the information in a way that it reinforces the rigid system. When this happens, she may relate to others, the world, and even herself, in an opinionated, dogmatic, unyielding, and harsh way.

As with A Tangled Ball of String parent, a parent who is emotionally domineering can also have difficulty tolerating and managing your attempts to develop as a separate, autonomous person. Your efforts can appear so threatening that they activate her rigid defensive attitudes. At best, she fails to support your attempts to be assertive—to speak up about what *you* feel, think, and need. At worst, she may actively resist or undermine your attempts to become independent. Both impinge on your developing autonomy and a sense of self.

Daniel encountered many challenges living with his aunt and uncle. One of the difficulties was that both of them had an In Your Face parenting style. They were clearly intrusive and over-controlling in a hostile, rigid, and domineering way. They had very little tolerance for Daniel's efforts to become autonomous.

Although Gina and Mike expressed some concern about how Daniel was coping with his mother's illness and his move to their home, they had little understanding of how he felt about the changes in his life. Nor did they have any insight into the toll their aggressive attitudes were taking on Daniel.

One day, about six months into therapy, I asked Daniel to describe what a normal day was like for him. Daniel glanced at me and then instructed me to sit on the other side of the room where I could not see the image he was creating on his sketchpad. After staring at the paper for a minute, Daniel began drawing intently as he described his daily life with frustration in his voice.

"From the minute I get out of school in the afternoon to when I leave in the morning, my aunt and uncle tell me what I can and can't do. It's 24-hours-a-day, non-stop—even on weekends! I have to ask them for permission to do *anything*—play with my toys, talk to my friends, move my clothes into a different dresser drawer, put a picture of my favorite *Star Trek* and *Star Wars* characters on my wall, watch TV—you name it. They try to control everything! They even tell me what I can and can't talk about in therapy. And, they try to make me tell them what we talk about, even though they know they're not supposed to!"

"Whoa! That's too much!" I protested with dismay. "No wonder you're upset!" We sat quietly for a moment, and then I asked, "How do you handle all of their attempts to control what you do?"

Daniel replied, "At first I didn't say anything because I didn't want to get yelled at. But then I couldn't take it anymore. I told them that I was frustrated and mad about them controlling everything I do, but they still didn't get why I was upset." Daniel's voice choked up as he continued, "They just said I had a bad attitude and was being disrespectful and that I should be grateful for everything they were doing for my mom and me."

Then, as Daniel began turning his drawing so I could see it from across the room, he commanded, "Don't say anything."

For a few moments, we sat silently studying his picture. Daniel had drawn the floor plan of his bedroom. On one side of the room was a small boy scrunched up inside a cage that had a large padlock on its door. Knees tucked under his chin and with another padlock on his lips, the boy looked out sadly through the bars of the cage.

On the wall across from him on the other side of the room was a huge clock with black hands. Underneath the clock was the boy's desk, which had another padlock on the main drawer. A TV cabinet was adjacent to the desk. Perched on top of a pile of books that were stacked haphazardly on the desk was a small, padlocked cage that was housing the remote control to the TV. Positioned against another wall of the room was a bare bed.

The edge of a picture frame was protruding out from under the bed. Distorted alien creatures were wafting out from under the glass of the frame, like ghosts rising from a grave. Without comment, Daniel turned the drawing tablet back toward himself and began drawing again.

My heart ached as I continued to watch Daniel and to look at the graphic scenario unfolding on the page before me. After a few minutes passed, I gently reflected, "Words cannot begin to capture how terrible it is to be trapped in a situation that you are powerless to change and where you're not even allowed to speak up for yourself to express just how helpless and angry you feel. It must be a living death to be imprisoned—with no way to get free."

Without looking up from his drawing, Daniel nodded in agreement.

An intrusive and over-controlling parenting style can contain an underlying hostility that permeates how your parent acts. She may reveal her hostile antagonistic attitudes overtly, such as by blatantly criticizing, demeaning, discounting, or rejecting you. Or she may express her hostility covertly, such as by subtly ignoring you or being unfriendly, dismissive, or arrogant toward you.

This hostility, overt or covert, is likely to overwhelm your psychological resources, which usually has a traumatizing effect on your developing mind.

To make relating to an emotionally domineering parent even more difficult is that a person with an emotionally domineering style has a poorly developed ability to empathize. This limitation makes it likely that she will disregard how her attitudes affect others.

In contrast, an empathetic person is able to "get out of her own head," put herself mentally in your position, and imagine what you are experiencing. She does not take on your experience as her own, nor does she become enmeshed with you. Instead, she is able to put her own attitudes on hold while she responds to you, based on who you are, not based on who she wants or needs you to be, thinks you should be, or wishes you were.

In Daniel's situation, although Gina and Mike were providing much needed care for Daniel and said that they loved him (and perhaps did in some ways), they also felt conflicted about the situation. They were distressed about Daniel's mother and her on-going battle with leukemia, which she appeared to be losing.

They also felt torn between the obligation they felt to care for Daniel and their resentment about doing so. They directed their obvious feelings of discontent and hostility at Daniel. Their actions were not just intrusive and over-controlling, they were antagonistic, provocative, and demeaning.

It is clear that their ability to empathize was impaired. They not only disregarded the impact of their attitudes on Daniel, but they also were unable to see the world from his perspective.

Let us consider for a moment how you, as a child, might cope with an emotionally domineering parent.

The Core Attitude You Develop: *Competitive–Controlling*

When a parent operates with an emotionally domineering In Your Face style of parenting, you, as an understudy to your parent, internally record your experience of the domination process. You internalize the way your parent feels and manages her emotions, how she thinks and what she believes, and how she acts. This occurs whether she takes a primarily dominating stance with you or operates so that you as a child dominate her. You also register how you feel, how you make sense out of, and how you try to deal with the domination experience.

In addition, you record how all of these parts work with each other. Over time, these emotionally domineering attitudes and relationship patterns become part of your attitude system and you develop a psychological attachment to them, which affects how you relate to others, the world, and even yourself.

Two common core attitudes that children develop to cope with this situation are a competitive attitude and a controlling attitude.

Coping by developing a competitive attitude. One way to survive psychologically in the face of a parent's domineering over-control is by developing an overly competitive "survival-of-the-fittest" attitude. This attitude attempts to protect you against the distressing feelings (e.g., inadequacy, shame, and vulnerability) that children commonly experience when a parent has an In Your Face parenting style.

A core unhealthy competitive attitude often involves a superior–inferior relationship pattern. In this pattern, you attempt to counteract your parent's frequent psychological impingements by competing to be in the superior role in your relationships, which will put others, in turn, in an inferior position. Your illusion is that being superior to others will make you secure.

Unfortunately, when you attempt to ward off painful feelings and to get your needs met by trying to be superior, you do not actually develop healthy attachments or a sense of self-efficacy, which are both necessary for true internal security. Instead, you maintain the illusion that you are superior to others. You also hold on to your psychological attachment to the internalized emotionally domineering parent system—in which you are in the inferior position.

The emotional component of your competitive attitude develops from both the internally recorded experiences of your parent's domination and your feelings of vulnerability as a child.

Although you may appear strong and powerful to others, under the surface you may actually feel helpless, fearful, anxious, or, at times, even worthless. You may not be aware of these vulnerable feelings. Usually you become aware of them when something puts your superior position at risk, causing you to feel in danger. This sense of being at risk can stimulate the body's fight reactions of anger and resentment as well as your strivings to have the upper hand.

Some common underlying thoughts and beliefs usually operate in an unhealthy competitive core attitude. To compensate for your vulnerable feelings, you can develop beliefs that make you feel superior. Underneath these defensive cognitions, however, beliefs that you are inferior still exist, and they can re-emerge when your competitive efforts to be superior fail.

- "I am safe and secure when I am superior in a relationship."
  "I am not safe and secure when you are the superior one."
- "I am only worthwhile if I am superior."
  "I am not worthwhile if you are superior."
- "I am acceptable and loveable because I am better than you."
  "I am not acceptable or loveable if you are better than me."
- "I have to win my competition with you in order to survive."
  "If you win the competition over me, I will not survive."

You can see that these ways of thinking not only have domineering elements, but they also reveal underlying core feelings of fear, anxiety, and inadequacy. These feelings are associated with the dualistic thought processes.

In a competitive core attitude (as in other attitudes), your feelings and beliefs are intricately tied to your actions. Because you do not feel emotionally secure and you believe your well-being lies in being superior to others, you tend to behave competitively in order to meet your emotional needs.

Consciously or unconsciously, you are constantly trying to determine if others in your life pose a threat to your emotional security and your sense of self-worth. If you feel vulnerable in any way, you are prepared to act in ways that keep others in a less advantageous position.

Your efforts to protect yourself from perceived danger may come out in obvious aggressive ways or in less obvious passive-aggressive ways. When your efforts to maintain superiority become overtly aggressive, you may be angry and hostile. You can find yourself criticizing, demeaning, and disrespecting others. When you are being covert, you express your hostility indirectly (e.g., by complaining about or sabotaging others in some way).

Over the course of Daniel's treatment, Daniel and I had talked many times about the different ways he was trying to manage his aunt and uncle's In Your Face parenting style. Daniel explained to me that before his mother had developed leukemia, he had always been a "good kid," compliantly doing whatever others wanted him to do.

Once his mother became ill (when he was seven), Daniel had begun to feel more frightened, confused, and helpless, due to the many changes and disappointments he was experiencing. At that point, the compliant attitude that he had developed as an understudy to his emotionally enmeshed widowed mother had already begun to shift, and his attitude had become more defiant. However, neither a compliant nor a defiant stance was helping Daniel deal with his losses or his aunt and uncle's emotionally domineering attitudes.

By the time Daniel started therapy, he had become determined to no longer be the underdog in his relationship with Gina and Mike. Daniel was not only being defiant, but he also had developed a competitive attitude in an attempt to deal with Gina and Mike's domineering parenting style.

Nine months into treatment, Daniel was able to verbalize remarkable insight into how he had been trying to cope with a very painful situation.

> "At first, I did what my aunt and uncle wanted because I thought that would help—but it didn't. They still tried to control everything I did. After a while, I couldn't take it anymore. They made me so mad that I decided to stop doing what they said and started doing whatever I wanted. We argued a lot! But mostly I just ignored them. I figured it didn't really matter what I did, because they were on my case all the time anyway. They punished me even when I did what they wanted!"

I commented, "It is very maddening and upsetting to be working so hard to figure out a way to handle a very difficult and painful situation, and then to find that no matter what you do it doesn't really make a difference anyway—that no matter how hard you try, you still feel like you are losing the battle."

Daniel nodded. "But I'm not giving up. What I'm doing now is trying to outsmart them. Every time they try to make me do something, I strategize a way out of the situation so I can outmaneuver them. Sometimes I can talk them out of whatever crazy thing they are saying or unfair punishment they are trying to give me. If that doesn't work, I'll do whatever it takes to keep them from being in control of me.

"One time I even keyed their new car when they weren't home. When they saw the scratch later, they were furious, but it made *me* feel good that I had figured out a way to get back at them!"

Daniel's look of determination deepened as he declared, "Sometimes they win a battle, but I am *not* going to let them win the war!"

I responded, "Even though you are sustaining injuries, you won't give up because it feels like your very survival depends on your winning the war—no matter what it takes—just like the person on your space ship felt when he was under alien attack and was fighting desperately for his life."

Daniel smiled, pleased that I had remembered his drawing from months earlier and had made the connection. "Exactly!"

As treatment progressed, Daniel and I continued working together on ways to navigate and survive the turbulent atmospheric pressures he was experiencing. We continued our efforts to help him develop effective ways of dealing with the alien entities that were inadvertently damaging and threatening to destroy his sense of self.

During this time, in response to questions from the ever curious and thoughtful Daniel, part of our discussion involved clarifying for Daniel the difference between a defensive competitive attitude and a healthy competitive attitude. A defensive competitive attitude is self-focused and does not strengthen relationships.

In contrast, healthy competitiveness values and supports those who are competing, which builds relationships. Healthy competitiveness encourages and challenges the participants to develop and strive toward personal goals that move them beyond their current capabilities.

A healthy competitive attitude involves focusing on what one is moving toward rather than on being superior to others or on pushing others down.

Coping by developing a controlling attitude. Instead of developing a competitive attitude, you may try to cope with a parent who is emotionally domineering by developing an attitude that focuses on power and control.

A central belief in this attitude is that you are only safe and secure if you have power—if you control others. Whether the control is overt or covert, the motivation and focus of this attitude is on obtaining power in order to dominate others.

Unfortunately, whether you are controlling others or they are controlling you, you still feel emotionally vulnerable—even though you may not be aware of it. In fact, you are more likely to be aware of your defensive anger and hostile emotions than your vulnerable feelings.

Your controlling attitude, however, reveals the way you think and what you believe. For example, you may have some of the following common core beliefs:

- "If I have power and control over others, I am important."
  "I am not important if others have power over me."
- "The only way to survive is by controlling others."
  "I will not survive if others have control over me."
- "Others must defer to my control, or I will punish them."
  "I must defer to others' control, or they will punish me."
- "Others are objects to use for my own purposes."
  "I am an object that others will use for their purposes."

These defensive beliefs and ways of thinking, along with your emotions, affect the way you act. You may play out your role as understudy to your emotionally domineering parent by becoming a "good fighter." You may fight to have control over both yourself and others as a way to feel safe and to survive in the world. This is not a competitive fight for superiority. It is a fight for power and control.

When you develop a controlling attitude as a protective strategy, you may, indeed, obtain and exercise power over others. And on some level, you may not feel so helpless and powerless when you are in this position. Unfortunately, your fight response feelings of anger and hostility usually increase, which feeds your sense of vulnerability. This cycle perpetuates your belief that this is the only way to survive. In the process of exerting power and control over others, unfortunately, both you and your relationships ultimately end up damaged.

Although Daniel initially had developed a compliant attitude to deal with his mother's enmeshed parenting style and had been operating with defiant and competitive attitudes to deal with his aunt and uncle's dominating parenting style, none of those coping strategies helped Daniel truly feel safe and secure.

As he gradually discovered this, Daniel began trying to control those around him by bossing them around, just as Gina and Mike were bossing him. He also attempted to control others with passive-aggressive behaviors that left others feeling powerless and angry, just as he was feeling with his aunt and uncle. During this time, Daniel, who had been watching *Star Trek: Voyager* for some time, gave me an "assignment" to watch the program—which I diligently (and pleasurably) did, week after week.

As Daniel continued struggling to deal with his losses and his internal conflicts about everything that was occurring in his life, he was actively engaged in communicating his experience to me. Although there were times that Daniel talked with me about his distress directly, he usually communicated his feelings and thoughts through his drawings.

At this point, Daniel began to re-create in session with me the dynamics of the controller-controlled relationship pattern that was occurring with him and his aunt and uncle. During these times, Daniel (in the controller role) would boss me around, telling me what I could and could not talk about and what we were or were not going to do during our time together. It was clear that my "job" was to take on Daniel's role—the controlled.

Initially Daniel was slightly bossy, and I compliantly "obeyed" his commands. As the enactment progressed, however, Daniel intensified his controlling behaviors, and I began to feel some piece of the oppression that I knew Daniel was feeling with Gina and Mike.

When the time seemed right, I began voicing (on my own behalf and by way of modeling for Daniel) my own feelings and thoughts about being in the controlled position, as well as those that Daniel had been expressing in his drawings and that I imagined he was experiencing.

"I hate it when you boss me around! You act as if you are the only one who is important, and it makes me feel small and unimportant. I feel sad all the time when you are being so controlling. It's like I don't count—I don't matter. You don't let me be myself.

"I feel like my life is getting choked out of me. How am I supposed to know who I am if you don't let me *be* who I am? How am I supposed to feel good about myself when you disrespect me?"

Daniel was delighted when I complained (with tongue in cheek) about my plight. He continued bossing me around for a few more sessions while I persisted in protesting loudly against his over-control.

One day, after a particularly vigorous replay of his experience, Daniel calmed down and sat silently for several moments. Then, looking at me intently, he smiled with chagrin and said to me regretfully, "I'm sorry. I just really wanted you to know exactly what I feel."

"I know," I responded with acceptance and my own sadness about what Daniel was suffering. "And I wanted to let *you* know that I understand how upsetting it is for you."

During one session shortly after this episode, Daniel was lying on the floor busily drawing, when the following interaction occurred.

I commented, "You know, Daniel, I'm glad you wanted me to watch *Voyager*. I really like it."

Daniel looked up, surprised. "What do you like about it?"

I answered enthusiastically, "Well, I *really* like the holodeck. It's a very interesting deck of the ship. It's like simulated reality. When the crewmembers are on the holodeck, everything seems real. Their experiences *feel* real, they *believe* their experiences are real, and what they *do* is experienced as real—*even though they are not.*"

Daniel looked at me thoughtfully, said nothing, and then went back to drawing again.

Over the next few weeks, I would make one comment during each session about the holodeck. I would say things such as, "Some parts of being on the holodeck are cool, but I don't think I would want to live there;" "You know, I think you've lived your whole life on a holodeck;" or "I hope we can help you find a way to get off the holodeck."

Daniel never commented on my remarks. He would simply look up at me for a moment from whatever project he was working on and then return to what he was creating.

One day after I had made a holodeck comment, Daniel finally asked, "What do you mean?"

I replied, "Well, I've been thinking about the situation you are in. It seems like others, especially your aunt and uncle, have all the power (just like the aliens in some of the holodeck programs). You feel so helpless and powerless, and you believe that the only way to survive is to battle with others *in the same way* that they are fighting.

"When I was watching *Voyager* one day, it hit me. When the crewmembers are on the holodeck, they don't realize that they don't actually *have* to keep thinking and acting in ways that keep getting them trapped and wounded by others' weapons and powers. They can actually choose to walk off the holodeck any time they want to.

"I think that the crewmembers and you are more powerful than you all realize. The trouble is, when you live your whole life on a holodeck, you don't know yet that there is another way to operate—even though there is."

Daniel looked at me thoughtfully for a moment and again went back to drawing without any comment.

Over the next several weeks, as Daniel and I continued our discussions of life on the holodeck, Daniel's battles with Gina and Mike at home intensified.

Then one day as Daniel was leaving the office, he slipped past Gina (who was standing in the doorway) into the hallway. Suddenly Daniel popped his head back around her, winked at me, and announced in a conspiratorial tone, "I'm off the holodeck."

Our eyes connected knowingly, and I nodded as I discreetly winked back.

Then, with a quick grin, Daniel ran down the hallway to the waiting room.

Daniel and I continued to process his experience together during the next nine months. We explored further how his life had been on his holodeck. Gradually, as Daniel began facing and conquering his fear of the alien forces that had invaded his young life, he began expressing his sadness and grief about his disappointments and losses more directly.

As a way to help Daniel stay mentally and emotionally connected with me during this time and not feel so alone, I gave him a small "communicator" lapel pin (like the ones the *Star Trek* crew would tap on when they wanted to communicate with each other). He could use the communicator to summon me mentally whenever he needed me. Daniel was delighted!

During this time, Daniel and I also worked to help him develop the capacities and abilities he needed to function effectively. He became more skilled at tuning in to his body's feeling signals and responding to them in helpful ways. He became involved in soccer and basketball as a way to discharge the negative energy and distress that tended to erupt with Gina and Mike's parenting limitations and with setbacks in his mother's health.

And, instead of expressing his feelings and thoughts only through his drawings or problematic, *acting out* behaviors—behaviors that revealed his internal dilemmas indirectly—Daniel began communicating his feelings and thoughts in words that others would be more apt to understand.

As Daniel continued to integrate his painful experiences in new and more meaningful ways, he began making peace with his situation. More aware of and confident in himself and better able to use his power and self-control in beneficial ways, Daniel had begun navigating the turbulence in his life and managing the alien forces with resilience and positive strength.

Summary: Enough Is Enough

When a parent provides Too Much—whether her style of parenting is emotionally enmeshed or domineering—it is difficult to develop healthy attitudes and relationship patterns as you are growing up.

A lack of adequate attunement and challenge interferes with the development of the psychological structures necessary for a clear and positive sense of yourself as a separate, autonomous person. It also makes it difficult for you to function effectively, specifically in relationships, but also in life overall.

In addition, like water dripping continually on a rock, leaving the stone pockmarked and perhaps even fractured, growing up with a parent who continually overloads you can emotionally damage you. It can leave you struggling in the aftermath of a multitude of life-shattering traumatic experiences.

If you, like Maria, Evan, and Daniel, had an emotionally enmeshed or domineering primary caregiver, it may be difficult for you to know who *you* truly are even as an adult. You may have difficulty tuning in to and managing your emotions, your thoughts, and your behaviors effectively.

You may find yourself struggling to regulate your emotions, to be self-reliant and autonomous, and to have a healthy sense of power and control over your life. It may be difficult to feel good about yourself or to function in your relationships in a healthy interdependent way.

If you grew up coping with a parent who provided Too Much, you may have developed attitudes grounded in compliance, defiance, competition, or control. Even so, you do not have to spend your life reinforcing those attitudes.

In fact, with adequate challenge and support from others and committed, informed, and focused work on your part, you can make changes in your attitudes. You can develop the psychological and neurological structures that will make it possible for you to develop internally, to transform your wounds into wisdom, and to live your life with healthier attitudes and relationship patterns.

CHAPTER 4

Attitudes that Develop
When a Parent Provides *Too Little*

It is only when parental feelings are ineffective or too ambivalent ... or when the mother's emotions are temporarily engaged elsewhere, that children not only feel lost but, in fact, get lost. —Anna Freud, *About Losing and Being Lost*

Imagine reaching out to connect with your mother as an infant or small child, and she is not there. Despite your best efforts to find and connect with her, she is not there to provide you with the emotional resources that you need in order to develop a strong, healthy emotional attachment to her. She is not emotionally present or available to engage with you or respond to your psychological needs.

Now, switch to another image. Picture yourself turning toward your mother for support and discovering that sometimes she is emotionally present and lovingly responsive, but at other times, she leaves you all alone in your distress.

Growing up with a mother whose parenting style is *emotionally unavailable* or *emotionally inconsistent* can leave you feeling emotionally alone, adrift, and insecure. These feelings can be exquisitely painful and are likely to occur if your mother provides Too Little of the relational experiences that you need for healthy development.

When a parent is emotionally unavailable or emotionally inconsistent, you fail to develop a secure emotional bond with her, which you need as an infant for both your development and your survival. The lack of adequate maternal emotional attunement and responsiveness also interferes with the development of your capacity to manage your emotions, thought processes, and behaviors in life-enhancing ways.

In order to survive in the face of these distressing gaps in parenting, your childhood survival system develops mechanisms to accommodate your experiences so you can continue to make your way through life. In order to cope with a parent who is emotionally unavailable, you may develop core attitudes grounded in *avoidance* or *detachment* to alleviate your pain. To cope with a parent who is emotionally inconsistent, you may develop core attitudes filled with *confusion* and *ambivalence*.

Before we begin our exploration of these parenting styles that provide Too Little and the effect they can have on the development of your attitudes, take a moment to remind yourself of one of the important principles inherent in how attitudes form.

A mother who provides Too Little is not intentionally trying to create problems for you, although, at times her behaviors may seem intentional to you. Her aim is not to confuse or distress you. And her purpose is not to starve you emotionally or dangle a carrot in front of your nose and then snatch it away.

Instead, in all likelihood, a mother who provides Too Little was not given the support that she needed as a child to develop attitudes that would enable her to meet your psychological needs or her own. She will tend to get caught up in her emotions, thought processes, and familiar ways of acting and have difficulty perceiving what is going on in you—even when she wishes she could.

Her doubts and fears will make it difficult for her to tune in to and support you in your psychological development. In effect, the ways your parent relates to you reveal her limitations and her unresolved internal conflicts.

Although these things may be true about your parent's experience, you must still come to terms with the impact they had on you as a young child, if you are to change your attitudes and save your life. It is important to face the reality that they affect how you live your life today.

Regardless of your parent's intent or desire,
your parent's feelings, thoughts, and actions affected the attitudes
you developed as a child and how you live your life today.

Let us examine how these Too Little parenting styles (emotionally unavailable parenting and emotionally inconsistent) function and how they can affect your early development.

When a Parent Is Emotionally Unavailable

Andre's Story

Andre, a 26-year-old man, came to see me some time ago because he was having difficulty getting motivated to do anything. He was failing some of his courses in night school, had few friends, and was having trouble keeping a job. At the time of the following conversation, we had been meeting for about six months.

"What I remember most about my childhood is feeling alone most of the time," Andre mused. "My mom and dad were always busy with one project or another. They were at work, fixing up the house, helping at church, or doing chores. In a way, they were in their own world of activity. I never felt like I was part of it."

Andre paused and looked directly at me. His whole body exuded the emptiness and sadness he was feeling. He continued, "Then, when Mom started getting sick all the time and Dad had to take on more responsibilities, I felt even more alone."

After a few more minutes of silence, Andre resumed. "I know they were honest, hardworking, and intelligent people. They made sure we always had food, decent clothes, and the other things we needed. They did a great job making sure we learned about all sorts of things like music, history, nature, science, and the world. You name it, we learned about it!

"That part of my childhood was awesome. I feel guilty about saying anything bad about them because they did the best they could. And, after all, they didn't beat us like some parents do."

A slight look of confusion passed across Andre's face, and his shoulders dropped in resignation as he stated flatly, "I guess I don't really have anything to complain about."

I replied, "Despite all the ways your parents cared for you, some part of you hurts when you think about how alone you were during so much of your childhood. And some part of you still feels sad and alone—just like you felt when you were little."

Andre simply nodded and looked off into space.

Andre was trying to make peace with his conflicted feelings about his parents' lack of emotional availability when he was a child. However, when he tried to acknowledge the negative impact of their attitudes on him and his life, he felt that he was betraying them. Unfortunately, Andre's internal battle between his different emotions was making it difficult for him to face and accept the truth about his childhood experience.

A dilemma like this often will emerge when you are working to identify the ways your parents' attitudes wounded you as a child and failed to help you develop psychologically. When this internal conflict occurs, it is helpful to remind yourself not to think in dualistic terms.

Remember, your parents, like all human beings, have areas of particular strengths, weaknesses, adequacies, and inadequacies. These different aspects of your parents contribute to you having a range of complex emotions about your experiences with them, and you may even experience several of these feelings simultaneously.

You can love and appreciate them—but be frustrated, disappointed, and hurt by how they have related to you—all at the same time.

Let us now look more closely at the experience of growing up with an emotionally unavailable parent.

The Parent's Style of Relating: *Missing in Action*

When a parent is Missing in Action, it indicates that she probably was not able to develop healthy attachments as a child. This lack of experience with a secure attachment makes it difficult for her to be emotionally available to you—and to herself—on some level.

It also can interfere with her ability to have empathy—intuitive understanding of feelings and needs—which is an important aspect of emotional availability. If your parent did not experience someone being empathetic with her as a child, she will probably have difficulty empathizing with herself and others, including you.

This unavailability can take the form of your mother being emotionally distant or absent. Whether she is too busy to relate to you, caught up in her own world, or absent, you are not a primary actor in her life's play. Instead, "busyness," distractions, and absence make her indifferent to or neglectful of your needs in some way. And, on some level, she leaves you to fend for yourself.

In addition, a parent with a Missing in Action parenting style often tends to disconnect emotionally from herself and others. If no one ever connected emotionally with your mother, it will be difficult for her to connect with you. This disconnection also interferes with her ability to regulate her own emotional states, leaving her easily and frequently overwhelmed.

When your parent has difficulty managing her emotions this will, in turn, interfere with her ability to help you regulate your emotions. Impairment in emotional availability and regulation can also appear in the form of a tendency to reject, shame, blame, criticize, or judge, which pushes you away and wounds you.

Finally, if your parent is physically not available because of chronic or severe illness, she will, in all likelihood, divert her energy and focus on caring for herself and her health needs.

The Core Attitude You Develop: *Avoidant–Detached*

When you spend your childhood with a parent who is emotionally unavailable, you internalize and record her emotional absence and your experience with her, such as aloneness.

Over time, your developing mind and body also records how you make sense of her absence emotionally and cognitively. As your attitudes form, you develop a set of emotional, cognitive, and behavioral tendencies that you draw from as you deal with her emotional absence.

Your parent's emotional absence operates like the white space in a picture: nothing is there, but the space defines the picture. It defines both your experience and who you become.

When your parent is not available to you emotionally when you are an infant and child, you fail to develop secure attachments to her. Therefore, the attitudes that you develop do not adequately connect your feelings and needs to the experience of being in a relationship.

This lack of connection prevents you from developing a sense of security. Instead of feeling safe and secure when you get close to others, you are more apt to experience distress. To cope with these distressing emotions, you will tend to develop attitudes that cause you to avoid or detach from yourself, close relationships, and life in general.

In my conversation with Andre, he responded to my observation of his deep sadness about being emotionally alone during his childhood. He described how growing up with emotionally unavailable parents affected him and his ability to function in relationships.

"I try not to think about how alone I feel in my relationships—but I can't help being aware of how hard it is for me to feel close to anyone," Andre acknowledged in a flat tone.

"I guess I feel sad too, but mostly I just tune out my feelings and needs. I've been doing it for so long now that a lot of the time it gets to the point that I don't even know *what* I feel. To tell you the truth, sometimes I just don't feel anything at all. My wife complains all the time that I don't deal with things—my feelings, her feelings, problems, needs, plans for the future—whatever."

Andre paused briefly, sighed, and then continued, "Usually I think all this hoopla about feelings is a waste of time. What you feel and need doesn't matter anyway."

Andre was silent for a moment, and then admitted, "My wife is probably right about one thing, though. I guess I do avoid a lot of things. I admit that sometimes I evade things on purpose, but usually I'm not aware that that's what I'm doing. Still, I know that when I put things off, at home or work, it creates problems.

"You know what's weird, though? At times I don't think I'm trying to avoid anything. It's just that things don't matter to me like they do to other people. I've noticed that I often feel detached from other people and from what's happening around me, and I don't care about what's going on.

"The truth is, I'm so used to operating alone that I think I actually prefer it (even though I'd never tell my wife that). Being in my own world can feel a whole lot better than dealing with all the outside stress!"

I responded, "Even though you often feel sad and distant from others and it causes conflict in your relationships, there's a way in which automatically shutting down kind of works for you. It keeps you from feeling so much pain."

If you grow up with a parent who is Missing in Action, over time, you, like Andre, may begin to avoid or to detach from your feelings. These protective mechanisms allow you to restrict or tune out your feelings and needs, just as your parent's lack of emotional availability did when you were an infant and child. That is why, even though these strategies may be helpful in some respects, the reality is that they leave you alone in your pain.

Although avoidance and detachment are related ways of coping, let us consider them separately for a moment.

Coping by developing an avoidant attitude. When your parent is emotionally absent as you are growing up, you fail to receive the resources you need to develop a secure emotional bond. The lack of this connection is anxiety provoking and very painful, so you may cope with her lack of availability by developing a core avoidant attitude. The illusory mantra is, "If I avoid situations that might cause me to feel distress, I will feel fine."

The emotional component of an avoidant attitude can appear in different forms. Because you did not receive adequate support in experiencing and caring for your emotions, you tend to perceive and experience emotions in a negative light and attach negative meanings to feelings. And because your parent was not available emotionally to help you learn to regulate your emotions, you have difficulty regulating them. So to cope, you tend to over-regulate your emotions through avoidance or under-regulate them by failing to provide yourself with the emotional stimulation you need. Like Andre, you may do this by not letting yourself know what you like or want, or by trying to make things not "matter" to you.

Unfortunately, these strategies can leave you feeling apathetic or unmotivated. While striving to avoid what you perceive as bad (e.g., emotional closeness, pain, or unmet longings), you miss the good (i.e., healthy emotional attachments and living fully).

In addition, when you are avoidant, it is difficult to engage emotionally with others. Connections with others, instead of being emotionally safe havens, become a source of anxiety, causing you to avoid emotional intimacy.

You may also find that you are hypersensitive to the influence and control of others, making it hard for you to trust and causing you to resist any sense of obligation to others. Being emotionally vulnerable is just too anxiety provoking.

If you observe yourself closely as you process these emotional experiences, you will begin to see how you tend to minimize emotions and the importance of relationships. And you will begin noticing beliefs that reveal your avoidant attitudes:

- "Feelings don't matter; they just make life difficult."
- "There's no point in wanting anything; you won't get it."
- "People don't *really* care about what you feel, think, or need."
- "People are more trouble than they're worth."

Your avoidant thoughts and beliefs, interacting with the emotions associated with them (e.g., anxiety and tension), affect how you tend to act. To cope with the absence of a secure attachment to your parent, you can become overly independent, disengaging from others and avoiding being dependent at all costs, since dependence evokes feelings of vulnerability.

Or you might find yourself focusing on the broader world because it is more distant and generally less anxiety provoking than relating to others who are part of your personal life. Avoiding your own issues, you may wrap yourself up in others' concerns.

Both scenarios result in relational patterns that involve avoiding emotional closeness.

Coping by developing a detached attitude. When you reach out to connect and no one is there in any useful way, it can be so distressing that you may begin not only to avoid emotions and relationships but also to detach from them.

If this happens frequently or long enough, you can try to survive emotionally by totally shutting down your awareness of your feelings and needs in many areas. You can "numb out," not feeling much of anything. This disconnection is protective on some level, in that it prevents you from being overwhelmed with distress, but it interferes with your ability to care for yourself and to function effectively.

When you have a core detached attitude, your mind attaches negative meanings to emotions and connections with others. Just as with avoidant attitudes, you have difficulty trusting and are uncomfortable with intimacy, vulnerability, and dependence. But if, and when, you become aware of your feelings, you realize that you feel disconnected from others. Inside you are deeply alone.

Because reliance on others has not met your needs and it is too painful to experience unfulfilled longings for emotional connection, you can begin to focus on yourself and the world in order to survive. This can appear cognitively in the form of conscious or unconscious thoughts and beliefs:

- "It doesn't matter what others do; I just do my own thing."
- "Others are needy, I am not; I am, therefore, superior to others."
- "I'm in my own world, and I prefer it that way."
- "Take care of yourself; others are unnecessary or a 'necessary evil.'"

If you stop tuning in to your emotions or reaching out to connect with others altogether, after a while, it may never even cross your mind to look for comfort or soothing from others, or even yourself.

Instead, you find yourself operating under unconscious assumptions that you are on your own and no one is available to care for you. You may develop strong needs for privacy, using these needs as a reason to disengage from relationships entirely.

You might even resort to fantasy relationships instead of real ones in order to protect your illusion of independence and control. Relating to others in your imagination can seem safer than dealing with here-and-now relationships.

This overly independent, detached style of coping reminds me of terrariums. A terrarium is a collection of houseplants grown in an enclosed, clear container. If the container stays sealed, terrariums need a minimum of care, because the plants develop their own ecosystem. The plants absorb moisture from the soil and release it through the leaves. The moisture then condenses on the glass walls and runs down to moisten the soil again. The atmosphere in the container also remains balanced through other plant processes. For plants to grow in a terrarium, all they need from outside the container is some light and warmth—and not very much of those.

When you cope with your emotionally unavailable parent by becoming overly self-sufficient, your "ecosystem" may maintain you for a time.

It can even seem like a great way to operate—for a while. Like Andre, you may find that detachment keeps you from feeling distress about your aloneness. You can also feel proud of yourself for being able to take care of things on your own. Others might even give you recognition and praise for your independence, not realizing it is unhealthy independence or even detachment.

At some point, however, whether you developed an avoidant or a detached attitude, the illusion of safety inherent in these attitudes may begin to crumble. You then begin realizing that you do not feel secure internally, despite your belief that you are safe when you are not relating. When this awareness occurs, it can be a very disorienting and even frightening experience.

True internal security emerges from the experience of having been in a secure relationship. This experience makes it possible for you to establish interdependent relationships with others—relationships that provide for healthy mutual engagement. Failure to develop this capability will take a toll on your life, just as it did for Andre.

Moreover, since you are not a terrarium, you cannot totally seal yourself off from those around you. Eventually, conflicts in your relationships develop because of the avoidant and detached attitudes you developed early in life in order to survive in the face of your parent's emotional absence. And conflicts are stressful.

In addition, the lack of a strong support network will have a negative impact on your physical and emotional health. Strong, supportive relationships help buffer the distress that is often part of life. They help diminish your stress levels which, in turn, enhances your body's ability to function.

When you become overwhelmed emotionally and physically, it depletes your vitality. If the primary way you operate in life is to avoid and detach from others and from engagement with life (flight responses), your ability to function at home and work will begin to suffer. A closed system cannot maintain itself forever.

Your unmet needs and wounded parts of yourself will continue to create pain in your life until you care for them adequately by grieving your losses and healing your wounds.

It is painful to spend your childhood with a caregiver who is emotionally unavailable and leaves you stranded on an emotional desert island. It is even more distressing to live with the pain of those early years of emptiness and aloneness reverberating throughout a lifetime.

So remind yourself that, although you could not choose the circumstances of your childhood, you can choose the paths you will travel on your journey as an adult.

You can choose the paths that make it possible for you to create a different ending to your life story by healing your wounds and changing your core attitudes of avoidance and detachment.

As you do, you will be saving yourself from a life lived in an emotional and relational wasteland.

When a Parent Is Emotionally Inconsistent

The Story of the Little Boy and the Hidden Ball

The little boy stood, mesmerized, in front of the magician's table. He watched as the magician tucked a ball under one of the cups—then watched that cup with eagle eyes as the magician shuffled it in and out among the other cups. As the magician whirled the cups around on the table, the little boy was sure he knew where the ball was hiding.

"Which cup is the ball under? Pick one," the magician ordered. He knew the little boy was longing to win the promised prize that came with the discovery of the ball's location.

The child confidently pointed to the middle cup. "That one," he declared.

The magician's skillful fingers deftly lifted the cup, but the boy had drawn a blank. There was no ball; there was just air under that cup. The child's body slumped with disappointment.

Determined to find the hidden ball so he could win the prize, the little boy rallied himself and insisted on playing the game again—over and over—round after round. "Now you see it, now you don't." But with each round, the child was becoming less and less certain of where the ball was—and more and more frustrated because he could not figure it out. The pattern of the movements was never the same.

Now and then, the little boy got lucky and picked the right cup. Most of the time, however, he did not. Part of him wanted to leave the game table, escape, and go anywhere else but there. Another part of him could not pull his eyes away from the cups and unseen ball as the magician continued to weave the cups and ball in and out. "Now you see it, now you don't."

The Parent's Style of Relating: *Now You See Me, Now You Don't*

Life with a parent whose parenting style is emotionally inconsistent is like the experience of the boy watching the magician maneuvering the ball— Now You See Me, Now You Don't.

Sometimes your mother is able to be aware of and be attentive to you emotionally, which makes it possible for her to respond to you in ways that match what you need. At these times, she is able to provide the affirmation, comfort, emotional connection, and healthy independence that you need. Because this nurturing feels so wonderful, you feel drawn to this part of her. Being with her in these moments is exciting, like finding the ball under the magician's cup. The care and excitement are irresistible!

Unfortunately, an emotionally inconsistent parent has two significant limitations. First, it is difficult for her to be aware of, tune in to, stay connected with, and regulate emotional needs and states consistently. As she was growing up, her ability to function in these ways emotionally and cognitively did not adequately develop.

This impairment leaves her with significant anxiety, fear, and tendencies to react to emotional states, rather than being able to regulate them. In addition, her thought processes—often erratic, with conflicting thoughts and beliefs—interfere with her being able to consistently be aware of and focus on what she or others need. Because of this, it is difficult for her to use the cognitive part of her mind to help care for emotions.

Second, it is difficult for her to perceive, discern, and identify emotions accurately and consistently. Because this part of her is not well developed, she often misreads and misunderstands her own and others' emotional states. Since she has trouble coordinating emotions with cognitions and interpreting and assigning meaning to her experience accurately, she will tend to attribute meanings to your feelings, thoughts, and actions that are inaccurate.

These misperceptions and inaccurate meanings interfere with your caregiver's ability to respond to you in a way that matches what you feel or truly need when you need it. Sometimes she "gets it right," and sometimes she does not.

You can observe these difficulties in the ways your parent acts:

- You need to play creatively and explore with your imagination; your parent might let you play the way you need, or she might make you play a game—according to the rules.

- You need comfort; your parent may give you some comfort, or she might leave you crying alone in your room, or tell you that you are not *really* upset.
- You need help to learn a new task; your parent may do it for you, or she may try to help you, or she may bark at you, telling you to figure it out yourself.
- You are withdrawn and sad; she gets angry with you and says you are being bratty and "just pouting."
- You make a mistake on your school project and feel bad about it; she may reassure you, or she may punish you for your "failure," or she might lecture you, saying you should have tried harder.

Life with a parent who is emotionally inconsistent is truly confusing and unpredictable. Sometimes she provides Too Much. Other times she offers Too Little.

At times, what she provides matches your needs, but other times her responses may be a mismatch for your needs. For example, on one occasion, she may be sensitive, loving, reasonable, and playful; the next, she may be irritable, angry, irrational, or punitive. She may be too involved with you at times and other times forget about you altogether.

Because your parent's attitudes are erratic, you cannot predict if, when, or how your parent will meet your emotional needs. Her capricious ways of relating to others—and to herself—leaves you not knowing what you can count on, or even if you can count on anything. This uncertainty leaves you feeling anxious because you simply do not know what her response will be.

Even so, like the little boy lured into trying to find the hidden ball, a force within draws you toward your elusive parent, which keeps alive your hope that you will eventually find the prize.

When you approach your parent in search of the emotional resources you need, you do not know what will happen—this time. You are not sure whether or not your parent will be there. Now You See Me, Now You Don't. And you are not sure whether she will know who you truly are. Now You See *Me*, Now You Don't.

The only thing you can predict and rely on
with an emotionally inconsistent parent
is that she will be inconsistent and unpredictable.

Your eye is on the ball—you *know* what cup conceals the treasure. Swish! The cups begin to move ... Your excitement mounts. Then you make your choice, and the magician lifts the cup. Suddenly, you are confused. Uncertain. Where did she go—the parent who was at least *trying* to be sensitive to you and to provide for your emotional needs in the best way that she could? She was just here! Now she is emotionally absent.

Your eyes shift back to the activity as it resumes. You are feeling more and more apprehensive. Again and again, you attempt to track the unseen ball while the cups are being maneuvered in and out. This time when the cups stop their dance, you hesitate over which one to choose.

In your uncertainty and doubt, you have difficulty trusting your ability to know what to do. You lack the security of knowing you can trust yourself. Unsure, you go back and forth, trying to decide which cup to choose.

What happens to you as a small child in this emotionally inconsistent world in which you live? What do you take in and record of your experience? What attitudes do you develop to survive?

The Core Attitude You Develop: *Confused–Ambivalent*

When a parent offers you the enticing promise of providing something you need emotionally but fails to deliver, she wounds you psychologically. This is not intentional but is due to the nature of the parent-child relationship.

Nevertheless, when your parent provides Too Little emotionally, your longings for an emotionally available, nurturing parent build up and then become dashed—over and over.

When this occurs, you end up experiencing multiple emotional connections followed by disconnections. Whether her promise is explicit or implicit, by virtue of her position as your parent, her failure to relate consistently breaks your heart.

Instead of becoming the base for secure relationships, your needs for consistent and predictable love and nurturing end up becoming the source of painful internal distress and conflict.

Because you are an understudy to your parent, as you internalize and record her inconsistent attitudes and your experience of her, you will tend to develop core attitudes of confusion or ambivalence to mitigate your distress.

Coping by developing a confused attitude. As you interact with your inconsistent parent, you take in all the confusion, anxiety, and internal conflict about emotional connections that prevent her from being emotionally available to you in a reliable way.

In the process of internalizing these aspects of her and recording your experience with her, you can develop a core attitude of confusion.

Emotionally, anxiety is the key driver of this attitude, and it causes you to feel uncertain much of the time. Even though you try to read your and others' emotional signals, you have difficulty tuning in to, recognizing, and staying present with your own and others' emotions.

You are not certain whether you do or do not feel or want something. You mistrust your feelings, especially your dependent feelings. Without a clear, consistent pattern of relating, you are unable to develop a safe solution to getting your needs met. Neither connecting nor disconnecting emotionally fulfills your needs. Life is often unsettling.

Cognitively, you have difficulty being aware of and thinking about what you feel and think and how you act. These limitations make it difficult for you to make sense out of your experience, making life seem very complicated.

In your confusion, you find yourself feeling off balance, bewildered, and lost. Pieces of different attitudes appear and disappear, leaving you to vacillate about what you feel, think, and believe about yourself and others. Life is often perplexing.

You are confused about how to interact with others because the relationship pattern you internalized provided no clear relational pattern. For example, you move toward someone or something, and then uncertainty and confusion flood over you and you hold back. Sometimes you fail to reach out, and you miss the opportunity for a positive experience. Other times you reach out and get hurt again. At times when you try to relate, you feel better. You just do not know how to read yourself or others or how to operate in a relationship.

You cycle unconsciously and repeatedly through these confused ways of relating. They are automatic and reflexive. Your mother's difficulties with her emotions, ways of thinking and believing, and her action tendencies, which resulted in her emotional inconsistency, have now become part of your attitude system.

Coping by developing an ambivalent attitude. Over time, as you internalize and record the painful, inconsistent experiences with your parent, you might develop a sense that the world is unpredictable and that it is unsafe to rely on others.

Instead of becoming emotionally secure, you are left feeling anxious, even fearful, about attachments to others. Anxiety and fear, which are at odds with your attachment needs, set the stage for a core ambivalent attitude.

Ambivalence occurs when you have both positive and negative feelings toward someone or something that pull you in opposite directions, such as when you feel both attracted to and repelled by something simultaneously.

The internal conflict between these opposing psychological demands or impulses usually creates intense mental tension. And, just as the young boy felt torn between his desire to find the magician's ball and his fear of disappointment, frustration, and failure, you may feel pulled between what you need and long for and what you fear.

Emotionally, the tension between opposing internal forces may cause you to be highly ambivalent about forming close relationships. On the one hand, you have significant feelings of anxiety. You may find yourself longing to be close to someone so that your anxiety will subside and you can feel safe and secure. On the other hand, your experience informs you that relationships are emotionally unsafe, so you fear closeness.

You may be especially fearful that others will abandon you. Reaching out, or even thinking about reaching out, to get your healthy needs for recognition, affirmation, and acknowledgment met can evoke the same feelings of insecurity that you experienced with your emotionally inconsistent parent.

Because of this, you may find yourself actively resisting forming attachments with others. Deep inside you two opposing powerful forces fight against each other. To be emotionally attached, or not to be emotionally attached? That *is* the question.

> *Ambivalence can become the driving force*
> *in how you feel, what you think, and how you act*
> *in your relationships and in the world.*

The ambivalence that develops as you experience your parent's emotionally inconsistent parenting also affects how and what you think and believe. Over time, as you internalize and record your parent's style of relating, you are likely to develop the strong belief that the world and everyone in it are as inconsistent and unpredictable as your parent is.

In addition, other related conflicting thoughts develop, whether or not you are aware of them. All of these discordant thoughts and beliefs can generate an internal tug-of-war with different cognitions and emotions pitted against each other (e.g., relate or do not relate; trust or do not trust).

Eventually, your thoughts and beliefs begin to reveal the tension between your conflicted feelings and thought processes:

- "I cannot count on anyone."
   "I must have someone to care for me."
- "I am weak and powerless and need someone to help me."
   "I do not need anyone; I can take care of myself."
- "I deserve to be loved, and I want to get close to others."
   "I won't survive if I get close to others."

Recall, for a moment, our discussion that the emotional, cognitive, and behavioral components of attitudes constantly interact with and reinforce each other. An emotionally inconsistent parenting style does not provide the experiences necessary for you to develop secure attachments. Nor do these experiences help you develop an internal confidence that you can care for yourself.

Instead, as you internalize and record your experiences, you develop deep feelings of vulnerability and inadequacy. You also form beliefs that you are powerless to get your needs met or that it is too painful to attempt to get them met in a relationship. You continually focus on what others feel, think, and do rather than on yourself and your attitudes.

In addition, when your feelings of helplessness and anxiety interact with these conflicting thoughts and beliefs, two common action tendencies may develop as part of your core ambivalent attitude. You may become overly dependent in your relationships, or you may become counter-dependent in how you relate with others and the world.

Because your needs for safety and security conflict with your fear of closeness and healthy attachments, you are likely to switch back and forth between these two survival modes. Let us consider these two action tendencies for a moment.

Overly dependent action tendencies. To handle all of the distress that emotionally inconsistent parenting evokes, you may become overly dependent on others as a way to meet your emotional needs. This excessive dependence can occur with both confused and ambivalent attitudes. Unfortunately, despite your hope that others will provide your unmet maternal needs and your belief that others can provide them, no one else can fill the void left from your early parent-child experiences.

Because you lack a core sense of confidence that you can care for your needs, this reality is frightening. Nevertheless, relying on others to meet your needs, even though it is painful when they fail to come through for you, can feel safer than feeling adrift with nothing, which can be terrifying.

Unfortunately, several problems tend to arise when you are overly dependent and look to others to provide the emotional resources that you failed to receive early on. When you try to please others and live up to their expectations instead of developing the ability to care for your unmet needs, you inadvertently reinforce and perpetuate your insecure, ambivalent attitudes. The more you fail to act in ways that care for yourself, the more anxious you become and the more you believe you cannot care for yourself.

Your passivity and lack of coping skills also leave you anxious, insecure, and hyper-vigilant in your relationships, and it may be difficult for you to regulate these emotions. Your constant internal pressure to have your early emotional needs met can result in your becoming clingy and possessive.

When this occurs, you continue to expect others to meet your needs, even though your needs are excessive and insatiable. Because clingy, demanding behaviors usually evoke distress in others, others may eventually push you away because they feel overwhelmed by your neediness.

In addition, your emotional hunger puts you at risk of being victimized because, in your desire for someone to meet your needs, you may unwittingly turn to those who prey on the weak and vulnerable. These emotional predators hold out the promise of love and power but then intentionally mistreat and harm you.

Counter-dependent action tendencies. Instead of attempting to resolve your distressing emotional tug-of-war by becoming overly dependent, you may become counter-dependent in your relationships with yourself, others, and the world. When you have a counter-dependent ambivalent attitude, instead of letting yourself experience your healthy emotional needs for affection and support, you may develop overly independent or oppositional life scripts in an effort to deny your needs and feel safe.

When enacting overly independent scripts, you may find yourself becoming fearful when others approach you or you are drawn to others. To alleviate your distress, you find a way to keep others at a distance, either by avoiding them or by actively pushing them away. When you distance yourself in these ways, neither of you gets your needs met. You also become isolated emotionally, which increases your need for closeness, which then draws you back toward the connection.

If you act out your ambivalence and counter-dependence through oppositional life scripts, you may find yourself angrily opposing, resisting and defying others overtly or covertly. These ways of coping with your fears, whether conscious or unconscious, keep you from functioning effectively in your personal and work relationships.

Your intent may be to ward off your feelings of anxiety and fear about being dependent, but these scripts alienate you from others, increasing your anxiety. In addition, your hostility, defiance, and rejection of others are likely to wound them as well.

Regardless of your behavioral style, counter-dependent attitudes reveal that you are holding onto the illusionary beliefs that you do not need others or that the only way to be emotionally safe is to resist emotional attachments altogether. These beliefs, based in denial, do not change what is real and true, however—emotional connections with safe people are crucial for your well-being. In addition, instead of removing your wounds, these beliefs exacerbate them, increasing your vulnerability and putting you at risk for further emotional injury.

Whether you cope with your emotionally inconsistent parent by developing attitudes of confusion or of ambivalence, these attitudes do not meet your emotional needs. In addition, although excessive dependence and counter-dependence can feel protective, in actuality, they reinforce your confused and ambivalent attitudes.

Fortunately, you can transform this unhelpful and unfulfilling childhood survival system. You can choose to begin developing the ability to stay present with your emotions and thoughts rather than avoid or detach from them.

As you learn to observe and tolerate your emotions and thoughts, they will become less confusing and frightening. Over time, out of the jumble of conflicting components, psychological structures will emerge that will support a true sense of internal safety and security.

Summary: Too Little Is Not Enough

When your primary caregiver provides Too Little (whether she is emotionally absent or inconsistent), you fail to develop core attitudes that promote secure attachments with others and healthy interdependence.

Instead, if your mother was emotionally absent, you may try to handle your feelings of vulnerability by avoiding or detaching from connections with yourself, others, and the world. Or if your mother was emotionally inconsistent, you may find yourself struggling with confusion or ambivalence in many areas of your life, especially those involving relationships.

You may try to cope with the feelings of vulnerability inherent to a relationship with a parent who provides Too Little by becoming inconsistent, due to your confusion, or by becoming overly dependent or counter-dependent, due to your ambivalence. Regardless of the modes of self-protection that you develop, they will keep you from functioning effectively in many dimensions of your life.

Each of these coping maneuvers sacrifices parts of you in some way. When a primary caregiver provides Too Little, your much-needed capacity for interdependence becomes impaired. If you are excessively dependent, your ability to function as a separate, autonomous person who can take charge of your life fails to develop adequately.

When you are counter-dependent, whether by being overly independent or oppositional, you fail to support the part of yourself that needs healthy attachments with others. Counter-dependence not only leaves you without the resources you need to develop who you truly are, but it also actively alienates you from yourself and others.

Whether you develop attitudes based on avoidance, detachment, confusion, or ambivalence to adapt to your parent who provided Too Little, your unconscious illusions frequently hold you hostage:

- the illusion that avoiding or detaching from yourself, others, or life will protect you from the pain experienced with an emotionally absent mother;
- the illusion that being confused about what you feel or think will keep you safe or get others to provide what you lack internally;
- the illusion that maintaining your ambivalence about closeness to others by being overly dependent or counter-dependent will fulfill your needs and keep you from feeling the pain of loss;
- the illusion that others are your only source of safety, security, and power.

Regardless of which core attitudes you may have developed growing up with a parent who provided Too Little, at some point, you start becoming aware that none of these illusions provides for your unmet emotional needs. Trying to be a self-contained ecosystem will not provide the nutrients you need nor heal your wounds. Continuing to play the magician's game in hopes that you can someday discover the prize you long for will never bring you peace or fulfillment.

Over time, you discover that illusions and temporary feelings of safety do not provide the long-term internal security that you need in order to live your life fully. You begin to glimpse the reality that you are sacrificing the truest part of yourself in your unrewarding efforts to be safe and secure.

The idea of developing safe relationships may seem frightening or even impossible. Nevertheless, these relationships will help you in your efforts to heal the emotional wounds you have incurred during childhood with an emotionally unavailable or inconsistent parent. These healthy attachments will also support you as you dismantle your unfulfilling emotional, cognitive, and behavioral patterns centered in avoidance or ambivalence.

Moreover, these connections, however fledgling, will begin to empower you as you do the work of developing new attitudes grounded in a secure and confident sense of yourself. Taking the risk to travel down this pathway on your heroic journey will make it possible for you to transform your wounds into wisdom and truly save your life.

CHAPTER 5

Attitudes That Develop
When a Parent Provides *Just Right*

Healthy parenting is an art that creates a safe, structured, emotionally attuned,
consistent, and reliable holding space in the heart and home in which each child
can flourish. —Audrey Seaton-Bacon, *Parenting the Self*

Ideally, from the moment of conception, your mother and you begin an awesome creative project. The goal of the project is to transform you from a minute speck of a fetus into a tiny, helpless infant, and then, eventually, into a secure, confident, fully functioning adult. You and your mother work *together* on this project as you are growing up, whether or not you realize it.

Your parent's mission—should she choose to accept it—is to both challenge and support you on your journey of emotional, cognitive, relational, physical, educational, and spiritual development. However daunting this may be at times, it is important that your parent provide the experiences that not only stimulate your growth in each of these areas, but that also sustain your movement forward, thus optimizing your development.

If your parent provides for your needs adequately, an internal core sense of security develops in your internal operating system during this process. This security enables you to take care of your needs with confidence and in ways that support mutuality.

The type of challenge and support you need from your parent varies based on your age and particular capacities. Regardless of the form it takes, however, it affects the formation of your attitudes. In turn, the functioning of the emotional, cognitive, and behavioral parts of your mind and body determines who you are and how your life unfolds.

This mission to be the facilitator of your development can seem impossible to your parent at times—but it is not! However unattainable this undertaking and goal may seem, what is true is that:

Neither your parent nor you need to be perfect for you
to develop a stable and healthy sense of internal security.

What *is* necessary, however, is that your mother provides you with sufficient (not perfect) psychological resources for you to establish a secure attachment with her in early infancy. In order for this to occur, she must be *emotionally accessible* to you in consistent, reliable, and predictable (but adaptable) ways.

A *secure attachment* with your mother as an infant and small child will enable you to form healthy attitudes and relationship patterns. The parenting provided by this type of mother is *Just Right.*[3]

As we continue our exploration of Just Right parenting and the attitudes that develop from it, let us consider Roxy's story.

When a Parent Is Emotionally Accessible

Roxy's Story

Roxy was a thirty-year-old single mother who first came to see me some years ago because she was struggling with multiple losses. Her recent breakup with John, her baby's father, as well the unresolved childhood losses that the ending of that relationship had triggered, had opened a Pandora's Box of unresolved grief.

The deluge of emotional pain Roxy was experiencing was more than she could handle. She was becoming more and more depressed and anxious. And she was finding herself increasingly angry in a way she had experienced in the past. Roxy was particularly worried about how her emotional distress might be affecting her two-year-old daughter, Adrianne.

Early in therapy, Roxy described her history and concerns this way.

"I've been having a really hard time coping with John leaving us. It has stirred up all my feelings from when I was a kid. For years, my dad had cheated on my mom, disappearing on us for months on end. Then, out of nowhere, he'd pop up at the house for several days, before taking off again.

---

[3] Donald Winnicott, a well-known British pediatrician and child psychoanalyst, refers to the mother who provides adequate emotional resources for her child's growth and development as a *good enough mother* (Winnicott, 1953, p. 89–97). I will be using the terms "good enough" and "Just Right" interchangeably.

The last straw was when I was ten years old and my dad moved to the Midwest with his new family, leaving our family for good. I was so mad at him! We needed him, and he wasn't there.

"My mom did her best to raise us all by herself, and she was there for us as much as she could be. But it was tough because Mom had to work long hours to bring in enough money to support the family. I could see that she needed help so I worked hard to take the load off her by being a good kid so she could be happy. I guess I also took on the mother role by taking care of the chores and my three brothers and baby sister."

Roxy paused briefly and then said in a forlorn voice, "When I was a kid, I knew my mom loved me. But I wish she had been able to be there more for me emotionally."

After a moment, Roxy continued, "In many ways, nothing in my life has changed except that now I'm the single mom whose partner has left her alone with a daughter to raise. My mom is still working hard, and I'm still trying to keep my mom happy and to get everyone to grow up and get their lives together. It's overwhelming!

"I'm sick of the others in my family not being responsible for themselves. Things are not totally bad, though. I guess the two things I feel best about in my life are that I'm doing well at my job, and I *think* I'm being a pretty good mother to Adrianne.

"But I *am* concerned that my moods since the breakup with John might be having a negative effect on Adrianne. I do *not* want her to have the same childhood I had! I don't want her to grow up feeling as if she has to take care of me and to keep me happy like I feel about my mom. It wasn't right that I was made to feel so responsible. In any case, I want to take care of Adrianne, and I know it's *my* job to take care of her!"

I responded, "You've experienced so many painful losses over the years and have been struggling to feel emotionally safe and secure in your family for so long. … But despite all that you have had to manage, you have always worked very hard to provide Adrianne with the emotional support she needs so that she doesn't have to suffer in the ways that you suffered—and still do."

Despite the past and present negative stressors in her life, Roxy was on a mission. She was determined to give Adrianne the emotional security she herself had not experienced when she was a child. She was working diligently to be a good enough mother to her daughter—the best she knew how.

Roxy had begun therapy with me to get help re-stabilizing emotionally so she could parent more effectively. She was aware that her difficulty dealing with the recent ending of her relationship with Adrianne's father was interfering with her ability to be emotionally available to their daughter.

As her treatment progressed, Roxy quickly came to recognize that she needed to work on her unresolved losses in order to help Adrianne develop a sense of internal security.

Indeed, the cornerstone of Roxy's work involved developing the ability to relate to both herself and Adrianne in emotionally healthy and reliable ways.

Let us consider what it means to be reliably available emotionally.

The Parent's Style of Relating: *Reliably Available*

There are four key capacities and skills—all hallmarks of Just Right parenting—that enable a mother to be Reliably Available to her child on an emotional level:

- The parent develops and nurtures her own internal security.
- The parent develops a secure attachment with her child.
- The parent regulates her own and her child's emotions.
- The parent manages the unavoidable disruptions in her emotional availability.

Let us look at these capacities and skills in more depth.

The parent develops and nurtures her own internal security. Remember for a moment the last time you flew on a plane. You squeezed your carry-on bags into the overhead bin and buckled up for safety. Then the flight attendant instructed those traveling with children that in the event that oxygen became necessary, they were to put on their oxygen masks before attending to their children. A mother cannot help her child if she passes out in the seat next to the youngster!

Like a parent traveling with her child on an airplane, your parent needs to be sufficiently psychologically secure in herself in order to help you develop an internal sense of security. It is important to remember that internal security is not an all-or-nothing state of being, however. A person may feel internally secure in some situations but find that other situations reveal areas of insecurity.

Nevertheless, it is important that a parent develop both her and your sense of internal security. She does this in two foundational ways.

The parent takes ownership of her own emotional growth process. A parent who provides Just Right parenting accepts the reality that only she can make the decisions and take the steps necessary to develop her sense of internal security. She also assumes responsibility for helping you become emotionally secure. For example, in Roxy's case, no one else could choose for her how she would deal with the multiple disappointments and losses she had experienced.

Only Roxy could repair the wounds she had incurred from the loss of her father and her mother's limited emotional availability. No one else could deal with Roxy's depression, anxiety, and anger that had developed in the aftermath of the breakup with Adrianne's father.

Finally, Roxy was the only one who could develop her ability to relate to herself and Adrianne in healthy ways. (We will explore the issue of taking ownership of your life in more depth later on.)

The parent becomes a good parent to herself. It is common for a parent to have a deep desire to provide her child with all the emotional support she herself had missed when she was a child. In order to progress toward this goal, however, the parent needs first to become a good parent to herself.

**To develop internal security as an adult,
you have to take ownership of your life and become a good mother
to yourself—to care for yourself emotionally.**

Unfortunately, when an individual grows up with a parent who provided Too Much or Too Little, she has not experienced adequate reliable emotional availability and responsiveness with her own parent. This limitation can make taking ownership of her life and becoming a good parent to herself (and to you) very challenging.

Remember, both the helpful and unhelpful attitude scripts the parent developed from her internalizations as a small child will affect what the parent is able to provide you.

In Roxy's case, Roxy had internalized many positive interactions with her mother. However, many of the emotionally supportive experiences she needed in order to feel secure in herself and in her relationships had been missing. Her parents' emotional difficulties, the trauma of her father's desertion, and the necessity for her mother to work long hours had all interfered with Roxy's ability to establish a strong sense of internal security.

Roxy was desperate to change the caretaking and aggressive attitudes she had developed as a child because she could see that they were reinforcing her agitated depression, anxiety, and angry outbursts. She could also see that they were disrupting her ability to care for Adrianne.

Because Roxy's experience with emotionally available and reliable parenting had been very limited, we frequently discussed the nature of good enough mothering. It was important that Roxy cognitively understand these characteristics. More importantly, it was crucial that I remain emotionally available and reliable so she could *experience* these qualities *in relationship*.

It was only as Roxy internalized the experience of healthier attitudes and relationship patterns that she was able to do the necessary work of changing her attitudes and developing a stronger, more stable sense of internal security. Only then could she become a Just Right parent to herself.

The contrast between what Roxy was coming to know about her past relationships and what she was experiencing in the relationship with me prompted her to revisit, confront, and, at last, grieve the reality of just how unreliably present her parents had been. As part of that grieving, Roxy was developing a renewed sense of appreciation for all her mother had given her.

The parent develops a secure attachment with you. In order to develop a secure attachment pattern with you, it is important that your parent interact with you in several important ways.

Your parent is emotionally available to you. In order to bond securely with your parent, it is important that she stay emotionally present, available, and accessible to you in consistent, predictable ways. Being present and available inconsistently or rarely is not sufficient to help you develop the internal sense of security you need.

In addition, it is also not enough for her simply to be present. To be truly emotionally available, she must also *focus her attention* on you, and *perceive* your physical and emotional feelings and needs.

As was mentioned earlier, being emotionally available does not mean your parent has to focus on and stay tuned in to you every minute of every day—that is simply not possible. Nevertheless, it is crucial to your development that she be emotionally available to you in *reliable, consistent,* and *predictable* ways—enough for you to develop a secure attachment with her.

When your primary caretaker is present for you in these ways, you, as her understudy, internally record the experience of being safe and secure in relationship. You also develop a sense of self. The internalization of these experiences becomes part of your core attitudes and relationship patterns, making it possible for you to be available to yourself and others.

Your parent is responsive to you. In order for you to develop attitudes grounded in security, it is also imperative that your parent be responsive to you and meets your needs. To do this, she has to be sensitive enough to intuitively perceive and recognize the signals you send that communicate you have a need. Then she must interpret what your verbal and physical signals mean.

When she perceives and interprets your messages accurately, she is in a position to respond to them adequately, whether that means engaging you in some way or allowing you some peaceful time alone. As your parent stays emotionally accessible and notices, interprets, and responds to your needs in consistent and reliable ways, you develop an attitude of emotional security.

Responding to you in these ways is not easy! Think about being a tiny baby for a moment. You scrunch your face—you fuss—you scream—you make demanding grunts. As you are doing all of this, your parent's task is to decipher and respond to what you are communicating and what you truly need at that moment.

Your fussing may mean that you are hungry or that you want your diaper changed. Your crying may communicate that you have a gas pain and need to burp or that something more severe is happening.

In contrast to physical needs, your vocalizations and body movements might be communicating that you need something emotionally.

For example, your parent has to discern if your cries mean you are frightened and need soothing or if you are lonely and need someone to relate to you. She must determine if your wiggling and kicking signal excitement, frustration and anger, fatigue, or over-stimulation, or if they simply demonstrate your newly discovered ability to kick.

Once your primary caregiver tunes in to and intuitively figures out what you need, it is her responsibility to respond to and meet your needs adequately. Regardless of what you need, you are dependent on your parent's ability to be responsive to you.

The parent regulates your emotions. A parent who is providing Just Right parenting is able to *stay present* with you emotionally and help you process and regulate your emotions *as you are experiencing them.* Consider a few of the ways she accomplishes this.

Your parent regulates your exposure to stimulation. In order to develop a secure attachment, it is important that your parent regulate your exposure to stimulation. To do this she must stay present with, and attuned to, you emotionally. This attunement makes it possible for her to assess your needs and adjust your exposure to stimulation so you can stay emotionally stable.

For example, when you are overly distressed, your parent needs to help soothe you. When you are an infant, this may mean she must provide the entire repertoire of talking reassuringly to you, bouncing you in her arms as she paces the floor, or singing so you will calm down. When you are older, she needs to develop age-suitable strategies to help you deal with distress so you do not become over stimulated.

In contrast, when you need stimulation, your parent needs to engage you in an energizing way. When you are an infant, her funny face making, babbling back and forth with you, and playing with you are crucial to your development. As you grow older, she needs to stimulate you in developmentally congruent ways.

Helping you regulate emotionally also means that when you have had enough stimulation, your parent needs to notice your signals that you need some quiet time. At that point, she needs to be calm and peaceful with you so you can develop the ability to calm yourself.

Your parent responds to your emotions in a reciprocal way. In addition to "up" and "down" regulation, it is also important that your parent respond to your emotions in a way that corresponds with yours. This response involves mirroring your emotions. A Just Right parent stays in sync with the intensity of, and shifts in, your emotional state, adjusting to and matching your emotions.

In turn, you track her emotional states and develop the ability to anticipate and predict on an unconscious level how she will be and what she will do. During these interactions with your mother, you not only internalize how she is responding to you, but you also begin to learn to regulate your emotions.

Infant researchers Beatrice Beebe and Frank Lachmann discovered in their studies that "[h]ow each partner's face attracts and responds to the other's is one of the foundations of intimacy throughout life. … These 'matching' experiences contribute to feeling known, attuned to, on the same wave length" (Beebe and Lachmann, 2002, p. 98).

When a parent is over- or under-stimulating or fails to match your emotional states it distresses you. For example, think about how the following mismatches in emotional intensity or nature could affect you.

- You are upset, crying, or frightened, and your parent laughs at, minimizes, or ignores your distress.
- You are happy and enjoying yourself, and your parent snaps at you with frustration or anger.
- You are sad or lonely, and your parent ignores you.
- You are a little nervous, and your parent works herself and you up into marked anxiety or fear states.

Regardless of your age, this mismatch of emotional experience is disruptive to your developing mind, although it is particularly disruptive during infancy and early childhood.

As your parent regulates your exposure to stimulation and responds to your emotions in a reciprocal way, she is helping you process and regulate your emotions. In addition, when she maintains both your and her emotions within an optimal range and adequately matches your emotional states, you develop the ability to relate to your own and others' emotions.

These abilities are necessary for secure attachments. Therefore, it is critical that your parent maintain both your and her emotions in a range that both of you can handle: not Too Much, not Too Little, but Just Right.

Your parent translates your emotions into words. A parent who is emotionally accessible and reliable continues helping you manage your emotions throughout infancy, childhood, and adolescence. During infancy, your parent primarily uses her emotional state and body language, including her tone of voice, to regulate your emotions.

As you get older, a parent who provides Just Right parenting helps you develop the ability to "translate" your body sensations into words. The better able you are to identify your emotions and use words to describe your internal world, the more effectively you can take care of your feelings and communicate them to others.

Simply translating feelings into words is not adequate for developing a secure attachment, however. A parent who is Reliably Available also needs to help you make sense out of what you are feeling. Because you are an understudy to your parent as you grow up, you internally record the meanings your parent gives your experience.

These meanings, whether positive or negative, become part of the emotional and cognitive components of your attitudes. You use them to filter and to make sense out of your and others' behaviors and the way the world works.

They also help you know who you are.

The meanings you put on your experience
determine how you experience it.

For example, imagine you are a child who is distressed about something that happened at school and is trying to get your mother's attention.

If your mother experiences your distress as "understandable and acceptable," you will attribute the same positive meanings to your distress.

If she computes your emotions and attempts to meet your needs as if they are "irritating or demanding," you will tend to internalize her perceptions and may become very irritable with or negative about your own emotions.

If your parent experiences your emotions and needs as a threat to her sense of worth and adequacy, and therefore labels your emotions and behavior as "bad, " you will also tend to experience your emotional self as unacceptable.

Early in her treatment, Roxy often had difficulty putting her emotions into words and attaching accurate and helpful meanings to her experience. Frequently she would come to sessions agitated, overwhelmed by her hurt feelings. She would begin by going over the details of all the things others had said and done the previous week that, as Roxy put it, "hurt my feelings and made me mad!"

On one level, Roxy had felt justified in her reactions. However, on another level, her childhood beliefs (e.g., "you are bad if you get upset; you should suck up how you feel") were evoking feelings of shame about being hurt and angry. And this internal conflict was causing her even more distress.

Over the next several years, Roxy and I set out to help her develop the ability to translate her feelings into words so she could both regulate and convey them more effectively. To do this, whenever Roxy would begin "venting," I would pay attention to the significance of what I sensed she was experiencing. Not only did I attend to her words, but I also listened for the meanings of what she was saying. And I was mindful of the vulnerable emotions that were lying beneath her frustrated, angry words.

In addition, when Roxy would express her emotions and thoughts, I would acknowledge and accept them rather than disregard, minimize, or judge them. Then, gradually, I would help her shift from simply emoting about what had happened to differentiating her various feelings and verbalizing the ways she had felt threatened by the experience.

Roxy would also work on identifying and articulating how she was processing her experience. It was important for her to make sense out of, and attach meanings to, her experience that were reality-based in the present rather than in distortions created in and by the past.

One day, after about four years of therapy, Roxy reported an incident that had occurred with Adrianne (now six years old) during the previous week.

"Boy, am I ever glad that I've been in therapy!" Roxy said as she rearranged the couch pillows and sat down. "I can tell that it's helping me handle things better. Yesterday, for example, after I came back from grocery shopping, I found Adrianne in the bathroom sobbing at the sink. When I asked her what was wrong, she told me (between sobs) that she had spent hours building a princess carriage but that her cousin had wrecked it.

"Apparently, when Adrianne had gone into the kitchen in order to get something to drink, her two-year-old cousin had started playing with the carriage and had dropped it. When Adrianne came back into the living room and saw her beautiful creation in pieces on the floor, she got very upset and started crying. (I could tell she had been *so* excited and proud of what she had accomplished, and she felt crushed by the accident.)

"As if that wasn't bad enough, Adrianne said that my mom and sister also had told her several times that she should stop being a crybaby because she could always make another carriage. At that point, Adrianne had run into the bathroom, sobbing her heart out—which was how I found her.

"I stayed with Adrianne in the bathroom so she wouldn't be alone while she was upset, and so I could try to console her. At first, when Adrianne was telling me what had happened to her project and what her grandmother and aunt had said to her, I reacted inside. I felt like wringing everyone's necks—not just for being so clueless about how to handle the situation—but also for being mean to Adrianne for crying. But I calmed myself down so I could stay focused on what Adrianne was feeling.

"At first, I didn't say very much to Adrianne. I just tried to be there for her and tune in to her feelings. After a while I said, 'It hurts really bad to work so hard on something that is important to you and then have it broken. I'm *so* sorry that happened to you and your wonderful project. It's very sad and frustrating.' I was stroking her softly on her back while I was talking. Adrianne kept crying, but every so often, between sobs, she would insist, 'I'm *never* going to make another one!'

"I waited until she was a little calmer and then said, 'You don't have to make another one if you don't want to.' I stopped talking for a minute in order to let that sink in. Then I gently told her, "Right now, you are sad and mad that your princess carriage was ruined, and the idea of starting over seems impossible. But, sometime, when you are feeling better, you may decide to make another one because you are very creative, and you enjoy doing crafts so much." I paused, and then said, 'But that's up to you.'

"After a few more minutes, Adrianne stopped crying and was calmer, and we left the bathroom. The next thing I knew, she was in her room building another princess carriage. I was so proud of her for bouncing back and not giving up! And I'm proud of myself for handling it like I did.

"Instead of creating a disaster out of how my mom and sister had handled the situation (which is what I used to do), I calmed myself down so I could help Adrianne feel better. I didn't want her to experience the situation as a catastrophe—and I sure didn't want it to traumatize her!"

Roxy's eyes misted up as she said, "It was an awesome experience!"

As Roxy was recounting what had happened that week, I felt moved by her narrative. Her ability to stay present with her own and Adrianne's emotions—and not become overwhelmed by them—showed Roxy's remarkable progress. In the past, Roxy would have reacted explosively in this type of situation and would have verbally lashed out at her family members for failing to support Adrianne.

This time, however, Roxy did not attach the meaning to the situation that it was a "disaster." Nor did she react as if her mother and sister were "all bad," which she had done so often in the past.

Instead, because Roxy had been able to calm herself down and pay attention to Adrianne's feelings of dismay and anger, Roxy was able to be emotionally present and available for Adrianne.

Roxy's ability to acknowledge and accept Adrianne's emotional experience and to put her own and Adrianne's feelings into words was invaluable in the situation. It had helped Adrianne experience, process, and express her feelings of loss and frustration without becoming overwhelmed.

In addition, because Roxy had interpreted the experience as a loss that was manageable and temporary, she had helped Adrianne do the same. Roxy had also empowered Adrianne by letting her know that she could choose how to handle her hurt and disappointment.

In the end, Adrianne was able to use her mother's support to bounce back and restabilize after a painful experience.

The parent manages the unavoidable disruptions in her emotional availability. It is extremely important for your parent to be emotionally accessible for you in a reliable, consistent, and predictable way. However, it is impossible for a parent—even a Just Right parent—to be perfectly in tune with you *all* of the time.

As you grow up, undoubtedly, there will be disruptions or failures in the emotional connections between you and your parent. Although these breaks in emotional connection may be stressful, perhaps even painful, your parent and you can use these failures in empathy to enhance your development.

For example, imagine for a moment that you decide to do strength training as part of your health makeover plan. You know that you should exercise different muscle groups on different days because the muscles develop micro-tears as you lift weights. Alternating exercise days provides your muscles a day of rest to let the tears repair.

When you increase the weight or the repetitions for the muscle group on the next training day, you again sustain micro-tears in your muscles. Strength training involves cycles of sustaining and repairing micro tears in the muscles. Tear-repair. Tear-repair. In the process, your muscles become stronger and bigger. If, however, you lift weights that are too heavy for your muscles to handle, or you fail to give your muscles adequate rest, you are likely to become severely injured.

In the same way, as you are growing up, you experience disruptions (tears) in your emotional connections with your parent. They are inevitable. How your parent and you respond to (repair) these normal disruptions determines their effect on you, just as how you handle the micro-tears in your muscles during weight training determines their benefit. The two of you can respond to these failures in her emotional availability in a way that damages you further or in ways that serve to make you stronger.

Moreover, just as lifting weights that are too heavy, doing too many repetitions, or failing to rest can severely damage your muscles, excessive and severe disruptions of your parent-child attachment can severely damage you. They can have a pronounced negative effect on how your attitudes and relationship patterns develop, impairing your ability to regulate your emotions, direct your thought processes and beliefs, and manage your action tendencies.

These disruptions in connection can be overwhelming since they can leave you feeling helpless, frightened, alone, and frustrated. If your parent fails to repair the breaks in emotional connection promptly and adequately, you will tend to attach negative emotional and cognitive meanings to the experience of attachment with others.

If you associate relationships with distress, you may find yourself consciously or unconsciously struggling with the roadblocks to what you want—a secure emotional connection—which can cause you to develop an internal sense of insecurity. You may also find yourself having difficulty accepting the reality that you cannot *always* get what you want, no matter how hard you try.

Because of the nature of the internalization process, it is imperative that your parent re-establish (repair) any breaks in the connection between you in order for the tear-repair process to enhance your growth and development.

A parent who provides Just Right parenting recognizes when there is a break in the emotional connection between the two of you, and she repairs the break as rapidly as possible. She calms herself, refocuses, tunes in to, and resynchronizes with you. As this occurs, all the stress hormones and other reactions in your body stimulated by the disconnection begin to subside. All these experiences help you remain stable.

As an understudy to your primary caregiver, you not only internally record the experience of the disruption in the relationship but also the repair of the break. You record the experience of calming down and re-stabilizing in stressful situations. Because this enables your capacity to tolerate stress without becoming overwhelmed to expand, you come to know that distress is temporary and that you can handle stress. During the tear-repair experience, you also learn that you are not powerless to handle conflicts or disruptions in connections with others.

Instead, you learn that you can maintain emotional connections even when there are tensions and mismatches in the relationship. You also develop a sense of self-efficacy as you learn that you can do something to repair breaks in the connections between you and others, even though you cannot control others or change their limitations.

Over time, the bond between you and your parent becomes stronger as you internally record your experience of the tear-repair process. You develop a sense of trust that the world is reliable, although imperfect. This process also serves to increase your sense of being loved, worthwhile, and capable in your own right.

Your self-confidence and your confidence in others increase and you become more resilient because of the positive meanings you attach to your tear-repair experience.

The meanings you attach to your experience, more than the nature of the experience, determine whether an experience becomes helpful or traumatic for you.

Recall for a moment the incident in which Adrianne's cousin damaged Adrianne's princess carriage project. Because Adrianne's grandmother and aunt not only failed to respond to her distress adequately but also increased her emotional pain, they injured Adrianne's self-esteem, confidence, and internal sense of security.

Fortunately, Roxy was able to intervene as a Reliably Available mother and restabilize Adrianne. Roxy was able to keep herself stable, to tune in to and be sensitive and responsive to Adrianne, and to attach positive meanings to her daughter's experience. Roxy's ability to function in these ways increased Adrianne's experience of being loved, worthwhile, and capable. Adrianne was able to use the experience to become more resilient and take charge of her response to untoward life experiences.

Repairing the damage from Roxy's childhood and enhancing her psychological capacities was an ongoing process. Nevertheless, because of her progress in therapy, Roxy was able to function generally as a Just Right mother to her daughter. Roxy was diligent in her efforts to be attuned, sensitive, and responsive to Adrianne, and she worked rapidly to repair any breaks in their emotional connection.

Because Roxy's mothering abilities at that point were good enough, Adrianne was able to develop a secure attachment with her mother. In the process, Roxy was not only changing her attitudes and saving her own life, but she was also providing a secure foundation for Adrianne that would save her daughter's life.

The Core Attitude You Develop: *Secure–Confident*

When a Reliably Available parent consistently and adequately provides for you psychologically, your internalization of your experience with her will help you develop core attitudes of *security* and *confidence*. And it will provide you with a foundational relational pattern based in a secure attachment. Both will help you function confidently and effectively throughout your life in many ways.

You develop a clear and positive sense of your identity and self-worth. When you grow up with a Just Right mother, you develop a clear sense of who you are: your needs, likes, dislikes, capabilities, and limitations. You learn to value and respect yourself and others as separate, autonomous individuals.

These internal strengths enable you to develop self-confidence and to set reasonable and flexible expectations for yourself and others. You learn that you can recover from setbacks and losses, develop good relationships, solve problems, and navigate your way through life.

A core sense of safety, security, and confidence will ground your beliefs about yourself, others, and the world, as well as how you act.

You are able to develop secure, loving, and fulfilling relationships. When a core sense of safety, security, and confidence grounds your beliefs about yourself, others, and the world, you come to believe that relationships can be generally safe and supportive. You are better able to trust yourself and evaluate what you can trust (rely on) in others.

The internal sense of safety and security also gives you the confidence to communicate your feelings, thoughts, and needs. And it makes it possible for you to develop relationships in which you both can give and receive support in dealing with your emotions.

All of these abilities make it possible for you to form secure, loving, and mutually fulfilling relationships.

You regulate your emotions, thought processes, and behavior effectively. When you develop secure and confident core attitudes and relationship patterns, you learn to regulate your emotions effectively. You can then process your experience emotionally and cognitively in ways that are relatively free from illusions and distortions. You can also adapt to changes that come into your life in healthy ways and can be resilient in the face of disappointment and loss.

In addition, you can handle conflict more effectively because the ability to regulate your emotions equips you to manage the incompatible needs, wishes, or demands that are inherent in both internal and external conflict. For example, when you find yourself struggling with someone over differing needs, you will tend to feel less threatened because of your sense of internal security. You will also have less need to respond defensively, which usually escalates conflict.

When you are able to manage your emotions, thoughts, and behaviors, you are better able to *keep yourself grounded in the knowledge of what is real and true about you and others.* During a conflict, this awareness helps you discern the effect your attitudes are having on you and how you are managing the conflict. You will be able to discern which emotions the conflict is evoking and what meanings you are attaching to the conflict.

This awareness also helps you consider how your attitudes are helping you or how they are hindering your ability to solve problems and control your behaviors. It helps you have more clarity about the parts of the conflict related to the other person's feelings, beliefs, and actions.

Many years after Roxy completed her therapy with me, she came back to see me because she wanted to give me an update on her and Adrianne's progress. During our meeting, Roxy described to me her thoughts about her past and the changes she had been making through the years. Then she talked about how affirmed she felt by a recent experience with Adrianne (who was now 17 years old).

"I think I've finally accepted the reality that my parents weren't able to help me as I was growing up because they had their own problems. It really *wasn't* because something was wrong with me. I also get why I coped by putting on a tough front, even though I was feeling insecure the whole time. Being tough was the only feasible option that I had at the time. But what's great is that I don't use the tough girl attitude very often any more because I feel safer and more secure most of the time now.

"I also have a better sense of who I am, and I am more confident that I can handle my life. My old insecurities and defensiveness do pop up at times, but I'm handling them much better. Plus, it's also a relief that I don't feel so alone any more. I know I can find help when I need it. In fact, I even got married several years ago—*at 48 years old*—to a *wonderful* man. A*nd we're not even living with my family!* It's a miracle!" Roxy chuckled delightedly.

As Roxy's excitement subsided, her eyes began to mist, and her voice was thick with emotion as she continued sharing the changes in her life with me. "What amazes me most is that even though I haven't been a perfect mother, by any stretch of the imagination, Adrianne has grown up to be an amazing, confident young woman. She can handle things a lot better than I ever could at her age!

"For example, just last week, Adrianne had a major setback. For the last two years, Adrianne has had her heart set on going to Scripps College. She was accepted and even registered for classes. But, at the very last minute, all of the financial support we had counted on fell through, and Adrianne had to withdraw. We were all heartbroken. But, after a couple of days of crying and talking things out, Adrianne regrouped herself and came up with a new plan for college that was affordable. I'm *so* proud of her!

"It's very comforting to know that even though Adrianne and I will have conflicts (like all normal mothers and daughters), we can handle our own and each other's feelings and work out our differences." Roxy nodded her head emphatically, as she declared, "Scripps College proved that!"

After a moment of silence, Roxy quietly commented, "I'm *so* grateful that Adrianne and I respect each other and have a secure, loving relationship. Our relationship is awesome!"

I responded, "Even though it's been hard work to change the old ways of dealing with yourself and others in your life, you're reaping the benefits of your efforts. You are feeling better about yourself, and you can see that your hopes and dreams that Adrianne would develop internal strength and security have come true.

"Not only that, but you also have been able to develop a loving relationship with your daughter ... and now with your husband. What you have accomplished truly *is* awesome!"

Through the years, Roxy had worked hard to change the attitudes developed in childhood that had been undermining her ability to provide the life she wanted for both her daughter and herself.

Although it had been incredibly challenging, Roxy had been able to be a Just Right mother to Adrianne, even while learning to take care of her own emotional distress and changing some of her ways of thinking and behaving.

It was true that Roxy had not been able to take notice of or care for her or her daughter's emotional needs all the time. Nevertheless, Roxy had provided Adrianne with sufficient emotional resources that Adrianne was able to develop fairly secure and confident core attitudes. In the process, both mother and daughter had developed an emotionally secure relationship with each other and with others.

Because they had experienced a secure attachment in their relationship, Roxy and Adrianne also had developed the ability to be more resilient when they encountered the adversities of life. They were able to bounce back from difficulties, re-stabilizing sooner and with less effort. Both of them had developed a core sense of confidence in their ability to manage their lives and reach their goals.

The work Roxy had been doing to transform her wounds into wisdom was coming to fruition. Moreover, in the process, she was helping to save her and her daughter's lives, as well as the lives of their family's next generation, from a future of perpetuating family wounds.

Summary: Mission Possible

When a Just Right parent provides for you emotionally in reliable and consistent ways, you develop core attitudes and relationship patterns grounded in security and confidence.

In order for her to adequately challenge and support you in your development, however, your parent must be able to tune in and be sensitive both to herself and to you. Her capacity for attunement and sensitivity make it possible for her to perceive, interpret, and be responsive to the developmental needs you both possess.

When your parent is Reliably Available, she is also able to help regulate both her and your emotions, maintaining them within a manageable range so that you do not become overwhelmed and thereby traumatized. When you become dysregulated emotionally, your Just Right parent helps you restabilize as soon as possible. And when there is a break in your emotional connection, your parent finds a way to repair the breach so your internal security and confidence will not be compromised.

Your parent does *not* need to provide these functions *all* of the time in some illusionary "perfect" way to be a Just Right parent. In fact, it is important that you experience a certain degree of frustration because it is *necessary* for your psychological growth and development! The process of repairing breaks in emotional connection actually increases your ability to tolerate frustration and disappointment, which can help you become stronger, more resilient, and wiser.

Over time, as your parent relates to you in reliably present, available, and consistent ways, you, her understudy, will internalize the experience of emotional safety, security, and stability.

This experience makes it possible for you to develop a secure attachment with her. And this bond, which provides you with a basic sense of trust and of confidence, will help you handle whatever comes your way in life. It will make it possible for you to act confidently on your own behalf and adequately care for your needs, both individually and with others.

In addition, the internal psychological structures you develop during this process will enable you to adapt in healthy ways to what is and is not available to you in your relationships with yourself, others, and the world.

Remember, however, that *attitudes and relationship patterns are not fixed; they are constantly evolving.* If your parent provided Too Much or Too Little of what you needed emotionally as a child, you *can* still change the attitudes that developed as part of your childhood survival system that are not serving you well.

You *can* develop attitudes and relationship patterns that will enhance your present life. Moreover ...

> ***You can do the work of transforming your life
> without having to be perfect!***

PART III

Attitudes Impact
How You Live in the World

CHAPTER 6

Re-enacting Your Parent-Child Scripts

If the structures of the human mind remain unchanged,
we will always end up re-creating fundamentally the same world,
the same evils, the same dysfunction. —Eckhart Tolle, *A New Earth*

Have you ever curled up on the bed with your children as they clamor for a bedtime story? It is not just any story they want, mind you. It is *this* particular story—the *same* story—the story they have heard umpteen times before, until you are sick of telling or reading it to them.

With the unrelenting persistence of children who will not give up their familiar nighttime story, you may find yourself reliving your childhood story repeatedly in your adult life. You can find yourself *re-enacting* [4] the attitudes and relationship patterns you internally recorded from your childhood experiences as you choose your friends and life partner, as you parent your children, and as you relate to life. You tend to replay these scripts with every person or entity in your life—including yourself—in some form.

Although as an adult you might be consciously aware that there are many varieties of attitudes and styles of interacting, you do not "know" any other way to be in the world. The core feelings, thought processes, and action tendencies that developed as you bonded psychologically with your primary caregiver are usually central to the parts you play and the scripts you follow in life.

---

[4] Many in the field of psychology consider a re-enactment to be the repetition of an early negative—especially traumatic—parent-child experience, because their focus is often on what went wrong in early relationships. Even though I will be using the term in this way as well, it is clear that we also repeat positive relational patterns from our Just Right parenting experiences. It is important not to lose sight of these positive resources.

Your attitudes and relationship patterns may arise from healthy or unhealthy psychological attachments. When you have sufficient Just Right relational experiences, you tend to develop attachments with others grounded in the healthy ways of dealing with emotions, thoughts, and behaviors that you experienced with your good enough parents.

However, when a parent provides Too Much or Too Little, you form dysfunctional psychological bonds and ways of relating that arise from the stored emotional, cognitive, and behavioral experiences that are inherent in interactions with such parents. These unhealthy ways of relating can develop when your mind is unable to process and integrate your experience in healthy ways and instead develops unhealthy attitudes and relationship patterns that impinge on your life.

Regardless of the nature of your early attachments, you are likely to find yourself replaying the childhood scripts in your adult life because you retain them in your mind-body memory system. Unless you have significant relational experiences that help you alter your childhood attitudes, you have no alternate internal models to filter, organize, and make meaning out of your life. Instead, the more you repeat the familiar early scripts, the more entrenched they become in your internal operating system.

Unfortunately, when you operate with the unhealthy attitudes you developed during childhood, you can find yourself reliving the same distressing dilemmas you experienced as a child. On one side of the emotional tug-of-war, you may hold on to what you know because you believe on some level that "familiar bad is better than unfamiliar good."

On the other side, you may cling to the hope that—this time—your story will have a different ending. As this internal conflict plays out, you may end up feeling, and perhaps even being, deprived or wounded as an adult in the same ways you were once injured as a child.

When you re-enact your painful childhood experience,
you feel the same distressing feelings, think the same undermining
thoughts, act in the same painful ways, and establish the same
self-destructive relationships, over and over again.

To transform your wounds into wisdom, it is important to understand how the re-enactment process operates in your life and develop the ability and skills necessary to change your attitudes and relationship patterns. Even so, simply understanding how your attitudes work and learning how to do things differently are not sufficient to bring about the changes you desire.

To be able to take care of your feelings, thoughts, and behaviors in new ways, it is particularly critical that you *experience* healthier ways of being in a relationship with an emotionally safe person.

The insights, capacities, and abilities you gain from these new experiences with an emotionally safe person will empower you to transform the unhealthy core attitudes you internalized as a child. They will make it possible for you to stop repeating the parent-child ways of relating that create problems in your life and to relate in new and healthier ways to yourself, others, and the world. As you engage in the necessary processes of freeing your life from your attachments to past wounds and developing new attitudes, you make your life less conflicted and more fulfilling.

Before we delve more deeply into the process of re-enacting your parent-child scripts, let us consider Amanda's story and see how she came to understand—and change—her attitudes and relationship patterns.

Amanda's Story

Amanda was a bright, caring, forty-seven-year-old woman who came to see me because she had been struggling with depression for many years. Her frustration with her relationships and life in general had been increasing during the two months prior to her appointment with me.

Initially, Amanda was reluctant to talk about her childhood. She spent the first several months of therapy focusing primarily on her frustrations with others and on "strategies" for managing her depression. Whenever we would touch on the topic of her early years, Amanda would become uncomfortable and revert to talking about her frustration with her life. She was clearly avoiding the deeper level feelings that were giving rise to her current distress.

Over time, and as she began to trust my acceptance of her more, Amanda began to open up about some of her childhood experiences. In the following discussion, which occurred about six months into treatment, Amanda described her relationships within her family. As she did, her ambivalence about her childhood and her family relationships became more apparent.

"When I was growing up, even though my parents took care of my physical needs, my emotional needs didn't seem to matter a whole lot. At times, they didn't even seem to exist, as far as my parents were concerned."

Amanda paused briefly, and then continued. "You know, it's not that my parents *never* did anything for me, but they were busy working most of the time. They expected me to take care of whatever needed to be done at home. That didn't just involve doing household chores, though. It was also my job to keep peace in the family and make everyone feel better when they were upset.

"What's weird is, when I was younger I didn't even think about or question what was happening. That's just how life was. When I was in high school, though, I started seeing what was going on, and it hit me like a ton of bricks. I was Cinderella! I remember being sad and lonely a lot of the time, and sometimes even pretty depressed." Amanda became silent, and she sank deeper into the couch as she began to experience her sadness. We could both feel its weight.

After several moments, Amanda continued, "I love my family, but I have a lot of mixed feelings about them and my childhood. I don't really get why I didn't feel loved most of the time when I was growing up and why I have trouble feeling loved now. My parents weren't *bad* parents. They did the best they could, given the circumstances. And … I know they loved me."

I responded, "You've been carrying a heavy load for a long time. And the pain and sadness you feel about not getting your emotional needs met as a child are fighting hard with your love for your family."

Tears trickled down Amanda's cheeks as we sat quietly with her sadness. Gradually her mood shifted. We then began to talk about her internal conflict between her love and attachment to her family and the emptiness, pain, and resentment she sometimes felt about her unmet needs.

At one point I asked Amanda, "How do you think your experience of being in the caretaker role as a child, and the distress you feel about it now, affect your current relationships?"

Amanda was thoughtful for a moment and then responded, "I'm the classic caretaker. I'm always trying to solve other people's problems and take care of their needs, just like I had to do as a child, even though I complain about it. I know I should take better care of myself, and sometimes I try, but before I know it, I find myself back helping everyone else again. Now others *expect* me to take care of them.

"The odd thing is that I do it, even when I know it's not my responsibility and even though I resent their expectations. I feel guilty if I don't. My parents used to tell me I was selfish if I didn't take care of everyone. But now, *I'm* the one telling *myself* I'm selfish when I don't do what everyone wants!"

Amanda paused and then admitted, "I like helping others, and I'm glad I'm a helpful person. But I don't get why others aren't helpful. I just wish someone would think about me *once* in a while. I have needs too, you know." She sighed and said, "I guess I'm just a moocher magnet, or, maybe, just a fool."

Your Life On the Stage

The Parts You Play

Like Amanda, the parts you play and the scripts you follow in life tend to emerge from the *repertoire* of core attitudes and relationship patterns that develop when you are a young understudy to your parent. (A repertoire is like a supply store that holds the parts or dramas an understudy can use when called upon to perform any role.) This storehouse maintains the ways of being in the world that are part of your internal operating system.

The tendency to operate with your familiar childhood repertoire of emotional, cognitive, and behavioral scripts is usually unconscious—you may not be aware of what you are doing. If you pay attention to your attitudes, however, you can become more cognizant of how you are re-enacting your internalized parent attitudes and their associated parent-child relationship patterns.

Three common themes tend to surface repeatedly in your life's story when you re-enact roles from this internal repertoire. You may experience what you know, attract what is familiar to you, and evoke what you expect from others.

Let us first take a broad look at how these themes may appear as you re-enact your life scripts. Then we will examine more specifically how they can emerge in the parts you play and the scripts you re-enact if your primary caregiver provided Too Much, Too Little, or Just Right.

You experience what you know. During a re-enactment, you will find yourself unconsciously experiencing the present *as if it were* the known and familiar past of your childhood. Because your repertoire of emotional, cognitive, and behavioral scripts developed as you and your parent were interacting, the central parts you play in a re-enactment are the roles of "parent" and "child."

You do not play one *or* the other part, however; *you re-enact both* parts, in some fashion or at some point. Although you may tend to replay primarily one role, you also can find yourself switching back and forth between the parent and child roles in a nanosecond.

In addition to the roles, your repertoire includes the attitudes and *relationship patterns* you developed. Because of this, in a re-enactment both roles (parent and child) must be experienced in order for the re-enactment to continue. Therefore, when you are enacting the parent role, someone else (or some entity) must be playing out the child role (and vice-versa).

As discussed earlier, you cannot be a victim without a victimizer—or a victimizer without a victim. The two roles operate as a relationship pair. Let me explain further.

When you are re-enacting your parent scripts (*active replication*), you operate with the attitudes and relationship patterns you internally recorded of your parent's experience *and* your experience of her. Once an understudy to your mother, you find yourself relating to others, yourself, and the world as you once experienced your mother relating to you.

At these moments, you may or may not be aware that you are feeling, thinking, or acting "just like your mother." Nevertheless, when you replay the Too Much or Too Little parent scripts, you end up treating yourself and others as you were once treated.

I once saw a wry saying on a pillow: "Mirror, mirror on the wall, I have become my mother after all." Everyone can identify with the quip on some level, but when you experience this in real life, it may not be quite as amusing. When you are re-enacting your internal repertoire, you end up re-living your painful childhood experiences in some way.

Not only will you be feeling as your parent once felt in some way, but also the person who is in the child role will be feeling as you once felt as a child (e.g., neglected, abandoned, overwhelmed, or discounted). In the process, you end up re-wounding yourself and others in the same ways that your parent once wounded you (active replication).

In contrast to the parent role, when you are playing out your child scripts (*passive replication*) you will tend to experience others as if they are your primary caretaker. For example, if your parent was primarily emotionally enmeshed or domineering, in a re-enactment you will experience others as providing Too Much—as if they are overloading you in some way. If your parent was emotionally unavailable or inconsistent, in a re-enactment you will experience others as providing Too Little—as if they are not providing adequately for your needs.

In the midst of such a re-enactment, you will tend to experience yourself as if you are the neglected, overwhelmed, or traumatized child of yesteryear. At these moments you will feel just as you did when you were a child (e.g., helpless, powerless, anxious, confused, frustrated, angry, or fearful).

You will also tend to think the same way you did as a child. Because young children do not understand that other people generate their own attitudes, you can find yourself believing that you are the cause of what others are feeling, thinking, and doing. You may also experience others as being more powerful or knowledgeable than you.

For some time Amanda worked on recognizing when she was re-enacting her familiar parent-child patterns as she related to herself and others. One day, about a year and a half into treatment, Amanda came to her session excited about how she had handled a situation with her difficult roommate, Marta.

"Something strange happened this week. I think it's what we've been talking about. I noticed that even though it was Marta's turn to clean the kitchen, she hadn't started yet because she was busy doing something else. I didn't have anything else to do, so I started washing the dishes. Before I knew it, Marta was in my face, and yelling at me. 'What are you doing? It's my week to wash the dishes!'

"I was stunned. No one had ever screamed at me for helping or 'doing what needed to be done.' To buy some time to calm down so I could think, I decided to answer her question literally and tell her what I had been thinking. So I said, 'You were busy, and I didn't have anything else I had to do, so I thought I'd be helpful and wash the dishes.'

"Marta glared at me even more and snapped back, 'No you weren't! You were *not* trying to be helpful!'

"I was really getting confused now. So I said, 'I wasn't?' Then I stopped for a second as I thought, 'Something's off-base here. Maybe Marta is doing one of those re-enactment things that Jolyn talks about, because Marta's reaction doesn't make any sense, as far as I can tell.' I decided to try to get more information about what was going on in Marta's mind, so I asked her, 'What did you *think* I was doing?'

"Before I knew what was happening, Marta got in my face and tersely spit out, 'You were trying to make me feel guilty!' Her anger was over the top!

"I had no idea what she was talking about! So I said to her, 'Well, I've got to tell you, that thought never crossed my mind. I don't think that way. How did you get that idea?'

"Marta started calming down. After a while she said to me, 'My mother expected me to do my chores immediately. If I didn't, she would start doing them herself, but the whole time she would either yell at me or criticize me. Or she would try to guilt-trip me by doing her whole martyr routine. She was good at that! I always felt guilty and blamed myself when my mom was upset, but I was also mad at her for yelling at me. I guess that when I saw you washing the dishes, I thought that you were doing the same thing to me that my mother used to do. And the anger I feel toward my mother just came out.'

"I said to Marta, 'No wonder you got so upset! If you thought I was trying to make you feel guilty like your mom used to do, I can see why you would get mad. You must have felt awful when she did that. ... But that's not what *I'm* like.'

"Then I told Marta, 'My mother was different. She expected me to take care of things. She would say, 'You have two eyes in your head. You don't need me telling you what needs to be done.' I learned that doing what needed to be done, regardless of who was supposed to do it, meant you were paying attention to others' needs and being helpful.

"I guess I went on automatic pilot when I saw that you were busy and the dishes hadn't been done yet. I wasn't feeling critical toward you when I was washing the dishes. In my mind, I was just doing what I was supposed to do. The thought never crossed my mind that washing the dishes might mean something different to someone else.'

"We sat there thinking for a couple of minutes, and then I said to her, 'You know, this situation is helping me realize something. ... Even though *I* learned that taking care of things that need to be done is helpful to many people, not *everyone* may experience it as helpful. So if you don't want me to help you, I can honor that. Or I can work on remembering to ask you if you'd like help *before* starting to help—whichever works best for you.'

"Marta looked surprised at my response. Then she said she would be comfortable with me helping her as long as I checked with her first, and she apologized for yelling at me. And I apologized to her for jumping into her business without asking her first or her asking me for help."

In this incident, both Amanda and Marta were experiencing what they knew from their childhoods. They were both re-enacting the child scripts they had learned and recorded as understudies to their mothers. They found themselves feeling, thinking, and responding to each other in the same ways they had responded to their mothers.

Marta's re-enactment clearly created a problem for herself and Amanda. When Marta saw Amanda washing the dishes, Marta filtered the situation through the attitudes she had developed when she was young and was relating to her guilt-provoking mother (child scripts). Because her unresolved experiences from childhood were distorting her current experience, Marta *experienced* Amanda as her enmeshed, controlling, and passive-aggressive mother.

This distorted perception caused Marta to misinterpret Amanda's helpfulness as criticism and belittlement. She then felt anxious, guilty, and angry—just as she had felt with her mother. When she yelled at Amanda,

Marta was acting out the anger she had felt toward her mother as a child and still felt toward her as an adult.

In a similar dynamic, Amanda had internalized her mother's expectations that she (Amanda) should both notice and do any uncompleted housework—without her mother having to ask or tell her what to do. Following her child script, Amanda automatically went into the helpful mode when she saw the messy kitchen. She began taking care of the undone chores without even considering whether Marta needed or even wanted her help.

In her re-enactment, Amanda was also managing Marta's outrage as she had once managed her mother's anger. Impacted by the past, Amanda tried to come up with a strategy that she hoped would take care of, and perhaps prevent, problems that might arise with Marta in the future.

In Marta's re-enactment, she had replayed parts of what she had internalized of her enmeshed mother. Enacting her parent script, Marta had expected Amanda to know what Marta was thinking and feeling, and she had made negative assumptions about Amanda.

In addition, although the ways of expressing anger were different, Marta had acted out her anger, just as her mother had. In the re-enactment of her mother's attitudes, Marta had inadvertently put Amanda in the same child role that she herself had been in when she was young. Because of this, Amanda had experienced the same sense of danger, confusion, and personal violation that Marta had once experienced with her mother.

Although Amanda had been unconsciously re-enacting her caretaker child script in some ways, this incident revealed the progress Amanda had made in changing her attitudes. She had been able to keep herself calm enough to observe and think about what was happening in an emotionally charged situation.

Because she took time to empathize with Marta's emotional dysregulation and distortions instead of reacting to them, Amanda had handled Marta's reactions in ways that kept the conflict with Marta from escalating. And she had been able to care for her own needs without attacking Marta.

You evoke what you expect. Another way you can re-enact the core attitudes and relationship patterns you developed as an understudy to your primary caregiver is to act in ways that evoke what you expect. In this type of re-enactment, you expect others to treat you just as your parent who provided Too Much or Too Little treated you when you were a child. You also expect that you will always end up in the same situation that you were in as a child—never adequately getting your needs met.

As a result, you will tend to deal with your emotions, thoughts, and behaviors in ways that elicit the expected parent response from others.

Their responses confirm your worst fears—that everyone will fail you just like your parent failed you. You then re-live your painful childhood experience in the present.

As we continued our work together, Amanda and I explored how her actions evoked the negative responses from others that she anticipated. Because Amanda's parents had not been mindful of her emotional needs, her unconscious expectation was that no one would ever meet her needs (child script). As a result, she had developed attitudes that required her to be both overly responsive to others' needs (child script) and neglectful of her own (parent script).

Amanda worked hard to see and understand how her underlying expectation that others would overlook her needs often resulted in what she dreaded.

Over time, Amanda became more aware of how the ways she tried to care for others frequently evoked responses from others that left her feeling alone, neglected, taken advantage of, and even mistreated—just as she had felt as a child. She also began experiencing the sadness that surfaced as she came to realize the extent to which her childhood scripts had taken their toll on her ability to care for herself in healthy ways.

One day, about two years into treatment, Amanda began to talk about her struggles in her relationship with her friend, Olivia.

Amanda complained, "You know, I've been thinking lately, Olivia used to try to be a good friend, but when I've needed her lately, she hasn't been there for me. I've been feeling really hurt because I've been thinking that she doesn't actually care about me." She paused, and then noted bitterly, "But I guess *that's* not a big surprise, though, because my friendships usually end up this way."

I responded, "It really hurts to think that Olivia doesn't care about you anymore, especially when you have had such high hopes that your relationship with her would turn out differently than others you've had in the past."

"Yes it does!" Amanda said. "And, it's been really confusing trying to figure out why Olivia started acting differently toward me." Then Amanda admitted. "At first I just felt angry about Olivia not caring about me. Then I began to notice that lots of old thoughts were popping into my mind, like, 'I knew this would happen! My friendships always end up this way. Why doesn't anyone care about what *I* need or want? Why doesn't anyone help *me*?'" Amanda paused and then continued, "Boy, did *those* thoughts ever make the warning bells start ringing in my head!

"Since then, I've been noticing my thoughts and feelings about my relationship with Olivia more, like you and I talked about. I've also been doing a lot of thinking about the situation, and I've decided that I am probably part of the problem—you know, that 'evoking what you expect' thing. I remembered that when Olivia and I first started doing things together, Olivia would ask me what I would like to do. I would always say, 'It doesn't matter; whatever you want to do is okay with me.' When she asked me what I thought or felt about things, I just shrugged my shoulders and said, 'I don't know.' Once, when I felt overwhelmed by projects, Olivia even offered to help me, but I told her, 'It's no big deal. You have enough to do.'"

I noted, "You are beginning to see how some of the ways you have been responding to Olivia's efforts to reach out to you may be playing a part in her not being as caring and helpful to you any longer." We were silent for a time, and then I asked, "I wonder, how do you feel and what thoughts cross your mind when Olivia *is* being thoughtful of you?"

Amanda considered this for a moment, and then replied, "When Olivia asks me what I think about things or what I want, I usually get really nervous, and sometimes I even start worrying. I think stuff like, 'What if Olivia doesn't like what I want or think? What if she doesn't want to be my friend any more? What if I accept her help and she doesn't follow through?' I would be devastated if any of those things happened!

"And, as if it's not bad enough that those thoughts and feelings start torturing me, when Olivia offers to help me, I feel inadequate and guilty! After all, it's *my* job to take care of *others*, you know." Amanda sighed deeply, and then said, "I guess I really don't know *how* to let people care for me."

I responded, "You so desperately want someone to care about you and your needs. But when someone *is* being mindful of what you think and feel (like Olivia was doing early in your friendship), it is very unfamiliar and uncomfortable. And when you don't know yet how to take in the caring that others do offer you, it can even be very frightening."

"I guess I got what I expected after all," Amanda said quietly. "I can see why Olivia not only stopped asking me what I wanted but also stopped offering to help me. I pushed her away whenever she tried to be considerate of me. I guess I've trained her to ignore me just like my parents would ignore me when I was young."

"And," I observed, "just like you now fail to tune in to yourself and to care for your own needs at times."

Amanda and I sat together for several moments, letting ourselves feel the sadness associated with her difficulty getting her needs met. Then Amanda sighed. "I feel really sad about how difficult it is for me to relate to others effectively, especially when I know all the changes I'm working on won't happen as fast as I'd like them to." Another moment passed, but then Amanda perked up slightly and declared, "I know what I'll do! I'll talk to Olivia about what's been happening between us and find out how *she's* been feeling about it all. Maybe we can work out a plan that will be helpful for both of us. At least it's worth a try!"

I smiled.

You attract what is familiar. In this form of re-enactment, you unconsciously seek out or attract others with whom you play out your familiar parent-child pattern. There are generally two possibilities for this type of re-enactment.

One is that you re-enact your child scripts by unconsciously developing relationships with people who operate with the parent scripts that are similar to your parent's style of relating. These people do not usually have the positive aspects of your caregiver. Rather, they often have the same, or similar, dysfunctional core attitudes and relational patterns that your parent had. These people end up failing you in the same ways your parent who provided Too Much or Too Little failed you when you were a child. When you form attachments to these people, you tend to be hurt just like you were as a child.

Another possibility is that you will gravitate to people with attitudes similar to your child scripts and end up replaying your internalized parent script with them. For example, you may operate as the emotionally enmeshed, domineering, unavailable, or inconsistent parent, treating others as your parent once treated you. In this scenario, you too end up operating in ways that hurt others.

As Amanda and I continued to work together, we began to see that Amanda did not just re-enact her childhood scripts by experiencing what she knew or by evoking what she expected. She also unconsciously attracted, and was attracted to, people who failed to meet her needs in the same familiar ways her mother and father had failed her.

This pattern became apparent about three years into therapy, when Amanda was struggling with making some important decisions. She described her dilemma to me.

"You know, I'm not comfortable at my church anymore because of all the problems that have been going on there. Even though the people there have been my church family for a long time, I don't think it's a good place for me to be at this point. I want to go somewhere else, but I'm afraid to leave because I don't want to hurt anyone's feelings—and I *really* don't want anyone to get upset with me. I keep hoping something will magically change and things will get better. So I just keep going to meetings and acting like everything is okay, when really, I feel like a ball of nerves when I'm there and sometimes even have mini anxiety attacks."

I highlighted her internal conflict. "Even though you know that being involved in your church at this point is distressing you, you keep hoping that the problems will disappear, and everything will go back to how it used to be."

"I wish!" Amanda said. "But it's not going to happen. Let me tell you, there's this woman at church who I've been friends with for a while who is one of the reasons why I want to leave. She's always bothered me a little, but I've just ignored how I felt and told myself I was being too sensitive. Lately, though, every time I even think about being around her, I feel uneasy. I'm in a bind. Right now, she is ill, and I know I should go visit her. It's the right thing to do. It's what my mom used to do when someone was sick. But everything in me is fighting the idea of going. I just don't feel safe with her. She creeps me out." Amanda shuddered.

I observed, "The intuitive part of you is telling you that she's not safe and to stay away from her, but the guilt-tripping 'shoulds' are kicking in and pushing you to ignore what you feel and know." As Amanda was speaking, I found myself going on high alert internally. I sensed that something very important was occurring that we needed to observe very carefully.

Amanda replied, "It took me a while, but I finally realized the woman is definitely not safe, because she doesn't have any boundaries. If I run into her during the week—like at church or even at the store—she scurries up to me, then starts dumping personal secrets about people at church on me before I know what she's doing. It happens so fast that I don't even have time to stop her. I don't know what to do, and I can't get away from her because she's talking non-stop. So I just stand there, feeling helpless and trying not to think about what she's saying until she finally leaves. It's awful!"

Hesitating, Amanda looked at me with embarrassment and began to disclose more of her experience. "You know, I've never told anyone this, but whenever I'm around her, the image of a huge, black widow spider comes into my mind. I immediately start feeling that we're in a very dark place and that she's been there lurking around just waiting for her next victim to arrive. When she sees me, she rushes over and starts wrapping me tightly up in her sticky silk. Then she injects her poisonous venom into me—and I can't do a thing!" She paused and then acknowledged, "I know it sounds weird, but it's really scary."

"It is *very* frightening," I responded. As we sat quietly for a moment, images from accounts she had shared of her childhood sexual abuse by her uncle came into my mind. I mused aloud, "I wonder if the spider image and feelings you get when you are around this woman, or even think about going near her, are like any feelings you have experienced before."

Amanda sat quietly for a few moments. Suddenly her eyes widened, and she became visibly distressed. "Oh, my gosh! I feel just like I did as a kid when my uncle would stay with my family on the weekends, and he would come into my room at night and molest me. I felt helpless and powerless, and I just lay there pretending I was somewhere else until he finally left the room. My uncle always threatened that if I told anyone, it would destroy the family because my parents would divorce, and it would be all my fault.

"The idea of losing my family was terrifying, and I believed that my only option to save my family and myself was to keep what he was doing secret and to act as if everything was okay. But the whole time I was pretending and trying to be a good person—obeying and being 'nice'—I felt guilty about what was happening." As Amanda's recollections tumbled out, her anxiety and fear were palpable.

Amanda took a deep breath and then continued her association. "That's exactly how I felt when the woman started telling me all the church secrets! As she was overwhelming me and injecting me with her venom, I froze and stood there, helplessly putting up with her intrusiveness.

"Ever since that day, I've been feeling guilty because I was a party to the vicious gossip because I didn't stop her. Also, I've been feeling caught in a bind—just like I felt when I was a kid. I've been thinking that if I tell the pastor or his wife that the woman had been telling me people's secrets, everyone at church will be hurt and upset—and it will be all my fault! So I've been telling myself, 'Keep your mouth shut. Just go to church and act like nothing's wrong so the church won't have any more problems to deal with than it already has.'"

Then Amanda protested, "I can't believe I'm going through this again. I thought I was over it! Why didn't I pick up that the woman wasn't a safe person earlier?"

Before I was able to respond to Amanda's frustration, Amanda looked directly at me and said decisively, "You know what? I am *not* going to do this *anymore*. It's crazy! It is *not* my responsibility to protect everyone else. And it's definitely *not* my responsibility to put up with everyone else's craziness! I'm going to a different church starting this Sunday!"

As I listened to Amanda describe her experiences with the woman from church, I could hear how she was continuing to develop her ability to observe herself and her relationship with others. She was more aware of the ways she was feeling, thinking, and interacting in her relationships.

Unfortunately, Amanda had not recognized early on in her interactions with the woman at church that she (Amanda) was unwittingly re-enacting her child scripts in her relationship with the woman—and the church. She had been attracted to (and had attracted) someone who had poor boundaries and was emotionally poisonous.

Fortunately, Amanda's recognition of what was occurring put her in the position where she was able to leave that church and eventually develop healthier connections in another church. In the process, she freed herself from continuing to re-enact her attitudes and parent-child scripts with the woman and even the church congregation.

It is common to play out these themes—experiencing what you know, evoking what you expect, and attracting what is familiar—when you are repeating relationship patterns. Unfortunately, when you re-enact your childhood survival scripts (parent or child), you, like Amanda, usually end up continuing to be hurt and deprived emotionally, just as you were early in life.

You also reinforce the distortion that others, you, and the world are as bad as you experienced them to be when you were young. Moreover, you fail to resolve the dilemmas created by those early experiences.

It is important to understand how you can unconsciously re-enact your childhood experiences in order to change the childhood scripts that are creating problems in your life. So let us look more specifically at common attitudes and relationships scripts that can be re-enacted as an adult when you grow up with a parent who provides Too Much or Too Little.

We will examine how you can replay these scripts—frequently filled with unresolved vicious cycles—on your life's stage. Then we will discuss the scripts that emerge when you grow up with a parent who provides Just Right.

The Story You Tell

A tale of Too Much. Two different storylines can emerge when your life is a tale of Too Much that are based in your primary caregiver's parenting style: A Tangled Ball of String and In Your Face. Both of these storylines reveal the internal conflicts that developed when, as a child, you attempted to survive with a parent who was either emotionally enmeshed or emotionally domineering. These storylines reemerge during re-enactments that occur in your adult relationships.

Replaying scripts with A Tangled Ball of String theme. In this scenario, you follow scripts based on your experiences growing up with a parent who had an *emotionally enmeshed* style of parenting. When you re-enact this storyline, your life resembles tangled up, balled pieces of string. Because your parent had difficulty separating her emotions, thought processes, and actions from others', her style of relating left the boundaries between you and her poorly defined. Unfortunately, because you were not able to establish yourself as a separate, autonomous person as a child, you may find it difficult to be your own person as an adult.

When you have a poorly developed sense of self, you will have a hard time knowing what you think and feel, or even who you are, as a separate person. These limitations usually leave you with internal conflicts between your needs for attachment and your needs for autonomy, both of which are healthy.

The undeveloped parts of you will also interfere with your developing healthy mutuality in relationships, because interdependence requires that both people be autonomous, not enmeshed. In addition, in a re-enactment, you may find it difficult to tell the difference between healthy accountability in relationships and enmeshed demands; both may feel the same to you. Any desire coming from others can feel like you are losing yourself in the relationship.

If you adapted to your parent's emotionally enmeshed parenting style by developing compliant attitudes, you could find yourself as an adult re-enacting *compliant child* scripts in your relationships, with others being your enmeshed parent counterpart. In this scenario, you, as the compliant child, try to figure out and then be what you think others want.

You also look for others who will tell you how to be, and then you take on their expectations and values as your own. Bartering for the illusion of safety and worth, you give yourself away, just as you did with your primary caregiver. It is just too frightening to do otherwise.

If you coped with your parent's enmeshment as a child by developing defiant attitudes, you will find yourself replaying *defiant child* scripts in your adult relationships at times. You will find yourself actively resist others' expectations, demands, and even simple requests in your relationships because you still believe that the only way to survive emotionally is to defy others.

On some level you are continuing to believe your sense of identity, self-worth, emotionally security, and self-efficacy depend on you continuing to fight against others. When you operate with the scripts of a defiant child, however, you will unconsciously press others into the enmeshed parent role. As the re-enactment continues, it taps into pockets of unresolved pain hidden deep within your psyche.

When you take on the enmeshed parent role in your relationships, however, the scripts you re-enact will reveal what you internalized of your parent's attitudes and style of relating. In this scenario, you do not realize your entanglement with others. Instead, you see others as an extension of you. You expect them to meet and care for your needs, and you take on their emotions or problems as your own.

Others in your life usually feel pressured and obligated to do what you want to make you happy, regardless of the cost to them. They feel guilty, fearful, or angry whether they comply with or defy your demands and frequently end up resenting you and their position. If others point out that you are overinvolved, you may justify your actions.

In the end, operating with the parent scripts of A Tangled Ball of String takes its toll on you, your relationships, and others in your life.

Replaying scripts with an In Your Face theme. In this storyline of a tale of Too Much, you follow scripts based on your experience growing up with a parent who had an *emotionally domineering* style of parenting. Because your primary caregiver did not have a healthy, well-developed, secure sense of herself, she attempted to deal with her vulnerabilities and inadequacies by trying to dominate you and others emotionally. Her style of relating tended to be harsh and punitive because of her own unresolved issues from her past.

If you adapted to your parent's In Your Face style of parenting as a child by developing controlling attitudes, you are likely to re-enact *controlling child* scripts filled with unhealthy over-control in your adult life. In a re-enactment, you may try to control everyone and everything in order to feel some sense of safety and security because your parent's domination left you feeling helpless, powerless, and perhaps even terrified as a child.

You can also attempt to counteract the feelings of inadequacy that you developed as a child by vying for control in your adult relationships in order to have a sense of worth. Your over-control may appear as overt control. It may emerge more covertly in the form of perfectionism, in which you try to make yourself, others, and the world operate without flaws. It may also appear in the form of passive-aggressive control maneuvers in which you attempt to disguise your over-controlling behaviors.

If you developed competitive attitudes to adapt to your parent's emotionally domineering style of relating, you are likely to replay *competitive child* scripts filled with unhealthy competitiveness in your adult relationships. You may believe that the only way to survive is to compete with everyone about everything. You end up playing a game of one-up-man-ship, in which you try desperately to be in the perceived superior position in order to have a sense of self-worth.

In the competitive child role of the In Your Face storyline, you tend to experience others as if they are domineering even when, in fact, they are not. You may be suspicious of others' motivations, "knowing" that they are trying to take away your power.

When this happens, you misread others' requests and desires for mutuality and interdependence as attempts to dominate or demean you. You may also act in ways that result in others actually trying to take charge of you. For example, if you are not taking charge of your responsibilities, others will tend to complain and try to get you to "do what you are supposed to do." When this happens, it confirms your fears that others are attempting to dominate you, just as your parent did.

What you fail to realize in this situation is that your actions actually evoked those reactions. You may gravitate toward people who are highly competitive and dominating and then feel controlled by them, just as your parent dominated you as a child. In this tale of Too Much, you find yourself, as an adult, re-enacting the controlling or the competitive child scripts, with others being your dominating parent counterpart.

In contrast, when you re-enact the domineering parent scripts of the In Your Face parenting style, you are the one in your relationships who dominates and controls others in harsh, punitive ways. Remember, however, that healthy relationships involve mutual regard and consideration, whereas domineering attitudes are inherently hostile and interfere with healthy relationships.

When you dominate others, you do not take others' needs or preferences into consideration. For all practical purposes, in this scenario, others do not have any importance or value and, in some sense, do not even exist, except to meet your needs. Even though these ways of feeling, thinking, and acting may seem perfectly understandable and justifiable to you, they clearly disregard others.

Whether you re-enact the enmeshed or domineering parent scripts or the controlling or competitive child scripts of a tale of Too Much, your relationships are negatively impacted. Just as your parent's dysfunctional attitudes once harmed her relationship with you, the undermining attitudes you internalized from your parent and those that you developed in response to them will interfere with your relationships. All of these attitudes make a mutually fulfilling relationship impossible.

These attitude scripts also interfere with your ability to operate effectively as an autonomous, confident adult. When a primary caregiver provides Too Much, the caregiver's needs and fears usurp your needs, capabilities, and boundaries. You then have difficulty feeling positive about yourself or feeling safe and secure in your relationships.

When you re-enact these child and parent scripts, you fail to develop the undeveloped parts of yourself that never received adequate challenge and support early on. Instead, you reinforce the wounds you experienced as a child.

To the extent that your primary caregiver's parenting style was emotionally enmeshed or domineering, you may try to protect yourself from anything that you experience as intrusive or controlling. All of these core attitudes—compliance, defiance, competitiveness, over-control—are attempts to protect yourself from being emotionally enmeshed or dominated in order to be safe and secure emotionally. Unfortunately, they fail to do so.

A tale of Too Little. When your adult life is a tale of Too Little, it may contain storylines evolving from experiences with a Missing in Action or Now You See Me, Now You Don't parent. If your parent was Missing in Action, themes of emotional unavailability and avoidance or detachment may run throughout your life's story. If your parent operated with a Now You See Me, Now You Don't style, your life story may be replete with experiences of emotional inconsistency and ambivalence or confusion.

Replaying attitude scripts with a Missing in Action theme. In this scenario, you follow scripts based on your experiences growing up with a parent who had an *emotionally unavailable* style of parenting. When you re-enact this parent-child relationship pattern, you tend to interact with others in a way that re-creates the experience of emotional absence.

In this storyline, one person will be in the role of your emotionally unavailable parent while someone else will have the experience of being the "not cared for, abandoned, alone, or needy one". Both of these reciprocal parts of the Missing in Action relational script leave you feeling insecure in your relationships.

In order to survive with a parent whose style of relating is emotionally unavailable, you may develop avoidant attitudes. When you re-enact the *avoidant child* scripts in your adult life, you may find that it is difficult for you to be open in your personal relationships. You may feel anxious and very uncomfortable around other people. You may think and even believe that something is wrong with you (e.g., you are inadequate, unworthy, or not lovable).

If you believe something is inherently wrong with you, you may avoid other people, emotionally or physically, because you fear that others will pull away from you. You may also worry that others will reject you, especially if you felt rejected by your emotionally unavailable parent. If you were in the position of *persona non grata* as a child, you might be terrified of being in that situation again. In order to deal with these distressing emotions, thoughts, and beliefs, you may become highly avoidant in your relationships.

If you adapted to your parent's emotional unavailability by developing detached attitudes, it might be difficult to form any significant emotional attachments to other people. When you re-enact *detached child* scripts, you may find that you have little to no desire to be close to people. You may choose to spend time by yourself because, after all, aloneness is familiar. You learned early on to survive without significant attachments, so they are of little value to you. In this type of re-enactment, if others criticize or complain about you, it does not substantially affect you since you do not have any internal connection to them.

When you are operating with attitudes grounded in detachment, you are not dependent on others for emotional resources. You may even function in a parallel universe, so to speak—present in some ways, but not emotionally interdependent in your relationships. The degree to which you cope by becoming detached varies according to your nature as a child and the extent to which your parent was emotionally unavailable.

When you are replaying the parent role of your assimilated Missing in Action relationship storyline, you will tend to find that you are emotionally unavailable in your relationships. Now *you* are the one filling your life with responsibilities that prevent you from being with yourself and others emotionally. You find yourself overloaded and too exhausted to talk to your family, much less your friends.

Even when you long, deep inside, to have close relationships with others, you have difficulty knowing how to relate and connect with them.

In this emotionally unavailable parent re-enactment, people in your life feel alone and distressed, just as you were as a child. They may complain that you do not spend enough time with them and that they miss being with you. They may feel disconnected and deserted. Eventually, they may give up trying to relate to you—just as you once did with your parents.

Replaying scripts with a Now You See Me, Now You Don't theme. If your primary caregiver's style of parenting was Now You See Me, Now You Don't, the main theme of your story will involve emotional inconsistency. In this storyline, the person who replays the child role will have the experience of being "the confused, anxious, uncertain, frightened, or emotionally empty one." For the re-enactment to continue, someone else must fill the role of the parent who provides Too Little by being unreliable or unpredictable.

As you coped with your parent's emotionally inconsistent style of parenting, you may have developed attitudes centered in ambivalence. Although part of you may want an emotional connection with others, part of you may also fear it because you do not know who or what you can trust. You believe and expect that others will not be available for you in any consistent, predictable way.

These feelings, thoughts, and beliefs make it difficult for you to rely on others or to develop secure attachments. When you are re-enacting *ambivalent child* scripts, you may find yourself trying to get close to others even though you have mixed feelings about it. But when you start to get close, your fear and anxiety of being close, or of losing closeness, can become activated, causing you to you pull away from relationships.

A different response to a parent whose relational style emotionally inconsistent is to develop attitudes grounded in confusion. When you are re-enacting *confused child* scripts, you may find yourself feeling anxious and overly needy in your relationships because you do not have the base of a secure attachment pattern.

You may be confused by, and have difficulty understanding, others' healthy autonomy needs, and you may misperceive autonomy as abandonment. You also expect and believe that others will be unpredictable and that they are likely to leave you. Your confusion and uncertainty can cause you to become clingy.

When you re-enact the parent scripts of the Now You See Me, Now You Don't style of relating, you tend to be unreliable. You can find yourself at times trying to be responsive to others' needs but at other times disengaging from them. You may spend a lot of time with others and then be too busy to get together.

People in your life may feel like they cannot count on you because of your unpredictability. They will tend to feel anxious and uncertain about their relationship with you and frequently look for reassurance that the relationship is working. In your own confusion and irritation about their insecurity, you may even find yourself wondering, "What is *their* problem?"

Whether you enact avoidant, detached, ambivalent, or confused attitude scripts in your relationships, the parts you play will be familiar. In these situations, because your attitudes may filter out attempts by other people to relate, you may experience others as if they are your emotionally absent or emotionally inconsistent parent.

In addition to feeling helpless and powerless to care for your needs, it may not even cross your mind that it is possible to have them met. After all, your parent was not there for you emotionally (or at least, not in any consistent way), so why would anyone else be?

Even if others are helpful, caring, and emotionally available none of their efforts may feel like concern because you believe that no one will ever be mindful of your emotional needs. Despite others' attempts to show they care for you, you can have trouble trusting that they will be there to support you emotionally.

In your relationships, you may find yourself frequently experiencing others as not being available to you in the way you want and need them to be. When this happens, you are left feeling alone, frightened, and in desperate need of emotional sustenance.

When you re-enact scripts involving Missing in Action or Now You See Me, Now You Don't relationship patterns, you act in ways that evoke others' emotional unavailability—just as you expected.

Because you anticipate and expect others to be like your parent who provided Too Little, you might relate to others in the same way you learned to relate with your parent—with avoidant, detached, ambivalent, or confused attitudes. Although meant to be protective, these ways of dealing with your emotions, thoughts, and behaviors will usually cause others to pull away from you, fulfilling your thoughts and fears.

In addition, when you re-create an emotionally absent or emotionally inconsistent relationship dynamic, you may attract, and be attracted to, others who provide very little relationally. You may try to form connections with others who are not willing or able to be emotionally available in any consistent way, reinforcing your beliefs and anxieties.

A tale of Just Right. If your parent had a *Reliably Available* style of parenting, the story of your adult life is more likely to evolve as a tale of Just Right. Although you, like everyone, will encounter the twists, turns, and upheavals inherent in life, the primary storylines woven throughout your life will have themes based on core attitudes of reliability, security, and confidence. These themes emerge because you have developed the capacity to function as a *secure and confident adult.*

Just as a strong immune system protects you from the pathogens you encounter in daily living, robust attitudes and relationship patterns developed early in life help protect you when you face life's hardships as an adult. Because they provide you with inner strength and the capacity to be adaptable, they enable you to deal resiliently with life's challenges.

These healthy ways of feeling, thinking, and acting will be apparent both when you are caring for yourself and interacting with others. Due to your parent's reliable attunement and help in regulating your emotions, you will be better able to observe both yourself and others and modulate your emotions and body states.

As a secure and confident adult you will be less susceptible to illusions and distortions. This allows you to deal with the present as the present, not the past—with others based on who they are, not based on who you or your parents once were. You will also have greater cognitive flexibility, modifying your thoughts and beliefs as you have new experiences and gain new insights. Utilizing a broader range of responses, you will be able to relate to others in mutual, collaborative, and interdependent ways.

Unfortunately, even if you were blessed to have a parent whose primary style of parenting was Reliably Available, you will still emerge from childhood with some attitudes and relationship patterns that may need to be revised. Some areas of your self did not develop adequately; some, perhaps, were wounded. (Remember, there are no perfect parents and no perfect children.)

Because of this, as an adult you may find yourself re-enacting dysfunctional scripts learned during times when your primary caregiver did not respond to you in an ideal way. These re-enactments are especially likely if you have not been able to work through the disappointing or hurtful experiences and integrate them psychologically in a healthy way.

Even so, you will tend to have fewer and less pervasive forms of painful re-enactments if your parent's primary style of parenting was Just Right than if her parenting style was Too Little or Too Much. You will also have a greater capacity to adapt to the different parts of yourself.

Remember, each time you find a way to effectively handle and adapt to the challenges you encounter, you will become even more capable, and more secure in your ability to manage the unfortunate things that befall you.

Summary: A Civil War Re-enactment

As you go about your daily life, you may discover yourself re-enacting your parent-child scripts on the stage of your life in some way. Initially, you may not notice that you are doing so because what is occurring will seem natural.

If, however, you pay attention to your body's responses to people and situations, you may notice you are experiencing *body memories* of your past painful experiences that alert you that a re-enactment is occurring. These body signals may involve feelings of distress (e.g., tension or hyper-alertness).

If part of your experience with your parent's Too Much or Too Little style of parenting was exciting, feelings of excitement might be the way your body signals the activation of old scripts.

When you pay attention to your body signals, you can choose how you will respond to them. You can take action to stop the re-enactment from occurring and protect yourself from being re-wounded. If you fail to recognize what is occurring or to disengage from the re-enactment, it is likely that you will end up harmed by it, just as your experiences hurt you when you were a child.

Unfortunately, as you become aware that you are re-creating scenarios that are apt to leave you wounded once again, a part of you may resist facing what you know deep within you.

If you observe your feelings, thoughts, and actions carefully, however, you will begin to notice that although one part of you may want your outdated attitudes changed and your wounds repaired, another part does not want to face the "monsters" that lurk in the recesses of your mind. You may find yourself desperately clinging to your familiar, and seemingly safe, ways of relating to others, yourself, and life—even though you can see they are not optimally adaptive.

You also may discover ways part of your psyche tenaciously works to keep you from doing what is necessary to bring about the changes you desire. For example, your attitudes may reveal that you want someone or something else to change your life for you, or you are clinging to the belief that others are responsible to make your life better. This discrepancy between desire and action alerts you to a great civil war waging internally: change versus the familiar known.

The unhealthy core attitudes you developed during your early years can prevent you from caring for your needs in other ways. Your feelings, thought processes, and action tendencies may maintain illusions and distortions that prevent you from taking accountability for your life. For example, your attitudes can promote the illusion that your needs are being met when, in fact, they are not. This illusion allows you to hold on to the mindset that your childhood survival strategies will protect you and will enable you to get—finally—what you failed to get from your parent during childhood.

Distorting your experience of yourself, others, and the world, you may cling to beliefs such as, "I can't do anything to change my life," or, "I don't know how to change my attitudes". These beliefs reinforce the idea that you are helpless and powerless to care for yourself. Distortions in how you feel, think, and act can also cause you to experience others as if *they* are your parent who provided Too Much or Too Little.

Unhealthy attitudes can also reinforce undermining self-fulfilling prophecies. When you expect and predict things will occur in a certain way, you tend to experience the very thing you predict. You may manage your emotions, beliefs, and behaviors in ways that evoke the very attitudes in others you anticipate. You may also gravitate toward, and attract, people who fail you in the same ways your parent once failed you, thus confirming your worst fears.

Challenging and dismantling this system of old attitudes and relationship patterns is often frightening and may seem impossible. After all, the old internal operating system is all you have ever known—a familiar defense in what you have experienced as an unsafe world.

With conscious and unconscious desperation, you may find yourself clinging tightly to the hope that you can make the ending of your story turn out differently—somehow—if you just try another way.

You realize that attempting to create a different ending to your story by pretending that others can meet your infantile needs does not make it possible. You can see how re-enacting old scripts that re-create the past in the present just leaves you with more pain and frustration.

So, consciously, or unconsciously, you may decide to try another strategy.

CHAPTER 7

Searching for What You Never Had

What should I possibly have to tell you ...? Perhaps that you're searching far too much? That in all that searching, you don't find the time for finding.
—Herman Hesse, *Siddhartha*

Part of the legacy of growing up with a mother whose parenting style provides Too Much or Too Little is attitudes that can leave you feeling lost, empty, and insecure. These attitudes can be confusing and incredibly painful. They can also be frightening and sometimes even terrifying. Because these emotions are so distressing, they can leave you "endlessly hoping that some day in some way it will be possible to find a niche in the human world, a connection that will enable [you] to feel human, to feel real" (Hedges, 1994, p. 110). They can also leave you clinging desperately to your life-preserving childhood hopes and desires for connection with someone who will provide for your unmet maternal needs.

Unfortunately, hoping for someone who will provide the emotional resources you failed to receive from your parent can draw you into a lifetime of endless searching for what you missed. These longings can also keep you holding tightly to what is available to you—the attitudes and relationship patterns you developed as a young understudy to your primary caregiver.

However, when you operate with the survival system you developed early in life, you unconsciously reinforce the familiar but undermining psychological connections to your internal parent-child scripts.

Regardless of how much or how long you search for someone who will provide all of your unmet childhood needs, ultimately such a person does not exist.

No one can provide what you needed emotionally (but failed to experience) in the first few years of life. Searching endlessly for the good enough mother of infancy in your adult relationships will not make up for what you lacked as a child. Maintaining a psychological connection to your parent by re-enacting your childhood scripts also will not meet your early infant emotional needs. Neither of these methods will help you develop an internal sense of security or a clear sense of your identity as an autonomous person.

That does not mean, however, that caring for your unmet needs is hopeless. The fact is, you have options for taking care of your unmet needs. You can develop your ability to observe your emotional, cognitive, and behavioral patterns and think about how the core attitudes and relationship patterns you developed as you interacted with your parent are affecting your life.

This ability to be mindful of and reflective about your internal repertoire will enable you to begin making more informed decisions about how you care for your unmet emotional needs and take the necessary steps to save your life from endlessly searching for the good enough mother of infancy.

Later we will look more closely at how you can free yourself from the grip of your childhood survival system and, in the process, change the undermining, recurring re-enactments of parent-child attitude scripts.

In this chapter, however, we will discuss how the never-ending search for someone to provide you with the emotional sustenance that you did not receive early in life can be entrapping. We will look at how your outdated attitudes and relationship patterns fuel the quest for someone who will provide your unmet needs and complete you. We will also examine what it costs to keep this endless search going.

Let us begin our exploration by considering how Leon unconsciously reinforced his parent-child scripts as he searched for someone who could fulfill his unmet childhood emotional needs.

Leon's Story

Leon, a 37-year-old divorced man, came to see me because he was feeling overwhelmed by conflicts with his girlfriend, Natalia, with whom he had been living for about two years.

In addition, in the month prior to starting therapy, Leon had begun to experience more anxiety and had gone to the hospital emergency room with panic attacks. After we had been working together for a few months, Leon summarized both his childhood and his relationship with Natalia this way.

"When I was a kid, I never really felt loved by my parents. My mom was very controlling and demanding in a whiny sort of way. She put subtle (and sometimes not so subtle) pressure on me to take care of her needs, even though she did it in a way that others didn't seem to notice. I used to think I was making the whole thing up."

Leon paused as tension rippled across his face. Then he continued, "Another thing ... my mom didn't see me for who I really was or value me for myself. Even though she often would brag about me to others, something about that felt weird. It took me a while to realize it, but I finally figured out that what she was doing was not about being proud of me. She was really using me to make herself feel important. I hated it!

"And, as if that wasn't bad enough, my dad wasn't there for me, either. He was the disciplinarian in the family and was constantly on my back about something or other. I never really knew what was acceptable to him. To tell you the truth, I am a little afraid of him. ... Well, actually, I'm afraid of *both* of them."

I responded, "It's painful when your needs are not being recognized or responded to and when you're not being related to as a person in your own right."

"It's horrible!" Leon said with angst in his voice. "It's made it really hard for me to know who I am; I've been trying to figure that out ever since I was a kid. My hope has always been that I'd find someone who would love me for myself. It's what's kept me going. I dated for a long time before I got married because I was trying to make sure I found the right person.

"When I finally did get married, I thought I had found the girl of my dreams, but my marriage didn't last. Since then I've been trying really hard to find someone who would be a good match for me, but my relationships have never worked out.

"Even now, I'm having problems in my relationship with Natalia. But when Natalia and I were first dating, everything seemed perfect, and I thought I'd finally found 'the one.' Natalia would show me lots of love, attention, and affection, and she seemed to have an uncanny ability to tune in to what I was feeling. And she seemed happy with me, too. I've tried really hard to show her I love her. I've given her whatever she's wanted, and I've never complained about it, even when I thought that she was being unreasonable."

I started to reflect, "It seemed that you had finally found the love you have been searching for all these years—"

"I'll say!" Leon burst out, interrupting me. "But about six months after Natalia and I moved in together, she changed, and things started going downhill. Now we argue and fight all the time. I'm still trying to give her whatever she wants, but she doesn't pay any attention to what I need anymore. She constantly criticizes me and rarely shows me any affection.

"Yeah, once in a while Natalia acts all lovey-dovey, and I start thinking things are going to get better. But I've decided that she's just pretending so that she can get something from me, because her 'niceness' doesn't last very long. I get really mad at her. I tell her, 'I'm being good to you—the least you could do is to treat me right. It's only fair.' But what I say doesn't make any difference. Natalia doesn't change, no matter what I say or do." Leon's eyes filled with tears as he continued, "I feel like such a sucker."

Mindful of Leon's distress, I said, "You've been searching a long time for someone who will give you the emotional care that you didn't get as a child. But, despite your hopes and expectations and your best efforts, you have been disappointed yet again."

Leon looked directly and intently into my eyes. "What am I doing wrong? Is it too much to ask that someone will love and care for me unconditionally? I try my hardest to be a good and kind person, but I never find anyone who comes through for me. I get mad about it, but what's the point?

"Lately I've started avoiding Natalia whenever possible. I guess I've given up thinking that things will get better. Instead, I'm trying to figure out how to get out of the mess I'm in right now with her. Once I do, you'd better believe you won't catch me being the good guy or trusting anyone again! I'm done with trying to find someone to care about me. I've decided that I don't need anyone! I've survived all these years without anyone, and I can make it by myself the rest of the way!"

I could see and feel the pain Leon was experiencing as he struggled with his internal conflicts. I reflected to him, "It hurts so much when others don't come through for you in the ways you want and feel entitled to ... and it's beginning to make you really angry! It feels so hopeless."

"You can say that again!" Leon exclaimed.

Leon had spent his life searching for someone who would meet his needs. Despite all of his efforts, others frequently had failed to come through for him in the ways he wanted and needed—just as his parents had failed him as a child.

Each time that happened, Leon had gone through periods of depression, re-experiencing the helplessness, disappointment, frustration, confusion, and anger that he had felt as a child.

Now, as Leon was dealing with the reality of what was not available to him emotionally in his relationship with Natalia, he was clearly experiencing all the old feelings again. In addition, Leon's underlying fears of being alone and not surviving emotionally were contributing to his panic attacks.

To protect himself from feeling the anger and heartbreak associated with his unmastered losses, Leon was unsuccessfully relying upon psychological defenses that were not serving him well. He was alternately desperately seeking a stand-in for the nurturing parents he had never had or falling back on a self-protective "I am a rock; I am an island" strategy. However, his defenses were only compounding his frustration, anguish, and rage.

Your Search for the Perfect Script

The normal, healthy emotional needs you have as a developing infant (i.e., love, emotional attunement and regulation, security, confidence, and self-worth) are called *infantile needs*. Because your parent (like all parents) was unable to provide for all of your infantile needs, you (like everyone else) emerged from childhood with some unmet emotional needs. As a young understudy to your primary caregiver, you recorded these experiences of *not* getting your emotional needs met.

It would be wonderful if you could just ask others to meet your infantile needs and get what you did not receive as a child. Unfortunately, your unmet emotional needs from childhood cannot be taken care of that easily. You must first experience and grieve your losses in order to free yourself from their negative impact.

It is hard, however, to face, grieve, and accept the emotional disappointments and losses you incurred as a child. Instead, you may try to protect yourself by clinging to the false hope that you can find someone who will perfectly meet all of your needs, thus correcting your experiences that wounded you in early childhood.

Your illusory belief is that the emotional resources you need are still outside you, in someone else, just like your parent was outside you. And your longings, felt needs, and beliefs propel you into searching for someone who will be, in essence, a Just Right parent stand-in.

However, reality is, however, that your unresolved losses and perpetual searching for these perfect emotional experiences are blocking your ability to meet your emotional needs and change your life scripts. In order to begin removing these blocks, it is helpful to observe and identify the patterns of your efforts to care for your unmet needs.

There are three common, predictable phases in the quest for these perfect corrective experiences, which I call the *search for the perfect script*:

- You look to others to meet your needs and complete you.
- You become outraged in your disappointment when others do not meet your needs.
- You give up in despair and retreat from your search.

Unfortunately, the feelings, beliefs, and behaviors that drive your search for good enough mother experiences interfere with the development of the security and confidence you truly need. So let us examine these phases in more depth.

You Look to Others to Complete You

Deep inside, you may long for someone who will supply the missing pieces that your primary caregiver was not able to provide reliably and consistently. Your hopes for such a person and your beliefs that such a person exists can drive you to search endlessly for someone who will make you feel complete.

Hope can have both an upside and a downside, however. On the upside, in general, hope is a positive and helpful emotion. Hope can help you develop healthy adaptations so you can survive difficult times. It is especially useful if it motivates you to pursue your goals. Under these circumstances, hope stimulates good feelings that, in turn, provide even more motivation.

On the downside, however, hope can be a way to avoid confronting reality. When you use hope in this way, you keep alive the illusion that someone *can* and *will* provide for all of your unmet needs, if only you search long and hard enough.

Martha Stark, MD, a psychiatrist-psychoanalyst on the faculty at Harvard Medical School, describes characteristics of this defense.

> [You may be willing] to suffer, to sacrifice, to work very hard, to accommodate, to do anything that is asked, as long as [you] can hold on to the illusion, the dream, the hope that someday, somehow, some way, if [you are] good enough, [work] hard enough, [persist] long enough, and [suffer] deeply enough, then the long-awaited goodies will be forthcoming. (1994, p. 267)

Although this illusionary hope may initially keep you from despair, it actually prevents you from taking care of your emotional needs. Instead, it strengthens the illusion that someone out there, somewhere, can provide what you failed to receive as a child. It reinforces the ineffective, and perhaps even harmful, attitudes that distort what is real and true in the present. If you spend your life searching for what you missed as an infant, in all likelihood you will fail to do what is necessary to meet your needs in the present.

At some point, the hope and illusion that others can meet your unmet infantile needs will begin to collapse—guaranteed. When your defensive illusions start to collapse, you may be flooded with the fear, anxiety, depression, and even anger that you have been warding off for years. You may also discover other emotions that you have never recognized or identified before, including your feelings of entitlement.

Along with these emotions, three key underlying beliefs often drive your search for someone to fulfill your unmet needs and complete you. These beliefs are part of your attitudes:

- You are *helpless* to provide for your needs.
- You are *omnipotent*; you have the power to make someone meet your needs.
- You are *entitled* to have all your needs met by others.

As long as you *believe you are helpless to provide for your needs*, you will feel helpless and act helpless. You may pursue people who you think will meet your needs—who you want and expect to provide for your unmet needs. You then attempt to elicit from them the good that you need.

Even though you may believe that you are helpless to provide for your needs, paradoxically, you can also believe that you are omnipotent. The unconscious belief that you have unlimited power and influence can operate in two ways. You may believe others can and will meet your infantile needs if only you persist long and hard enough. In this script, the theme becomes, "I Try Harder." Using the relational pattern you internalized as a young understudy to your primary caregiver, you then try very hard to get others to give you what you think only they can provide.

In your omnipotence, you may also *believe you have the power to make others meet your needs*. In this script, the theme becomes, "I Can Make You." This belief reinforces the illusion that your expectations and demands are so powerful that you can force others to act the way you want them to act. It also strengthens the notion that you can *only* feel secure and confident if others operate according to your expectations and demands.

In both of these scripts, your core attitudes are comprised of feelings and beliefs grounded in omnipotence. The sense of omnipotence is developmentally normal in toddlers who think they are the center of the universe and have yet to come to terms with their limitations. When a sense of omnipotence operates in an adult, however, it reveals unresolved areas of internal conflict. These conflicts often occur between what you know is true about others, yourself, and life and the hopes you have that you will find what you need.

Even though it is an illusion to believe that you have all power to make others, and even yourself, do whatever you want and demand, you may cling to it desperately. The illusion is a defense against the helplessness and powerlessness you felt with your parent who provided Too Much or Too Little and that, on some level, you still feel as an adult.

Along with a feeling of entitlement, you may also *believe you are entitled to have others meet your needs*. This belief is founded in your entitled sense that it is your right to have your infantile needs met today because you did not get the emotional resources you needed as a child. You believe others and life should make up for the losses you incurred as a child, because, after all, it is your due.

Unfortunately, these feelings and beliefs keep you trapped in the never-ending cycle of searching externally for what you never received as a child.

An endless search for someone to provide for your unmet emotional needs—combined with the belief that you are helpless as well as omnipotent and entitled to have others meet your needs— is a recipe for problems in your life.

As Lawrence Hedges, a training psychoanalyst and founder of the Newport Psychoanalytic Institute, puts it: "By nurturing the belief or fantasy that everything should be, nay must be, perfect, ideal, blissful, happy … [you] ensure ongoing and unending unhappiness, misery, suffering, and unrest" (Hedges, 1994, p. 167). Ultimately, these attitudes interfere with the necessary process of caring for your needs in healthy ways. They also reinforce the outdated attitudes and relationship patterns that keep you from creating a secure and confident life.

How you look to others to meet your needs and complete you depends on your parent's style of parenting—whether it provided Too Much, Too Little, or Just Right. Consider the following ways you might look to others to meet your needs and complete you.

If your parent's style of relating was emotionally enmeshed. When a parent has an emotionally enmeshed style of relating, you may develop attitudes and relationship patterns based on *compliance* or *defiance* in order to survive emotionally.

If you adapted to your parent by becoming compliant, you might re-enact these scripts by trying to please others as an adult. Feeling helpless, you may look to others for approval by trying to be perfect or by striving to measure up to others' expectations (at least what you think and perceive their expectations to be).

You hope and expect that your efforts will provide you the love, worth, acceptance, and emotional safety you long for if you try hard enough. The helpless belief that you can only have your emotional needs met by others may also make it difficult for you to establish personal boundaries. You may fear others will reject you if you operate with a separate, autonomous sense of self. Therefore, you try to accommodate others as you once accommodated your parent.

If, however, you adapted to your parent by developing defiant attitudes, you may relentlessly re-enact these scripts. Even though defiant attitudes may not appear to be an attempt to provide for your unmet emotional needs, surface appearances can be deceiving.

Consciously or unconsciously, you may become involved in activities that resist societal norms to obtain a sense of identity, worth, and belonging. Your unconscious hope is that by involving yourself with others who have the same defiant attitudes and relationship patterns you will get your needs met.

In addition, to meet your need for an autonomous sense of self, you may try to prove that you are not like others. You might try to justify your attitudes by developing a cynical, critical, and oppositional style of relating to yourself, others, and the world.

If your parent's style of relating was emotionally domineering. If your parent's style of relating was emotionally domineering, it is likely that you often felt helpless, powerless, and inadequate as a child and coped by developing *controlling* or *competitive* attitudes. If you adapted to your parent by developing attitudes based in control, you might try to get your infantile needs (e.g., for belonging, acknowledgment, and affirmation) met by controlling others.

In this situation, your underlying hope and belief is that if you control others like your parent controlled you, you will get the sense of worth and personal power that you failed to develop as a child. After all, that is how your parent tried to care for her needs.

Controlling attitudes can appear in different forms. For example, you may develop a rigid code of living, believing that if you can make yourself and others conform to these standards, others will love and accept you. You may believe that if you can make yourself be "perfect" you will be worthwhile. You may try to force others to operate according to your expectations and demands, perhaps even to the point of being abusive in some way. In your attempts to convince yourself and others of your worth, you may also try to control others' perceptions of you.

In contrast, if you tend to believe there are limited amounts of love, acceptance, and worth available you may try to meet your infantile needs for love, self-worth, security, and confidence through unhealthy competition, which focuses on being superior to others or on pushing others down.

In this type of competition, you may believe that if you do not win the prizes you seek, they will go to others, leaving you with nothing—once again. Notice that this is an either-or equation. Either you get to feel and be important or the other person gets to feel and be important. In this type of competition, both of you cannot end up being valuable. One person has to be in a less-than position.

Unhealthy competitive attitudes can also appear in different forms. For example, you may create and attempt to win arguments or conflicts in order to feel powerful and adequate. Or you might focus on trying to be smarter than others are in order to feel important. You may feel delighted when you can outsmart and outmaneuver your "opponents" and render them as helpless or inadequate as you feel.

Your competitive efforts also may focus on competing with others by owning expensive things or having high-status affiliations in order to gain a sense of self-worth and personal power. The tenaciously held underlying belief is that these associations will compensate for what you failed to receive from your parent.

Efforts to obtain internal security and confidence by controlling or competing with others, however, are misguided. Either scenario only provides the illusion that you are important and powerful. You can live the lifestyle of the rich and famous and wallpaper your house with academic diplomas.

You can win every power struggle and every competition. You can outsmart everyone you know. Still, you are not likely to feel emotionally secure internally.

If your parent's style of parenting was emotionally unavailable. If your parent was emotionally unavailable, you might have adapted to her absence by avoiding closeness or even detaching from others in order to prevent yourself from experiencing the pain of her unavailability.

If you are able to overcome your attitudes of *avoidance* or *detachment,* even for a time, you may begin searching, consciously or unconsciously, for someone who will provide your needs for love, acceptance, and a sense of worth. When this happens, you may find yourself wanting, expecting, and perhaps even demanding that others be what you want them to be—until this search for someone to provide your infantile needs fails. At this point, your defenses of avoidance and detachment may take over once again.

Alternatively, if your search for someone to be emotionally available fails, you might try to meet your needs through fantasy relationships. In fantasy, your longings and fears can co-exist without too much conflict because the action is in your mind, not in the real world. This can make fantasy relationships appear safer than real relationships. But because the safety of fantasy is an illusion, eventually the imaginary security will dissipate, leaving you with your unmet needs.

Whether the fantasies are solely in one's imagination or acted out in the outside world, the hope and illusion is that the imagined experiences will enable you to feel loved and worthwhile—while still maintaining your defenses.

If your parent's style of parenting was emotionally inconsistent. If your parent's style of relating was emotionally inconsistent, you might have adapted to her inconsistency by developing attitudes infused with *ambivalence* or *confusion*. These attitudes usually interfere with your ability to get your needs met in the present.

When you have ambivalent attitudes, your search for someone to meet your needs may be inconsistent. You may attempt to relate to others and then disengage for a while, especially if others disappoint you. You may look for someone to meet your needs but develop relationships with those who have a limited capacity to do so. It can be very difficult to establish committed relationships when you have core attitudes of ambivalence.

If your attitudes reflect confused ways of feeling, thinking, and behaving, it will be hard to take care of your needs. When you are confused, you may not even know what you want or need. This lack of insight interferes with your motivation and leaves you floundering.

To solve this dilemma, you may look to others both to tell you what you want and need and then to provide what you want and need. Unfortunately, attitudes of confusion and ambivalence usually reinforce feelings of helplessness and the belief that you cannot care for your needs. They can also set the stage for attitudes of entitlement to develop, which makes it hard to act on your own behalf because you cling to the illusion that others can, will, or should take care of all you needs.

But regardless of your efforts to get others to meet your infantile needs and complete you, your search is doomed to fail. Even if you are able to you develop some type of connections with others, you may ultimately disengage because you have a sense that something is missing in the relationship, although you are not sure what is wrong.

You Become Outraged When Disappointed

At some point in your search for the perfect script, you will come face to face with the reality that others ultimately fail to meet your expectations that they should provide *all* of your unmet needs. When this occurs, your hopes are dashed. You may feel shame because your efforts have failed. You may also feel disappointed, sad, and betrayed.

At this point, your feelings of loss, shame, disappointment, sadness, betrayal, and entitlement can converge, and you can become outraged. Martha Stark puts it this way:

> In those moments of clarity, when the person sees that the rewards for his unstinting efforts are not going to be forthcoming, he responds with a crushing sense of devastation and outrage. He experiences himself as having been unappreciated, misunderstood, deeply wronged, treated unfairly, violated, victimized. In fact, part of what fuels the person's outrage is his conviction that he has been abused. (1994, p. 271)

These core beliefs—that you are helpless to care for your infantile needs and that others not only can but also are *obligated* to provide them because it is your *right*—set you up to be disillusioned. The anger and resentment aroused by the shattering of your unrealistic expectations reinforce the underlying "I can't"—"you can"—"you should" beliefs of your childhood survival system, which in turn increases your feelings of entitlement. These beliefs, which drive your search for someone to fulfill all your needs and make you feel whole, seal everyone's fate. In reality, others are neither obligated nor able to provide for your unmet childhood needs, and you do not have the power to make them do so.

Your outrage following a failure to get your needs met is directed at those you believe betrayed your "trust"—your trust that they would provide what your Too Much, Too Little, and even Just Right parent failed to provide. You may, like the Queen of Hearts in *Alice's Adventures in Wonderland*, stomp around demanding others' heads be lopped off. After all, you believe, they are supposed to meet your expectations.

How could you *not* feel angry and resentful when those who are supposed to be stand-ins for the Reliably Available parent you never had fail in their charge? When you are in the midst of experiencing and unleashing your outrage at your failed expectations, it can be extremely difficult to recognize and reality check your illusions and regulate your emotions.

You may also aim your anger at yourself for failing to extract the good you need from others. You may be infuriated that you are not perfect or omnipotent (and never can be) and find yourself mentally flagellating yourself for your failures. At these times, your belief that you can—and should be able to—make others meet your needs because you are all powerful is warring with the reality of your own limitations, as well as the limitations of others.

Some people have difficulty being aware of their anger and resentment. If it was not emotionally safe for you to express (or even feel) anger when you were growing up, you may find that you have repressed or detached from your angry feelings.

It can be frightening to let yourself experience your anger if you think others will disapprove of or reject you for being angry. It can also be terrifying to feel (or to think you might feel) your anger taking over, getting out of control, and becoming destructive. Nevertheless, whether or not you are aware of feeling angry and resentful, you still may *be* outraged, even if the feelings exist at an unconscious level.

The search for perfect corrective emotional experiences is usually tenacious. With unyielding determination, you can refuse to accept your own real limitations, in addition to the limitations of others, and continue to hold on tightly to your underlying (perhaps unconscious) beliefs that you are omnipotent and can make others meet your needs.

You may also refuse to let go of your demands that others can and should meet your needs. Even if you do give up trying to get your needs met by a particular individual or in a certain situation, the cycle will not end. If you do not grieve your losses and do the work necessary to transform your attitudes of entitlement and perfectionism, you will eventually begin searching for someone else to provide for your infantile needs.

When you are stuck in a state of interminable outrage, you may also aim your anger and resentment at life in general. Everyone and everything can become stand-ins for the parent who failed you. You can spend your whole life being resentful that the world does not operate the way you think it should.

One thought to consider, however, is that "every minute spent fretting about what [you] cannot get from a relationship is a moment spent not enjoying what is available and breaking whatever contact might be established" (Hedges, 1994, p. 248).

Whether you direct your anger at yourself, at others, or at life in general, you reinforce the attitudes and relationship patterns you developed from your early experiences. Your emotional wounds and unmet needs continue to drive your parent-child re-enactments and your search for someone who will provide for your unmet needs.

In addition, in this never-ending cycle of looking to others to meet your needs and make you whole—becoming outraged when you are disappointed in your efforts—and giving up in despair and retreating from others—you put the life you desire in jeopardy.

When others fail to meet your unrelenting demands, you can become
outraged, acting out against yourself and others in ways that can
damage and perhaps even destroy your connections with others.

Leon struggled for weeks with the conflict between his anger that
Natalia was not meeting his expectation that she should provide for all of
his emotional needs and his fear that he was losing his connection with
her. We talked at length about the cost of his unrelenting demand that
Natalia feel, think, and act in all the ways that he wanted.

We also worked together on the conflicts between his desire for the
good he had never received as a child, his demands that Natalia provide
them, and the reality of what she was able to offer. Even so, Leon
remained stuck in his relentless outrage and adamant demands.

At one point, I told Leon the following personal story that others had
found helpful when wrestling with their expectations and demands.

Several years ago, I spent the day driving through a wild animal park with
some friends. I was particularly eager to get to the zebras because I think
they are cute. However, I soon discovered that, in reality, zebras are also
aggressive. When we drove up to a herd, several zebras pushed their
humongous heads into the car, trying to get food from us. It was so exciting!
One friend then commented, "By the way, I read a warning sign that said not
to feed the zebras because they're mean and might bite our fingers off!"

Startled into reality, we began "encouraging" the zebras to get their heads
out of our car. The zebras, unfortunately, had trouble getting our hints and
were not about to give up their search for the food pellets. The herd began to
surround the car. It was clear that the zebras expected us to feed them and
were now demanding that we give them exactly what they wanted!

Fortunately, we finally forced our way through the mass of determined
zebras and reached the lovely giraffes. What a delight *they* were! One of the
giraffes ate gently out of my hand and even let me stroke its coat. I was
thrilled!

Later that evening I was reflecting on my experience with the zebras and
giraffes. I *thought* the zebras were cute. I *wanted* them to act like the
giraffes. Unfortunately, just because I wanted the zebras to be friendly and
safe did not mean they *were or even could be*. I could stick out my hand with
food all day long; I could pout, plead, and demand. But no matter how much
I wanted or expected zebras to be like giraffes, or even acted as if the zebras
were giraffes, none of my efforts could ever turn a zebra into a giraffe.
Zebras will always be zebras; they will never be giraffes.

After I told him this story, Leon and I sat in silence for some time. It was clear that Leon grasped the metaphor. I could see him struggling internally. Gradually, Leon began to release some of his anger and to experience some of the sadness that he felt about his losses.

In the weeks following this session, Leon's internal conflict between his needs and the needs of others intensified. He also was becoming more and more aware of how his attitude system and relationship patterns were keeping him from getting his legitimate needs met. Occasionally, Leon was even able to be more accepting of people and life's limitations.

Although his core attitudes and relationship patterns were beginning to change, Leon was not yet able to let go of his illusions, expectations, and demands entirely. Instead, his defensive solution to his internal conflict at this point was to move into the next phase of his infantile search for the perfect script—give up in despair and retreat.

You Give Up in Despair and Retreat

When all of your searching and demanding fails to get you what you long for, you, like Leon, may give up trying to get your needs met. Although your anger and resentment are still present, they may subside and go underground, so to speak.

In their place, hopeless attitudes can emerge, and you can become flooded with despair. In this stage of searching for the emotional resources you never adequately received when you were young, hopeless and helpless thoughts may run through your mind.

- "No one will ever come through for me in the way I need."
- "No one cares about me."
- "It's impossible to get my needs met."
- "I can't trust anyone anymore, so I won't even try."

Even though the feelings of futility and powerlessness underlying these thoughts are very strong and real, they are linked to distorted beliefs based on either-or thought processes. Either "I get all of my needs met" or "I get none of my needs met."

As Leon was fluctuating between looking to others to meet his needs and becoming outraged when they failed to do so, he began observing that his negative, despairing thoughts were increasing. He also noticed he was experiencing episodes of giving up in despair and retreating from Natalia so that he could feel safe.

About two and a half years into therapy, Leon described a recent experience.

"I realize that I've spent the whole time I've been with Natalia doing everything I can think to do to make our relationship work and hoping that she will change ... but she never does. It's so frustrating! I know it's pointless to keep hoping Natalia will care about me, because she really is a self-centered zebra.

"I've been trying to get free from her emotionally, but doing that has been like struggling to get out of quicksand. Part of me keeps getting sucked back into hoping that maybe I'm wrong ... maybe a miracle will happen, and Natalia will start acting like she did at the beginning of our relationship." Leon sighed with defeat. "But hoping for *that* is a deadly trap."

Then, in a tone of resignation tinged with bitterness, Leon continued, "I know I've said it before, but this time I *really* mean it ... I'm done with Natalia, and I don't even care anymore! I don't have enough energy left to care. And I'm sure not going to waste the energy I *do* have trying to turn her into someone she's not and then being mad at her because she isn't who I want her to be. It's ridiculous!"

Leon shifted around uncomfortably in his seat and then continued matter-of-factly, "It's depressing, but the truth is ... Natalia will *never* be who I want her to be, whether I like it or not! I've finally given up. In fact, I moved out of our apartment this past weekend, and I'm *not* moving back in. The challenge is going to be not isolating myself from everyone like I've always done in the past after my relationships have ended."

Like Leon, you may have spent your life searching for someone to be a stand-in for the idealized parent you never had and then raging when you realize that all of your efforts have been in vain. In your pain, you may have pulled back from relating to others.

Unfortunately, when you give up in despair and retreat from others, you not only turn away from those who have failed to live up to your expectations, but you also might find yourself avoiding all intimate relationships.

When you surrender to despair, you find you have resigned yourself to a life that feels pointless, and worthless. In this space, your infantile needs for love, acceptance, and worth intensify.

Eventually, your unmet needs, which are very powerful, will compel you to re-engage in the familiar but painful and fruitless cycle of searching for what you never had.

To transform your wounds into wisdom and save your life,
you must change your attitudes, freeing yourself from childhood
adaptations and defenses that are doomed to fail in the end.

Summary: Wishing and Hoping

At times, you may have found yourself on the stage of your life singing plaintive, hopeful refrains that echo from fairy tales.
I'm wishing (I'm wishing) for someone to give me all the love I never got as a child ... for the one who will finally approve of me ... for the one who will keep me safe ... for the one who will make me feel valuable ... for the one who will tell me who I am and how to be.

If you have, you are undoubtedly aware that you have searched desperately, perhaps your whole life, for someone to fill in the missing pieces of your unmet emotional needs.

You are also very familiar with the outrage you have felt when others have not given you what you wanted and felt you needed. As you recall those moments in your life, images of yourself unleashing your outrage onto those around you (and even yourself) may play across your mind. If so, you are acutely aware of the pain and harm you, others, and your relationships have suffered because of your difficulties regulating your emotions.

You may even remember times when your unrelenting anger and sense of entitlement have impaired your ability to reason. At these moments of being flooded with rage, the fear that you might go crazy if your anger intensified further may have knocked menacingly on the door of your mind.

You may also recall times when your hopes for someone to provide all of your needs were dashed yet again. In the aftermath of this realization, you may have collapsed, giving up your search to find someone who would provide what you so desperately need. Trying to protect yourself from further pain, or perhaps even from fears that you would not survive further blows, you may have withdrawn from others and even life.

You may have cut yourself off from closeness with others (and yourself) for a very long time. Over time, however, your self-imposed isolation may have become so exquisitely painful that you eventually mustered up the energy and motivation to begin the search once again.

As you stand alone on the stage of your life, you may eventually find yourself longing for the unrelenting cycle to end. You realize that searching for someone to meet your needs, raging when no one does, and detaching from others in despair when they do not meet your legitimate (and outrageous) needs (and demands) is futile.

In the forefront of your mind, you may have the painful awareness that you have spent your whole life re-enacting your parent-child scripts and searching for someone else to fulfill all of your unmet needs. You may not have let yourself realize that the window of opportunity for having someone else meet your infantile needs for love, attunement, and emotional regulation closed long ago.

The vicious cycle of relentlessly searching, raging, and retreating does not change what was real and true about your parent in the past. Nor does the cycle of searching endlessly for what your parents did not provide you emotionally as a child change what is real and true about yourself and others in the present.

To change your attitudes and save your life, it is important that you allow yourself to face and come to terms with the following truths about your parent:

- Your parent was limited in what she could provide you. She could never be the totally reliable, consistent, and all-nurturing parent that you needed.
- Your parent was a separate, distinct person from you and not an extension of you. She had core attitudes that filtered and made meaning out of her experience. She had relationship patterns that she internalized as a child. Some of these were helpful; some were not.
- Your parent could not be changed, regardless of what you did or did not do. You had no control over her attitudes or her relationship patterns, nor were they your fault. You could not force her to change and become someone she was not.

It is also important that you come to realize the following truths about yourself so that you can begin to deal with your losses in a way that truly frees you from the power of your unresolved past.

- Your fantasy that you can make others be what you need if you are good enough, try hard enough, demand it, or plead for it is an illusion.
- Your belief that your wounds can only be healed and your needs can only be met if you can make others be what you want them to be is a distortion.
- Your failure to find the perfect script is not due to a lack in you. Perfect scripts do not exist.

Fortunately, even though you may wish you could turn a zebra into a giraffe and be frustrated that you cannot, there *are* reality-based ways to take care of your unmet needs and your emotional wounds.

Moreover, you have the ability to create a healthier emotional life and healthier relationships, with the guidance and support of someone who can help you with the process of transforming your wounds into wisdom.

Transforming your wounds into wisdom and caring for your unmet needs is determined by your very real power to choose how you will deal with your and others' very real limitations.

PART IV

Transform Old Attitudes
and
Save Your Life

CHAPTER 8

Grieving Your
Disappointments and Losses

*"Every great loss demands that we choose life again. We need to grieve in order
to do this. The pain we have not grieved over will always stand between us and
life. When we don't grieve, a part of us becomes caught in the past like Lot's wife
who, because she looked back, was turned into a pillar of salt."*
—Rachel Naomi Remen, *My Grandfather's Blessings*

In order to develop an internal sense of lovability, security, and
confidence as a child, it is important to have consistent and reliable
emotionally nurturing experiences with a primary caregiver.
Unfortunately, when a parent provides Too Much or Too Little, the
experiences you need in order to develop in these areas are often not
sufficiently and consistently available.

In addition to impairing the development of parts of your
psychological system, your parent's interactions with you may actually
wound your developing self. When this happens, you will experience
significant loss, perhaps even traumatic loss.

These losses can have a profound impact on your developing attitudes
and relationship patterns and your ability to function—unless you are able
to confront and grieve the reality of what was.

***Grieving your disappointments and losses frees you
from self-sabotaging ties to the past.***

Mourning the unresolved disappointments and losses that emerged in
the aftermath of your interactions with a parent who provides Too Much,
Too Little, or even Just Right makes it possible for you to change outdated
and ineffective ways of feeling, thinking, and behaving.

Working through the mourning process reduces your inclination to re-
enact (unwittingly and compulsively) childhood dramas that re-create the

wounds of yesteryear in your present life and empowers you to stop re-enactments that are occurring.

It also releases you from the internal pressure to keep searching for what cannot be—a way to undo the painful experiences of the past and find someone who will meet all your infantile needs. Grieving opens the door for you to begin developing the emotional security and confidence you long for so that you can create a fulfilling life.

In this chapter, we will consider what grieving involves and then discuss the tasks of grieving. In particular, we will explore crucial areas to experience and work through so you can release old ways of relating to the past and embrace newer, more adaptive ways of being and doing.

To begin, let us look at Anthony's experience with grieving. As we continue our exploration, we will catch glimpses of how Anthony engaged in his grieving process so he could free himself from his emotional ties to past losses.

Anthony's Story

Anthony, a 49-year-old man, had made an appointment to see me several years ago at the insistence of his wife. She had been pressuring him to seek help because she was increasingly frustrated with their difficulties communicating. The following interaction occurred with Anthony during our first session.

Anthony swaggered into the office and sat down on the couch across from me. His eyes darted warily around the room, checking everything out, including me. After a few minutes, Anthony announced, "I don't need to be here. Nothing's wrong with me. It's a waste of money. I'm just coming because my wife threatened to leave me if I didn't go to therapy."

"It must be aggravating to have your wife give you an ultimatum that you get therapy when you don't see any need for help. Why does she think you need therapy?" I asked.

Anthony looked out the window and then said matter-of-factly, "Oh, she complains about me being mean to her and emotionally distant. She thinks it's because of my past."

As he continued to look outside, Anthony elaborated, "My father was a druggie and died from an overdose when I was ten. He was crazy. A few years later, my mom, who was rarely around and who never got up the courage to leave him, got stomach cancer. I took care of her for about two years, but nothing helped her. She died when I was fifteen, and I had to go live with my grandparents."

I responded to his apparent detachment, "All of that happened so long ago that you're not convinced that looking at how it might be affecting you now would be helpful or make any difference anyway."

Anthony turned to me and said adamantly, "It was hard, but I'm doing fine. None of that really affected me. What's past is past, and I don't want to talk about it."

So began Anthony's and my journey together. For the next few years, despite his reluctance to revisit his early painful losses, Anthony slowly and gradually became more open to exploring the impact of some of his early experiences. He began to acknowledge that there was some connection between his past and his problems in his marriage.

What Grieving Involves

Grieving your losses is central to changing your attitudes. As I have worked with clients through the years to help them transform their wounds into wisdom, invariably, they have asked me two questions: "What does grieving loss really mean?" and "How do I do that?" Therefore, before we begin to examine the work of grieving, let us define some words related to grieving, as I will be using them.

Loss, Grief, and Grieving

Loss. Whenever you do not obtain, maintain, or retain something you need, want, or have, you experience a *loss.* Loss can appear in many forms. When you do not get what you want, or think you need or deserve, such as recognition or a relationship with someone, you can experience the loss as deprivation or disappointment.

Loss can be frustrating because it may involve roadblocks, such as your internal defenses or external circumstances that prevent you from obtaining what you need or want. If you discover that your perceptions or beliefs are inaccurate or false, you may experience loss as disillusionment.

A loss also occurs when you lose something or it is no longer part of your experience, such as the loss of hope, emotional connection, or a person. Grieving can involve any form of loss.

Grief. Grief is the emotional pain that results from past or current experiences of loss. It is a normal response to any type of loss. Although people commonly use the word *grief* to denote the sorrow and heartache you feel after the death or loss of a physical relationship, grief can also occur after any psychological loss.

In addition, because loss occurs as a normal part of the human experience, everyone experiences grief at some point. It is not something you choose. *Suffering*, however, is the unhealthy emotional distress you experience when you do not work through grief adequately. Not everyone ends up suffering because of loss.

Grieving. *Grieving* and *mourning* are the active processes of working through loss and grief. They involve several tasks that occur over time. (We will examine those tasks later.) Although some writers differentiate these two terms, I will be using them interchangeably.

Salman Akhtar, a professor of psychiatry at Jefferson Medical College in Philadelphia, points out, "Mourning is useful because it permits us to relinquish attachments and attitudes that have lost their realistic usefulness. It therefore facilitates growth and development" (Akhtar, 2001, p. 109).

Grieving opens up the psychological space and energy needed to form new ways of connecting to who or what you have lost and to move forward in your life.

In large part, the attitudes you developed from your early experiences with your parent who provided Too Much, Too Little, or Just Right determine how you experience loss, grief, and grieving.

Because your attitudes are the core filters through which you process all of your experience, they affect your emotional response to loss, your beliefs about loss, and the ways you act when you experience a loss.

For example, if you feel, believe, and act as if your loss is an "end-of-the-world disaster," in all likelihood, you will experience the loss as more traumatic than if you compute the situation as "a sad and painful loss." If you tell yourself the painful loss is "no big deal," you will have difficulty grieving your loss and resolving it. The meaning you place on your loss is critical to how you experience a loss.

Let us look more closely now at the nature of grieving.

The Nature of Grieving

Grieving your losses is work. Grieving is work because it involves actually remodeling your inner world. In a way, grieving is like remodeling a house. Remodeling jobs are costly and labor intensive. They are usually messy, confusing, and time-consuming. They are often frustrating because, invariably, some problem arises that slows the project down or puts it on hold for a while. Because remodeling jobs are also often unpredictable, they can seem overwhelmingly impossible, intimidating, and sometimes even frightening.

In the same way, it takes time and effort to remodel your inner world. During the grieving process, you have to dismantle old ways of connecting to what you have lost. The mourning process involves rerouting neurological and psychological connections and establishing new connections and structures. Because this process involves reconfiguring your internal operating system, attitudes do not change quickly or easily.

As you are doing the remodeling work of grieving, you usually experience a range of emotions (e.g., frustration, confusion, sadness, fear, disorientation, uncertainty, and loss). Because it is uncomfortable to experience these emotions, you may want to avoid doing the work of grieving. It is necessary, however, to experience and process your emotions in order to work through your grief.

Grieving your losses involves change. Whenever you experience a loss, your old ways of relating to what you have lost do not exist anymore. Losing the part of you that no longer exists *in the relationship* is part of what makes loss so painful. But it is important to remember that although loss requires that the nature of the relationship change, you do not lose who you have become because of your experiences.

In essence, they have become a part of you. For example, if your best friend moves away, you have to change how you will relate to the person, but your earlier experiences with the person have become part of who you are—you do not lose them.

If a traumatic experience damages your sense of self-efficacy, you will not be the person you were before the experience. You will need to repair your sense of self-efficacy. However, the experience of being able to care for yourself prior to the trauma is still a part of your sense of yourself, even though it may not be apparent at a particular point in time.

Although you retain the experiences you have had and the person you have become by virtue of the relationship that existed, the nature of the relationship changes with loss. This requires you to develop a new way of knowing yourself and relating to who or what you have lost. You will need to stop focusing on and investing your energy in the other *in the same way* that you have in the past.

The work of grieving involves letting go of the ways things have been, tolerating the tension that occurs with unfamiliar experiences, and establishing new attitudes and relationship patterns. As you remodel old attitudes during the grieving process, new, more emotionally rewarding ways of relating gradually develop.

Grieving your losses involves choice. Any time you consider starting a project that involves change you have to make choices. You have to decide whether you will leave things alone and live with them as they are or create something different. You have to decide whether the outcome of the project will be worth all the work and cost and, if so, commit to the project.

In the same way, you have to choose what you will do with your losses and the pain and suffering you have experienced (and are experiencing) in the aftermath of the storms and tsunamis of your life.

This choice usually involves an internal tug-of-war. Part of you may want to cling to your familiar ways of operating that are part of your childhood survival system—even though they cause you distress.

Another part of you may want to be free of the tyranny of this early defensive system and the suffering it has caused by compelling you to re-enact old parent-child patterns and to search for and demand what you missed as a child. It is important to remember, however, that this tug-of-war is never about *whether* you will choose to grieve.

The fact is, every day you *do* choose between staying attached to your old self-sabotaging ways of being or grieving your losses so you can move forward. The question before you at each moment is, "Which option will you choose?"

You must choose to grieve your losses if you wish to let go of old, ineffective attitudes and relationship patterns and create new attitudes and ways of relating that help you function more effectively.

Although grieving is a natural process that occurs after you experience a loss or disappointment, you may become aware that you may not have grieved some of your losses adequately. In fact, because grieving is a painful process, you may find yourself resisting mourning in several ways. For example, you can be so overwhelmed by your emotions and the losses associated with change that you consciously or unconsciously avoid grieving—or even refuse to grieve—your losses.

In addition, you might detach from your feelings about your losses, which blocks you from making the changes that are necessary for your growth and development. You might resist dealing with your losses and disappointments in several of these ways (or others) simultaneously or at different times. If you fail to work through your grief and the mourning process, however, you may end up suffering.

When you choose not to mourn the losses incurred as you grew up with parents who provided Too Much or Too Little, however, you are choosing to stay attached to childhood scripts. You are choosing to continue life with the old attitudes and relationship patterns that you developed as a child and have reinforced as an adult that are creating problems in your life today.

Re-enacting the past in the present, however, does not undo the past or keep you from experiencing the pain of loss. Whether you experience the present as if it were the past, evoke what you expect from others, or attract what is familiar to you, none of these re-enactments will help you create the life you want. Neither will a relentless search for someone to make up for what you failed to get from your parent as a child.

So, let us examine what grieving entails.

The TASK of Grieving

It takes time and a great deal of energy to grieve your losses and disappointments, whether they occurred as you were growing up or as an adult. Because grieving is not a linear process, it does not occur in a step-by-step fashion. Instead, grief takes different forms, appearing in one form at one point in time and emerging later in a very different form. Each time your grief emerges, you have the opportunity and challenge to process the many aspects of your losses once again.

Four major tasks are central to the process of grieving:

- **T**ell yourself the truth about what you have lost.
- **A**llow yourself to experience the range of your emotions.
- **S**top clinging to old attitudes and relationship patterns.
- **K**eep your focus on accepting your losses and on moving forward.

Let us look at each of these tasks more closely. As we do, remember that these tasks are not items that you check off a to-do list. They are processes that are ongoing and ever changing, and they affect each other.

Tell Yourself the Truth about What You Have Lost

Acknowledge the reality of your losses and grief. One of the necessary tasks on the journey to transform your wounds into wisdom is to tell yourself the truth about what you have lost, which involves acknowledging its reality. This can feel very threatening psychologically.

When you face the reality of your losses, the painful feelings of grief that you may have avoided or disconnected from for years usually begin to emerge. Although it is critical to let yourself experience the emotional pain and vulnerability associated with your losses, these distressing emotions can easily activate your mind's internal protective system. This system often works to keep you from being aware of what is real and true about your losses and your grief.

During the first year of therapy, Anthony had battled fiercely against acknowledging the reality of the pain he had experienced—and was continuing to experience—because of his childhood losses and disappointments. In sessions, he would focus primarily on current conflicts with his wife and day-to-day aggravations with his children. Because he was fearful of losing control of his anger, his pattern of dealing with conflict was to retreat and shut down instead of rising to the challenge of dealing with problems.

Anthony's detachment and avoidance patterns were interfering with his ability to engage with his wife and children in meaningful ways. Instead of interacting with them, Anthony would retreat to his bedroom and spend hours working on the computer. His disengagement also made it difficult for him to harness his energy to work on his life-long dream of building a sailboat.

For a long time, whenever I would make a comment that might connect his current dilemmas to his past losses, Anthony would ignore the link. As time went on, however, he gradually began to talk about his struggle with facing the full extent of the pain he felt about his early losses. One day Anthony was feeling particularly conflicted and began talking about his dilemma.

"I know I need to deal with my childhood, but it hurts too much. I'm scared that if I let myself think about everything that happened, I'll never stop hurting. I'm afraid that my feelings will take over and that I'll go crazy like my dad. Or, even if I don't go crazy, I'm afraid that if I keep continuing like I am now I'll end up in a humdrum existence like my mom had. It's as scary as hell. It seems a lot easier and safer just to avoid the whole mess."

I responded, "Even though you know that, at some point, you will probably need to face the reality of your childhood losses, at the moment, it's terrifying to think that if you did, your pain might never stop—or that you might end up crazy … like your dad."

"My childhood was pretty bad, and if I open up that can of worms, I don't know what I'd do with what might pop out. I'm afraid I wouldn't be able to handle it." Anthony paused, sighed, and then said, "I'm so tired of my past lurking around every corner. I'm always on guard, just waiting for it to jump out and destroy my life."

Anthony thought for a moment. Then he continued, "I hate to say my wife is right, but she's probably on to something when she says my childhood problems are already messing up my life."

Mindful of his inner conflict, I reflected, "Although you're recognizing that you might be paying a high price for not confronting the devastating losses you experienced as a child, it still feels too dangerous. And you're not sure it would be worth the pain and the risk."

Anthony replied, "I know I have a lot of demons to face from my past. I just hope I'll be able to figure out a way to deal with them. I'm so tired of living in my own little world. I feel so alienated from everyone—and so alone."

"Safe, but so alone," I reflected.

As our work together moved forward, Anthony and I talked many times about the dilemmas he was experiencing. Even though Anthony wanted to resolve his early losses, there were times when he would not let himself see the truth about his childhood because it was so distressing. Other times, he was acutely aware of feeling torn between two powerful but conflicting feelings. His desire to be free from the negative impact of his past moved him toward grieving, but his fear of facing the reality of his disappointments moved him away from mourning.

Although Anthony's grief and fear were extremely painful, over the next year he persevered, bravely telling himself the truth about how his parents' dysfunction had torn him apart inside as a child and teenager. Very slowly and carefully, we paced our work with his growing inner strength and capacity to confront the reality of his unmet emotional needs—his childhood wounds—and the truth that he was suffering because of both of them.

Identify and face your disappointments and losses. Part of telling yourself the truth about what you have lost involves identifying and facing your disappointments and losses. If you fail to identify your losses and the impact they have had and are having on your life, it will be extremely difficult to make any helpful changes in your attitudes.

When you identify what you have lost, however, you know what you are mourning and what you will be letting go. This knowledge can guide you throughout the grieving process.

You may also put yourself at risk if you do not identify your losses or your grief accurately. At best, vague or inaccurate identification of your losses can keep you stuck in your emotional pain. At worst, it can lead you inadvertently to act in ways that aggravate your wounds or create even more problems in your life.

If Anthony were to decide that his parents' failures only damaged his self-esteem and that his parents were the only source for its repair, he would probably not work to develop his self-esteem. His partial identification of his losses and his beliefs about them would interfere with his healing.

During the grieving process, as you identify your losses more clearly, you are better able to grieve them. You are in a position to create an effective and healthy plan that will help you care for yourself and your needs.

Common psychological losses result from growing up with a parent who provides Too Much or Too Little. All of these losses can leave you feeling disappointed in others, life, and even yourself. For example, you are likely to experience the loss of an internal sense of safety, security, and confidence in others, which interferes with your ability to function effectively in relationships.

In addition, when your ability to connect securely with others is impaired, you usually experience losses in the areas of identity, self-esteem, and self-confidence. Interactions with a parent who provides Too Much or Too Little also tend to create losses in your ability to regulate your thoughts and emotions and to empathize with yourself and others.

As Anthony persisted in his efforts to identify and face his losses, his psychological defense system was actively attempting to keep him from acknowledging, identifying, and facing his losses. It was also trying to prevent him from experiencing his grief about his past.

But Anthony kept on wrestling with the frightened part of himself that did not want to deal with the reality of his childhood wounds lest it be too much for him to bear. He also kept struggling with the part of him that was trying to protect him from the awareness that he was not receiving the recognition and care he so desperately longed for in the present.

Another part of Anthony knew, however, that he would have to deal with his losses if he hoped to have a more emotionally authentic and engaged relationship with his wife and children.

As Anthony increasingly came to appreciate the price he was paying for refusing to see the truth about his disappointments and losses, it became harder and harder for him to remain entrenched in his self-protective defensive stance.

Although still conflicted, Anthony gradually began to talk more about the anger, anxiety, and loneliness he had felt growing up with an abusive drug- and alcohol-addicted father and an emotionally disengaged mother.

One day Anthony reported some reflections he had had during the previous week about his internal demons.

> "I've decided it's time to stop playing games with myself and tell myself the truth. Even though I tried to stay away from home as much as I could when I was a kid to avoid what was going on, the truth is, I was miserable.

"I resented that I didn't have parents who paid attention to me like some of the other kids had. I got in trouble for fighting with kids at school or in the neighborhood at least once a week because I was mad all the time. I didn't really care about what anyone thought or what happened to me or other people. I figured no one cared about me, so why the hell should I care about anyone else?"

I responded gently, "It is terribly painful to be feeling so alone, desperately needing and wanting your parents to notice you, love you, and be there for you. The pain goes deep when you have no one to provide the nurturing you need. … Sometimes it is so unbearable that striking out at others seems like the only recourse."

Anthony's eyes brimmed up as he continued to acknowledge the painful truth about his isolation and despair. "It's really hard to admit it, but my childhood was very lonely. In fact, I don't think I ever felt loved as a kid. And I sure didn't feel good about myself, even though I tried to act like I was a big man by throwing my weight around. But I was only tricking myself into thinking that I didn't care about my parents or anyone else.

"The truth was, I felt totally lost and alone—especially after my mom died." As he spoke these last words, the tears began to roll down his cheeks; his anguish was palpable.

Anthony was beginning to let himself know the intensity and depth of his losses: his lack of a secure attachment to his parents when they were alive, the devastating loneliness after they died, his difficulty forming healthy and engaged relationships, and his lack of a solid and grounded sense of identity, empowerment, and self-efficacy.

Although it was painful and frightening for Anthony to let himself experience his grief about the price he had been paying for these losses, it was a critically important part of his grieving process.

As he was mourning, he was beginning to transform his wounds into wisdom and to change his maladaptive attitudes so he could become more authentically engaged in his life.

Work through your reluctance to feel the heartbreak. As Anthony discovered, when contemplating losses and feeling grief becomes too painful, your unconscious mind may try to protect you from emotional pain by activating *psychological defense mechanisms.*

The mind's defenses aim to protect you from experiencing the potentially overwhelming reality of your losses. *Repression* (forcing feelings into the unconscious), *rationalization* (making excuses), and *intellectualization* (separating emotions from ideas) are just a few of the defense mechanisms that may become active during grieving. One of the most common defense mechanisms that you may experience after a loss is *denial*.

Denial, in this situation, is an unconscious and sometimes conscious refusal to admit the truth about your disappointments and losses so you will not have to feel the heartbreak related to them. It promises to protect you from emotional distress if you operate with the illusion that you did not suffer any loss, or the loss you experienced was not significant, or the loss had little to no impact on you.

Although denial may be a helpful buffer against being emotionally overwhelmed when you initially experience loss, in the end it interferes with the functioning of your inner feedback system.

Imagine for a moment denial as three monkeys sitting in a row on their haunches: one with its hands over its ears, one with its hands over its eyes, and one with its hands over its mouth. The illusionary message of these *Three Denial Monkeys* is that you will not feel the heartbreak of your losses and that you will be emotionally secure if you "hear no truth—see no truth—speak no truth."

Denial keeps you from mourning your losses because unconsciously, if not consciously, denial makes it hard *to hear* the truth about your losses. It keeps you from paying attention and listening to yourself—how you truly feel and think.

When denial is operating, it prevents you from being able *to see* what you have lost and how your unresolved losses are interfering with your life. You may not be able to (or even want to) see the truth that in your personal world limitations, failures, bad, and even evil exist.

Denial also makes it difficult *to speak* the truth about the losses and wounds you have experienced, both as a child and as an adult. When you speak the truth about your experiences, somehow, they feel more real.

Although denial and other psychological defenses give the illusion that they are protecting you, in actuality, they are not. Instead, they keep you operating with attitudes and relationship patterns that leave you feeling insecure, emotionally unsafe, and lacking in self-confidence.

Moreover, when you do not hear, see, and speak the truth about your losses, you are more at risk of being re-injured because your wounds have not healed. To protect yourself effectively in healthy ways, it is necessary that you repair your wounds and develop mature and strong psychological structures.

By the end of the third year of therapy, Anthony had made considerable progress in his efforts to acknowledge and identify the truth about his losses. In addition, he had allowed himself to experience some of his heartbreak about the parts of himself that had failed to develop and the parts that had been wounded during childhood. Even so, there were times when Anthony's psychological protection system temporarily would gain the upper hand in the battle for the truth.

One of these episodes occurred about two and a half years into therapy, when Anthony was processing deeper levels of his grief. This day Anthony was grappling with his reluctance to feel his devastating heartbreak about the role his emotionally unavailable mother had played in his young life.

"My grandparents told me that when I was really little my dad started hanging out and using drugs with his friends after work. What *I* remember is that when my dad would finally get home, he would usually zone out drinking and endlessly watching his stupid TV shows, though sometimes he would yell at me or hit me for no good reason.

"My mom was very passive and didn't do anything to protect me. She didn't really pay attention to me, either. It wasn't her fault, though, because she was working two jobs to keep up with the bills and was tired all of the time. I still don't get why she didn't just leave him and make a better life for us.

"And what I *really* don't understand was that even after my dad died and I settled down a bit, my mom still ignored me. I figured that I had blown my chance to get close to her, somehow. Sometimes I blamed my dad or myself that my mom was in her own little world most of the time. We shouldn't have been so selfish and made life so difficult for her.

"But it wasn't until my mom got breast cancer and died and I had to move in with my grandparents that I started thinking I was getting a raw deal in life. I nipped that thinking in the bud, though, and tuned out my feelings and thoughts about the past. 'It was what it was,' became my motto."

I noted, "It has been so difficult for you to deal with the reality of how your father's failures have negatively impacted you. But it's even harder still to let yourself know the truth about how your mother's limitations have negatively impacted you. And it is still very painful—and confusing—to think about what a disappointment she was and how she failed to protect you and make your world feel safe."

Anthony's eyes were filling with tears. After a few moments he added, "It is very hard to admit that something was wrong with my mom's ability to give me the love and care that I needed. It's a lot easier to make excuses for her or to blame my dad or even myself for how she treated me. I wanted her to love me so much.

"Over the years I have tried so hard not to think about how much I missed out on as a kid and how devastating it was for me that she really wasn't there for me in the way a kid deserves to have his mother there. I have tried to act like it doesn't matter by glibly saying, 'the past is the past'—but it does matter." Anthony became quiet as the tears trickled down his cheeks.

I quietly responded, "There is so much you didn't have, and it breaks your heart."

Anthony's reluctance to experience the heartbreak of his multiple losses and disappointments had kept him barricaded and isolated inside himself with his grief. His pattern of detaching from the reality that his parents had failed to provide for his emotional needs had prevented him from experiencing his grief and mourning his losses.

Over the next year, however, as he continued to grieve, Anthony was gradually freeing himself from the undermining ties to his past. He was developing a more solid and grounded sense of himself and a more emotionally fulfilling relationship with his wife and his children.

Your childhood survival system, like Anthony's, may try to keep you from confronting the reality of the losses you experienced as a child growing up with a parent who provided Too Much, Too Little, or even Just Right. It may try to keep you from identifying your losses and make you reluctant to feel the heartbreak you experienced in their wake. It may cause you to distort who is responsible for your losses, past and present, and who is responsible for doing the work to repair your wounds and to develop psychologically.

Denial and other psychological defenses, however protective they may seem, keep you from hearing, seeing, and speaking the truth about your experience. They offer the illusionary promise of protecting you from pain, but in reality, they obscure the truth about your losses, creating additional distress.

Denial is a way you maintain your illusions
and distortions in the face of reality.

You can choose to maintain your seemingly protective illusions and distortions, but they prevent you from healing yourself. Beliefs that you had no losses, that the losses you had did not affect you, or that you and others have no responsibility for your losses all impede your ability to grieve. It is difficult to care for the wounded and vulnerable parts of yourself when your defenses are wrapped tightly around them.

In order to end your suffering, however, it is important to work through denial and other defenses. As you confront and let go of the illusions and distortions that are part of your old attitude system and that undermine your life, you will be in a position to move forward to create a fulfilling life.

Allow Yourself to Experience the Range of Your Emotions

Stay connected to your feelings. As you do the work of grieving, it is important to stay connected to your feelings. It is crucial to experience and express the full range of emotions connected to the losses you have experienced. When you fail to let yourself experience all the emotions evoked by your losses, repressing or disconnecting from them instead, you inadvertently quell *all* of your emotions, both painful and positive.

When this happens, it becomes difficult to experience pleasure and to enjoy the good parts of your life. It is also hard to create new and healthier attitudes and relationship patterns when you avoid or shut down your emotions and thought processes.

Staying connected to and letting yourself experience your distressing emotions during mourning, however, is not sufficient to resolve loss. You must also process your emotions in order to integrate your losses in a meaningful and positive way.

Processing your emotions allows them to integrate into new ways of feeling, thinking, and behaving that are healthier and stronger. This integration helps you move forward with a greater capacity to experience and manage your emotions and losses in the future.

Moreover, processing and integrating your emotions helps develop resilience. (We will discuss emotions and emotional processing in more depth in the next chapter.)

Be mindful of the variety of your feelings. As you mourn your losses and disappointment, it is normal to experience a wide range of emotions that fluctuate in intensity and frequency. Common emotions experienced during the grieving process are anxiety, fear, yearning, heartache, sadness, regret, despair, emptiness, anger, and guilt.

Although these feelings are uncomfortable and even quite distressing at times, it is important that you stay present with and attend to the different aspects of your feelings of loss. As you do so, you develop your capacity to tolerate grief. You also increase your awareness of your patterns of grieving. Understanding your experience of the grieving process and increasing your capacity to tolerate the emotions you encounter enables you to be resilient in the face of loss.

Let us explore a few of the emotions that emerge during the grieving process.

Anger. When you experience a loss, it is normal to feel anger in some form because anger is part of the body's protection system. When your sense of self, self-worth, safety, and security depends on who or what is being lost, you can experience your losses and disappointments as threats to your psychological well-being.

You may even feel your very survival is in jeopardy. This sense of emotional vulnerability can activate the body's fight response. During the grieving process, you may find yourself more irritable, resentful, angry, or frustrated as a protective response to feelings of vulnerability.

Although anger is a normal part of grieving, if you do not work it through, it can entrap you, just as quicksand can snare an unsuspecting wanderer. When this happens, you may aim your outrage about your losses at yourself, others, or the world in general.

Internalizing or acting out your anger, however, will not alleviate your pain. It will not undo your losses, heal your wounds, or help you take care of your needs. Even though anger can be useful in many ways, it will not protect you if misdirected. In fact, if you allow anger to flood your mind and body, it can erode your feelings of security and self-worth.

In addition, if you do not take care of your anger adequately, it can cause you to act in ways that end up alienating others, which leaves you alone in your pain. You may end up not only harming yourself but also provoking others to harm you.

To free yourself from the negative power of anger, you must feel your anger, process it, express it in healthy ways—and then let it go.

Allow yourself to experience the full force of your anger about your losses without attacking yourself or others. Grieve what you have lost. Mourn that you and others are who you are—people with wounds, limitations, and failings.

Then choose to let go of your anger so you can direct your energy toward continuing the work of changing your old, ineffective attitudes and relationship patterns and creating the life you want.

Although working through your anger takes time, you cannot change your attitudes or save your life if you hold on to and feed your anger.

Sadness. As you stop denying your losses and shaking your upraised fist in anger, the reality of your losses begins to sink in. You may experience a profound sense of sadness, helplessness, emptiness, and weariness as you face the reality that you cannot undo past losses or prevent future loss.

Even though these emotions are distressing, it is important to allow yourself to experience the feelings that emerge as you face the truth about what you have lost.

If you do not let yourself feel, express, and process your sadness and related emotions, you may become overwhelmed by the sense of loss and begin suffering from depression. The depression can then become chronic and leave you feeling mired in quicksand.

Heartache. Grieving your losses frequently involves feeling the pain of heartache. In fact, heartache is perhaps the most common feeling experienced during the grieving process. People experience heartache in many ways. You may experience it as an actual pain in the chest.

Most often, however, people experience heartache as a painful yearning (longing or desire) for what was lost. Sometimes your heartache can take the form of regret for something you did or failed to do that relates to your loss.

As you grieve your losses, you need to both feel and process your heartache, whether it takes the form of yearning for things to be different or regretting actions taken or not taken. You cannot alleviate your heartache by longing and wishing for things to be as they once were or the way you imagined them. Nor can you resolve your grief by clinging to expectations about the way you think things should be.

Anxiety. One of the functions of denial and other psychological defenses is to keep you from feeling anxiety. Because of that, as you let go of your defenses and face the reality of your disappointments and losses and their impact, you may experience anxiety.

Although this anxiety can be very uncomfortable, it is normal, and it will subside. In a way, anxiety during the grieving process is a type of separation anxiety that occurs as you let go of your attachments to the old familiar scripts and psychological connections and begin to create new ones.

Because anxiety is uncomfortable, you may experience a strong pull to hang on to old attitudes and relationship patterns, even when they create pain and chaos in your life, in order to avoid the anxious feelings. Nevertheless, it is important to let yourself experience and work through the anxiety that is part of grieving. This will enable you to integrate aspects of what you have lost in a way that enhances your psychological maturation.

Grieving is a process that occurs incrementally, in random cycles. It is influenced by your physical and emotional state, the developmental stage you are in, and your past experiences with loss and mourning. The emotions you experience will also move in and out of your conscious awareness.

As you grieve your losses, you may experience your emotions and then move away from them for a while. Then you will re-experience them and work on them again. As you mourn, the losses and the emotions that go with loss are metabolized, bit by bit.

Each time you process your emotions, your mind works to repair the damage from your losses and strengthen your capacity to deal with loss. This repairing process enables you to change old, ineffective attitudes and relationship patterns and create new ones that allow you to live your life in healthy ways.

<u>S</u>top Struggling to Create a Different Outcome

The ways of dealing with emotions, thoughts, and behavior that you developed as a child may have helped you cope with (and survive) some very difficult and painful circumstances. However, they can often undermine your ability to live your life in healthy ways as an adult.

Therefore, to move forward in your life, changes are necessary. It is important that you stop trying to make your past different from what it was and that you relinquish ties to self-sabotaging attitudes.

Stop trying to make your past different from what it was. Even though your childhood attitudes may not serve you well in the present, you may still hold on tightly to these ineffective patterns, under the illusion that you can undo the past.

You may cling tenaciously to the hope that you can get today what you could not get early on from your parent who provided Too Much or Too Little. Day after day, year after year, you may struggle to create a different outcome to your early life story by persistently using the familiar but outdated childhood scripts that once helped you survive.

In an attempt to make your past different from what it was, you may continue re-enacting the past in the present—consciously or unconsciously. You may find yourself longing and searching relentlessly for what you did not get as a child, even though the old, unhealthy scripts perpetuate and compound your pain in the present. But to save your life you must release yourself from these illusionary ties.

Relinquish ties to self-sabotaging attitudes. In addition to perpetuating the illusion that you can undo the past, you may cling to the illusion that the familiar attitudes and relationship patterns you developed as a child can save you in the present. They cannot.

They may seem more secure than letting go of your attachment to your familiar pain and working to repair your wounds. They can feel safer than letting go of the illusion that the old systems will protect you and working to develop the capacities and necessary connections that will enable you to create a fulfilling life. Nevertheless, it is still an illusion to operate as if the unhealthy mindsets that you developed as a child can serve you well in the present.

Consider this scenario. Imagine you are on a boating trip on the ocean. During the trip, it becomes clear that there are some problems. The boat is not very seaworthy, and water is rapidly seeping into the boat through cracks in the hull.

You search frantically for a way to save yourself. You grab a nearby tattered life preserver, put it on, and try to hold on to the boat. After a while, you see a rescue boat cruising around nearby, but you are frightened. You have been clinging to the life preserver and boat for so long that you refuse to let go of them. You refuse to let go and swim to the rescue boat that can save your life.

It is important to stop trying to undo the past
and stop clinging to old attitudes and relationship patterns
that put your present life in jeopardy.
Let go—so you can do the work necessary to save your life.

To let go of the illusions that you can undo the past or stay safe by clinging to undermining childhood attitudes and relationship patterns, you need to grieve your losses. This entails recognizing both your childhood losses and the losses you have inadvertently perpetuated on yourself as an adult in your attempts to cope with the impact of those early losses.

Engaging in the process of changing old, ineffective attitude scripts also involves facing the reality that the old system is interfering with your ability to live your life fully in the present—and that you are paying a steep price for holding on to the old system.

Although the core attitudes and relationship patterns developed during childhood may have been life preserving at one point, there is a cost attached to them. *The price you have paid and continue to pay for holding on to these attitudes is the loss of who you really are and who you can become.*

Keep Dealing with Your Losses and Moving Forward

Part of dealing with your losses and disappointments during the grieving process will involve accepting that they are part of your experience. Because acceptance is crucial to your ability to move forward in your life after loss, let us consider for a moment what acceptance means and how it evolves.

What acceptance is and is not. People frequently think that if you accept something you are saying it is okay. This distortion causes people a great deal of internal conflict. When someone wrongs another person, it is, in fact, not okay. Violations of relationships or ethical and moral codes are *not acceptable*. It is not healthy to pretend, to try to believe, or to act as if they *are* acceptable.

When you say something is acceptable, you are passing a judgment on the situation. Is it okay or not okay? Allowable or not allowable?

For example, most people do not consider it acceptable behavior for a child to have tantrums for hours or to kick other people. People expect the adult responsible for the child to make a judgment call about the out of control behavior, determine that the behavior is not acceptable, and do something to stop it.

In Anthony's situation, clearly, his parents' behavior was not acceptable. They needed to change their attitudes for their own and Anthony's well-being, or they needed someone else to intervene and stop the emotional negligence and mistreatment. Unfortunately, that never happened, and they were all psychologically injured.

Acceptance, however, is not the same as *acceptability*. In the above tantrum example, before the adult could take responsibility for the child's inappropriate behavior and determine that it was not acceptable, she would have to *accept* the reality that the child was misbehaving.

As an outcome of the mourning process, acceptance involves knowing and coming to terms with what is real and true about the nature of your loss. It allows the fact and impact of your loss to be true without trying to deny it, pretend it is something else, or make it be something it is not.

Acceptance involves letting go of efforts to create a different outcome and making peace with the reality that there is nothing you can do now to change what happened to you in the past.

You cannot undo the past.

Acceptance is letting go of trying to change
something that is unchangeable.

Acceptance develops as you work through the grieving process. As you mourn your losses, letting go of your denial and efforts to create a different outcome, you will begin to accept the losses you have incurred. In turn, this increasing acceptance of your disappointments and losses will make it possible to continue mourning your losses, psychologically integrating aspects of what you have lost. This synergistic process frees you to live more fully in the present.

As Anthony continued working through the tasks involved in grieving, we often discussed what acceptance of his losses and their impact on his life entailed. The following conversation occurred after about three years in therapy.

Anthony admitted, "It is really hard to face the truth about my life. Sometimes I don't want to accept what happened in the past, and I *really* don't want to admit that I am responsible for creating some of my own problems in the present. It's a lot easier to blame my wife, kids, co-workers, boss—anyone but me—for my screw-ups. But most of the time now I try to stop that and remind myself of what's really going on—that it's really a story about me."

Anthony's eyes began to well up with tears and his voice choked as he continued, "I'm trying to accept that those were the cards I was dealt as a kid. Being angry about it and wishing for a different hand isn't going to get me different cards. It's my job to figure out how to play the hand life dealt me so I can win the game.

"I am getting better at spotting when I'm taking on the parent and the child roles that I learned growing up. When I get into arguments with others, I can see how someone always ends up in the role of the "mistreater," and someone else is the "mistreated one." I've decided that neither role is okay, any more than they were when my dad was mistreating my mom and me or when I was getting into fights at school. My other brilliant strategy of zoning out in order to escape conflict isn't okay either because it doesn't solve any problems or protect me from anything."

I responded, "Even though it's hard, you're starting to let yourself see and accept the truth about what you missed growing up. You're also beginning to see how the old ways of coping keep you from what you want and need today."

Anthony leaned forward and, looking directly into my eyes, said, "The truth is … whether I'm fighting or disappearing, both make things worse. So now I'm trying to do things differently.

"The other day, for example, my wife made a sarcastic comment after dinner that I was probably going to spend the evening hanging out with my 'best friend, Dell the Computer' again. Instead of ignoring her or making some caustic comment, I said, 'Well, I thought about it. But I decided it would be more fun to hang out with you and the kids and play a game.' She almost fell off her chair. The kids were so excited, and we had a really fun evening playing Monopoly."

Anthony's eyes misted up as he said quietly, "I'm grateful to you for helping me turn my life around."

What you need to let go. In order to accept the truth about yourself, others, and life, you need to let go of any illusions that may be interfering with your ability to move forward.

Daniel J. Boorstin, a distinguished social historian and Pulitzer Prize winner, comments about illusions: "We suffer primarily not from our vices or our weaknesses, but from our illusions. We are haunted, not by reality, but by those images we have put in place of reality" (Boorstin, 1992, p. 6).

It is important that you identify the illusionary images you have created that are making your life more difficult. For it is only as you let go of these illusions that you can accept what is real and true and move forward.

Let us consider a few illusions common in unhealthy attitudes and relationship patterns.

Let go of the illusion of oneness. The illusion that you and others are one—that others feel, think, and act the same as you—is a natural and normal infant experience. And it is easy to continue operating as an adult as if this misperception were true.

However, because you and others are, in fact, different, the illusion of oneness will eventually create problems for you. This assumption sets up unrealistic expectations that can result in internal conflicts as well as conflicts with others.

For example, you may find yourself thinking and saying things that reveal these conflicts:

- "I feel hurt or angry when others don't do things the way I would do them."
- "She shouldn't feel that way; I don't."
- "How could you possibly think that?"
- "I would never do that (so neither should others)."

The core belief underlying these comments is, "Because *I* do not feel, think, or act a certain way, others *should* not feel, think, or act that way." In essence, "We are (or should be) the same." To save your life from painful re-enactments of your understudy scripts and an endless search for what you never had, you need to let go of the illusion of oneness.

Let go of the illusion of total power. In the process of grieving your losses, it is important to let go of any illusions you may have that you have total power and control over yourself, others, or life. Letting go of the illusion of total power does not mean you have no power or ability to influence your life. However, you need to let go of any illusions that you have the power to make yourself, others, and the world ideal.

The illusion of total power can evidence itself in endless efforts to try to make people and situations be what they are not. This illusion is based on false beliefs that you are in charge of the universe; you have the power to pass out edicts about how to be, and others are required to follow your commands. The illusion of total power appears any time you try to undo the past or to control others.

Let go of the illusion of entitlement. An often-treasured illusion is that you are entitled to have others take care of you. In fact, in addition to this you may believe that others are responsible for you and are *obligated* to take care of you. When people operate with this illusion, it is common for them to express these core beliefs of entitlement in word or deed:

- "I deserve to be taken care of—to be treated as 'the special one' who is above the limitations and responsibilities imposed on others."
- "Others are responsible to make decisions for me."
- "Other people and life owe me; they are responsible to make up for what I have lost."
- "Others are obligated to prevent me from having difficulties and to rescue me from any problems created by my decisions or from life's disasters."
- "Others are responsible for how I feel and what I do."

In all of these examples, you can see that the illusion of entitlement is filled with themes of "*I can't, you can, and you should or must.*" "I can't do what is necessary to care for myself." "You are the only one who has the power to provide my needs—and you should, indeed, must take care of them." Feelings of helplessness, insecurity, and lack of self-worth often accompany these beliefs and demands, and you can act in ways that reinforce them.

In order to save your life from these self-sabotaging attitudes, however, it is important to let go of the illusion that you are entitled to have others feel, think, and act as you think they should. It is crucial as an adult to accept that others are not responsible for taking care of you, including taking responsibility for your life.

Reinvest in the new reality and move forward. As you grieve your losses and stop investing your energy into expectations, demands, and efforts that do not yield the positive outcomes you desire, you can use your energy in ways that enhance your life.

You can choose to do the work necessary to change your attitudes and save your life from the harmful effects of unmet infantile needs and past psychological wounds. You can reinvest your energy and other resources into efforts that will create a new and healthier reality.

It is important that you base this new reality on an acceptance of the truth about separateness, limitations, and accountability.

Accept the reality of separateness. As you let go of the illusion of oneness, you can begin to accept the reality of separateness—the reality that you and others are separate, unique individuals. You and others will never be one person. Although you may long for the experience of oceanic oneness with someone else, it is simply not possible.

You may have difficulty accepting this truth and find yourself struggling with the reality that you and others have different emotional responses, thought processes, and ways of handling things. Nevertheless, regardless of your wishes, expectations, and demands, you and others do not, and never will, have the same attitudes.

You also have different past experiences, different minds, and different bodies. It is important to your well-being and the health of your relationships that you face and accept the reality that you and others are, and always will be, separate beings.

As you accept the truth that you and others are separate, unique individuals, you can choose to begin accepting your differences and learning to manage them effectively. You can develop your ability to keep yourself emotionally stable even when others are not stable, knowing that you do not have to absorb their distress.

You can develop your ability to empathize with others without losing your sense of yourself. And, you can learn to value and accept yourself when you observe your differences even if others do not have that ability.

Accept the reality of limitations. In order to be free from the past so you can create the life you want, it is also important that you let go of the illusion of total power and accept the reality of limitations. Reality is that you, others, and life have limitations and flaws.

No one can measure up to anyone's idealistic wants or beliefs about what "should" be. No one has the power or ability to undo the past or to make it be something different from what it was. No one can keep you or anyone else completely safe—at all times—forever. Nor can you save your life by clinging to ineffective childhood attitude and relationships patterns.

Part of accepting the reality of limitations involves accepting (allowing it to be real and true) that limitations and flaws are part of the human experience.

And because of these limitations and flaws, you not only experienced losses as a child, but it is likely that others wounded you in some way.

Moreover, because of the lack of perfection in you, others, and the world, you will undoubtedly experience disappointment and hurt as an adult.

Accepting the reality of limitations requires that you come to terms with the fact that nothing you or others can do in the present can ever make up for past disappointments, suffering, and loss. And because of this reality, you can never be *the* center of another's "universe."

As you accept the reality of your, others', and life's limitations, however, you will be free to accept the truth. The truth is that regardless of your limitations and flaws, you can transform your wounds into wisdom. You may not yet feel like, or believe that, you have the power to change your attitudes, *but you do.*

Although you do not have the power to make yourself, others, or life perfect, you can do the work that is necessary for your psychological growth and development.

Accept the reality of accountability. Instead of holding on to the illusion of entitlement, it is important that you accept the reality of accountability if you are to transform your wounds into wisdom.

Accountability involves accepting that you are not entitled to have others take care of you, give you everything you want or need (or think you need), or act like you want them to act. Instead, it requires that you take ownership of your life, just as Anthony was learning to take ownership of his life.

Ownership involves accepting that something belongs to you and you are responsible for it. As the owner of your life, you need to accept the reality that your life belongs to *you*—no one else—and that you are accountable for what you do with your life.

You are accountable for whether or not you repair your wounds and develop the areas of your life that did not develop adequately as a child. You alone are responsible for establishing and working toward goals for your life. Only you can make the choices that will care for and help protect your life in healthy ways.

You are the only one who can change your attitudes and relationship patterns and save your life from the damage and disrepair that you have incurred throughout the years. As you choose to accept the reality that you are accountable for your attitudes, you can do the work needed to take care of your wants and needs in healthy ways.

As you develop new attitudes and relationship patterns grounded in these new realities, you will be able to transform your wounds into wisdom and move forward to save your life from the negative impact of childhood scripts.

Summary: Integrating Losses and Gains

After a loss, some people may try to help you move on with your life by saying, "Forget about the past," or "Never look back." However, remembering, or looking back, is not what causes problems in your life.

It is what you do with your memories of your past that determines whether you are stuck in unhelpful attitudes and relationship patterns or whether you move forward in healthy ways.

Remember—*you have choices.* You can choose to look back constantly with longing, regret, or anger at what you have lost. If you refuse to deal with the disappointments and losses you have experienced and the way they continue to affect your life, you may turn your life into a memorial of loss. This refusal can leave you with rigid attitudes and relationship patterns that undermine your life and hamper your ability to move into and create a new future.

You can choose, however, to accept ownership of your life and to develop a new and fulfilling life script. To save your life, do not forget your past but make peace with it by grieving your disappointments and losses. As you grieve your losses, you begin to transform your life.

Tell yourself the truth about what you have lost. The truth is you did not receive everything you needed emotionally as a child, and, in all likelihood, others wounded you. Work through your denial, avoidance, detachment, and other defenses, so you can accept the truth about your life.

Allow yourself to experience the full range of your emotions about your losses. Identify your emotions and losses and process them in safe and manageable ways.

Stop struggling to undo the past. Neither re-enacting old attitudes and relationship patterns nor searching endlessly for what you never received as a child can ever undo the past. Let go of your illusions that you can. Accept the reality that you are a unique and separate person, with very real and human limitations, and are accountable for what you do with your life.

Keep your focus on accepting your losses and on moving forward. As you working through the grieving process, you will gradually integrate your losses into a new sense of who you are—now. As you mourn your losses, you release the negative power attached to them that keep you tied to the past in hurtful ways.

Grieving opens up the opportunity for you to integrate past disappointments and losses into a new life script grounded in what is real and true in the present.

This new script, however, needs to integrate not only your disappointments and losses but also the reality of the care you *have received* from others as a child and as an adult. It is common to focus on what you did not get and what wounded you in the past and to believe dualistically that you have not received anything positive in life.

Nevertheless, as you do the tasks of grieving and let go of attitudes and relationship patterns that undermine your life, you open the door to take in and experience the good that you also received.

Ralph Waldo Emerson, an American philosopher, essayist, and poet, writes, "For every thing you have missed, you have gained something else; and for every thing you gain, you lose something" (Emerson, 1926, p. 71).

Let yourself know on a deep level what you have missed and lost and what you have gained from your losses. Learn to identify, accept, and integrate the reality of the strengths you did develop due to your losses as well as the positive experiences in your life.

As you do, you free yourself from the past so you can create powerful, meaningful, and enriching experiences in the present that move you forward into a new future.

CHAPTER 9

Regulating Your Emotions

Most powerful is he who has himself in his own power.
—Seneca, *Moral Letters to Lucilius*

In the beginning ...
As you are developing as an infant and young child, an intricate and elaborate internal operating system evolves in your mind and body that affects how you regulate your emotions as an adult. This operating system develops as you record all your experiences of emotional regulation—whether your parent provides you with Too Much, Too Little, or Just Right emotionally. Your attitudes and relationship patterns are part of this internal operating system that governs how you regulate your emotions.

Because the parts of the brain dealing with emotions are the first to develop, one of the earliest relationship patterns you form is the way you relate to feelings. If your primary caregiver provides sufficient Just Right experiences involving emotional regulation, you are likely to develop the ability to experience, identify, tolerate, and regulate your emotions. However, if your parent provides Too Much, you will tend to internalize the experience of being emotionally overwhelmed. Or if she provides Too Little, you will tend to record the experience of being dysregulated or inadequately or inconsistently regulated.

Fortunately, regardless of your parent's style of parenting, you can enhance your ability to regulate your emotions even as an adult because of the brain's ability to form new neural pathways and synapses (*neuroplasticity*). Significant emotional experiences with others who attend to you emotionally and support your developing mind can also buffer some of the negative impacts of dysregulated emotional experiences. As changes occur, new attitudes begin to develop.

Learning to regulate your emotions is critical to your well-being. Daniel Siegel, a clinical professor of psychiatry at the UCLA School of Medicine, puts it this way: "How we experience the world, relate to others, and find meaning in life, are dependent upon how we have come to regulate our emotions" (Siegel, 1999, p. 245).

Think about that for a moment!

All of your experiences and relationships, as well as your ability to find meaning in life, depend on how you regulate your emotions.

The emotional parts of your mind-body system are operating all the time and they affect how you experience and function in your life—whether or not you are aware of or acknowledge them. They help integrate how you perceive, experience, and create meaning from your experience. Whether your feelings are enjoyable (e.g., joy, happiness, or peace) or distressing (e.g., sadness, anxiety, or frustration), they influence how you think and how you behave.

Taking ownership of your emotions and becoming accountable for their impact on your life will help make it possible for you to change your problematic attitudes and save your life from the negative impact of emotional dysregulation.

As you learn to regulate your emotions more effectively, dysfunctional attitudes and relationship patterns will begin to change. As they do, you will begin to develop an internal operating system that is stronger and has a more unified and coherent sense of your self. This newly emerging system will be more adaptive, flexible, and resilient. You can use these essential qualities to create a life that is more emotionally secure and fulfilling.

In this chapter, we will explore how the ways of relating to emotions that you developed in childhood affect how you tend to deal with emotions as an adult. Then we will discuss what regulating your emotions effectively involves, focusing on what you can do to enhance your ability to care for your feelings and to develop internal security.

As we begin our exploration, let us consider Sofia's experience. Throughout the chapter, we will see how Sofia's feelings, thoughts, and behaviors began to change as she was better able to regulate herself emotionally.

Sofia's Story

Sofia was a fifty-six-year-old woman who came to see me some time ago because she was having difficulty managing her emotions. Her lack of control over her anxiety, anger, and depression was creating problems for her at both home and work. When others failed to respond to her needs,

Sofia would feel helpless and increasingly frustrated. As her distress intensified, she would become overtly angry, sometimes even pushy, in her attempts to force people to respond. When her efforts failed to elicit the desired response, she would then shut down and retreat, and would eventually become depressed.

One day, about four months into therapy, Sofia talked in-depth about her difficulty regulating her feelings.

"We don't *do* feelings in our family," Sofia announced to me in a flippant tone. "Feelings just mess up your life." She hesitated, and then continued with a touch of uncertainty. "At least, that's the message my siblings and I got loud and clear from our parents as we were growing up. In fact, the unspoken rule in the family is still: 'Thou shall not have feelings, much less express any emotion.' We learned early on that it isn't safe to talk to one other about what we feel—only what we think."

As Sofia was pausing to reflect, I noted, "The consistent message you got growing up was that it's not acceptable to have feelings. Not only is it not *acceptable*, but it's also *wrong* to have feelings."

Sofia became quiet, and her initial energy began to dissipate. She acknowledged sadly, "My parents were not very good at dealing with emotions. Most of the time, they didn't express any feelings—unless, of course, they were really upset. Then they'd say something harsh and walk away. Or, sometimes, they would get on a tangent—ranting and raving. When my dad got on a roll, sometimes he would even grab our arms and jerk us around while he was yelling at us. Then he would stomp out of the house. It was dreadful."

I said, "So your experience was that it could become very confusing and frightening—even dangerous—when emotions got out of control?"

Sofia replied, "It was very frustrating and scary trying to figure out how to deal with my parents. I never knew how they were going to react to things. I remember hiding in my room a lot just to get away from them—I felt safer there—out of sight and out of mind (I hoped). I was upset with them, but most of the time I just felt anxious and afraid. Sometimes the anxiety got so bad that I felt like I was going to fly out of my skin. It was awful!

"When I was *really* anxious and angry, I would usually pace around my room trying to calm down. I would do anything I could think of to get rid of my feelings. I'd usually end up lying on my bed and crying." Sofia sighed deeply and then noted sadly, "What hurts the most is that my parents *never* came in to comfort me."

As I listened to Sofia, I found myself feeling sad and remembering the following quote, which I shared with her. "Alone, alone, all, all alone, Alone on a wide wide sea! And never a saint took pity on My soul in agony."[5]

Sofia looked startled for a moment. Then her eyes brimmed with tears as she replied, "I *did* feel alone—*all* the time." We sat together in silence for several moments. Then Sofia continued, "You know, it makes sense that I felt so alone ... I *was* alone with my feelings. The bottom line message my parents gave us was that our feelings didn't matter or simply didn't exist.

"We knew they wouldn't *really* listen if we tried to say anything when we were upset. On the rare occasions that they did let us talk, they would tell us either to 'get over it,' 'stop being a cry baby,' or 'toughen up.' Other times they just made fun of us. It was all very painful."

Sofia paused and then said, "I used to think they didn't care about us and were being mean. I still think that sometimes. But most of the time now I think they acted that way because they had no idea about what to do with their emotions, much less ours. ...

"You know what's weird? Even though my parents gave us the message as we were growing up that emotions were taboo, there sure were a lot of out of control emotions being thrown around all over the place."

Sofia had grown up with little support from her parents as the emotional parts of her mind were developing. In effect, her parents had deserted her emotionally, leaving her all by herself to cope with the various confusing, anxiety-provoking, painful, and frightening situations in which she found herself.

The message Sofia had recorded as a child during these experiences was that emotions were scary and harmful. She had learned that the only way to deal with feelings was either to let them become overwhelming (and then they might, of course, spill out onto others) or to avoid feelings altogether.

Sofia's story is familiar to many people. When your parents have trouble relating to emotions, it is difficult for them to regulate both their emotions and yours, which negatively affects the parent-child relationship. Overwhelming feelings, even positive ones, can be very frightening. The emotional dysregulation makes it difficult to feel safe or to bring all of yourself into your relationships.

When this occurs, there is also a tendency to attach negative meanings to emotions, relationships, and life in general. These problematic

---

[5] This is from *The Rime of the Ancient Mariner,* by Samuel Taylor Coleridge, Part IV, lines 233–236.

meanings then become part of your attitudes and relationship patterns that affect you throughout your life.

The Impact of Outdated Attitudes on Your Emotions

Some of the attitudes you developed early in life are undoubtedly still helpful. Others, however, may need to be changed. Let us examine briefly some ways of dealing with your emotions that may be interfering with your relationships with yourself, others, and the world.

When You Disregard Your Emotions

If your early relational experiences were with a parent who provided Too Much or Too Little, you, like Sofia, would have experienced significant disregard and disrespect for the emotional part of you. Because you would have internalized and recorded these aspects of your parent's attitudes in infancy and early childhood, you probably developed the same attitudes toward your emotions that your parent had toward them.

These internalizations can result in your re-enacting your parent-child experiences with yourself and others later on. You may find yourself as an adult failing to notice or to consider your and others' emotions. You may also find yourself acting in ways that evoke negative responses from others or gravitating to others who fail to consider your feelings.

Failure to receive adequate emotional attunement and regulation as an infant and young child interferes with the development of your internal operating system, including your attitudes and relationship patterns in other ways. You may not learn to observe or regulate your emotions.

Not only that, but if your parent relates to the emotional part of you in a way that leads to your being emotionally overwhelmed, it is also likely that your mind will record those experiences, and even the relationship, as traumatic in some way.

Unless someone provides you with—or helps you learn to provide yourself with—the emotional resources to repair these limitations and wounds, you may have difficulty keeping yourself on an even keel as you move further into adulthood.

In addition, instead of developing the capacity to tolerate and effectively manage the bodily sensations that go along with emotions, you can develop a fear of (or other adverse reactions to) those sensations.

To protect yourself from these distressing emotions, you, like Sofia and her parents, may develop patterns of relating to feelings such as avoidance, denial, detachment, minimization, and rejection. You may also find yourself defensively projecting and shifting your distress onto others.

Ultimately, however, these efforts do not protect you emotionally nor do they provide the care that you need for psychological growth and repair. In fact, this ongoing disregard or disrespect for the emotional part of you sets you up to be re-wounded.

One of the goals Sofia and I initially established was for her to become more aware of her patterns of relating to her feelings and bodily sensations. As Sofia continued to deal with her issues in our second year of treatment, she began to discover ways in which she would re-enact her parent-child emotional scripts in her current relationships.

For example, when Sofia began treatment, she was unaware of the tension that mounted in her body whenever she was anxious or frustrated. As she practiced paying more attention to her body, however, she discovered that she tended to ignore or to hold in her feelings. Then, as the pressure inside intensified, Sofia's feelings would emerge, and she would become demanding and resort to making snide or sarcastic comments.

When the pressure became too great, Sofia would become overtly hostile, sometimes even shouting at others. Through these angry reactions, Sofia was unconsciously re-enacting some of her parent scripts. In contrast, when Sofia was re-enacting the child role of her early understudy experience, *any* uncomfortable bodily sensations or emotions would easily overwhelm and frighten her. She would then find herself withdrawing, just as she had done when she was young.

Gradually, however, Sofia was becoming more skilled at identifying her affects and recognizing when she was re-enacting her parent-child emotional scripts in her relationships. She was also becoming more aware of how her lack of mindfulness about her own and others' emotions was resulting in conflicts with her family and co-workers.

One day Sofia shared a significant experience that had occurred the previous week.

"This week I had an 'Aha!' moment," Sofia announced at the beginning of our session. "I have been *very* frustrated that my husband hasn't been telling me how he feels about things. When John doesn't tell me what's on his mind, I get afraid that he might leave me and that I'll be left alone.

"When he shut down the other night, I started pressuring him to talk to me. The more I got upset and pressured him, though, the more withdrawn he became—which, of course, made me more anxious and frustrated. The more upset I got, the less I could handle my emotions. I ended up yelling at him. But I finally gave up and went to the bedroom and cried myself to sleep. It was terrible!"

I commented, "It's so scary and frustrating to want so desperately to feel connected to someone and not be able to get the closeness you need. To make matters worse, the anger that's supposed to protect you actually leaves you feeling more alone, overwhelmed, and helpless ... and sometimes, even, collapsed."

"Exactly!" Sofia responded. "But this time (after I calmed down a little bit) it hit me—I hadn't been paying attention to or taking care of my feelings at all! I hadn't been noticing my body sensations that I'm *sure* were probably sounding alarms. I also hadn't tried to reality check my fearful feelings and thoughts like we've been talking about doing or to do anything to relieve my frustration. I was just reacting.

"I wasn't considering my husband's feelings, either. I just wanted John to listen to me and make me feel better. I was ignoring the fact that I was overwhelming him *and* me. It didn't feel good to realize that I had been disregarding *both* of our feelings—just like my parents used to do. And I *sure* hadn't stopped to think that maybe he was afraid to tell me how he felt! I feel very sad and embarrassed about that." Sofia sat quietly for a moment; her body seemed to deflate. Her sadness was palpable.

Then I noticed Sofia's shoulders moved back slightly as she sat a little taller. Her mood was also shifting as she continued, "The part I feel good about is that I was able to recognize what I had been doing and to work through what had been bothering me—even though it was after the fact. I told John what I had figured out and apologized to him.

"Amazingly, we talked for a long time about how we both had learned to deal with our emotions growing up. We also agreed to work on paying attention and responding to our own and each other's feelings instead of just ignoring or discounting them or letting them build up inside like we both usually do."

Sofia paused and then, with emotion choking her voice, she said, "We both felt a lot closer to each other after that. It felt *so* nice!"

I commented, "Even though you don't usually observe or respond thoughtfully to your own and others' feelings, you're discovering that you can do a better job of regulating them when you do."

As I listened to Sofia, I could hear how the meanings she had attached to emotions as a child were negatively affecting her relationship with her husband. In her childhood survival system, emotions were troublemakers. Emotions meant unbearable fear, helplessness, shame, vulnerability, and feelings of inadequacy. The expression of emotions was also very psychologically threatening to Sofia because she associated it with lack of control and disruptions in her relationships. These perceptions caused her to either lose emotional control in or avoid conflict situations, creating a break in her connection with John and reinforcing her attitudes about emotions.

Although these meanings were still part of her internal operating system, Sofia was letting herself know the truth about how her childhood losses and disappointments were interfering with establishing rewarding relationships. This awareness was making it possible for her to begin grieving the losses of emotional safety, security, and self-worth that she had incurred during childhood because her parents had not been mindful of her feelings.

She also began grieving that she had not learned to regulate and control her emotions effectively because her parents had difficulty managing their emotions and, therefore, they failed to help her learn to manage hers.

In addition, Sofia was learning to notice her body's sensations and let herself experience her emotions more fully. She was also striving to pay attention and be responsive to both her own and others' emotions.

Although stressors might still activate the childhood protective system that was part of her attitudes, Sofia continued working on transforming her old system.

And even though her old patterns of letting her fear and despair get out of control and berating herself reared their ugly heads periodically, Sofia was learning to focus her energy on regulating her emotions more effectively and moving forward in her life.

When You Are Overwhelmed by Your Emotions

As you grow up, you develop the ability to tolerate your emotions within a particular range. Daniel Siegel refers to this range as a "window of tolerance" (Siegel, 1999, p. 253). Your window of tolerance is the range of emotional arousal that your body and mind can manage without disrupting your ability to function.

Some people can handle a wide variety of emotions at different levels of intensity. Other people have a narrower window of tolerance—even small amounts of emotional arousal can overwhelm them.

Many factors influence the range and intensity of emotional arousal your mind can process without becoming overwhelmed and disrupting your ability to function.

- Your biological makeup at birth (your inborn temperament) can make you more or less sensitive to and capable of handling your body's emotional signals.

- Your physical state can affect your emotional state. Your health and even your eating and sleeping patterns can affect your ability to process your emotions.
- The number and type of stressors you experience on any given day, week, or year can affect your window of tolerance. The more stressors you have, the closer together they occur, and the greater their frequency and impact, the harder it becomes to manage your emotional response to stressors.
- Your early childhood experience with your parents affects how you deal with your emotional load.
- The type of emotional support system available to you can also influence your ability to tolerate your emotions. Rather than trying to manage your emotions alone, it is easier to regulate yourself when you have a stable, supportive, and caring network of people in your life.

The primary focus of attention here, however, is how your experience (especially your early relational experience) affects your attitudes, your window of tolerance, and your ability to regulate your emotions.

Your core attitudes play a significant role
in how your window of tolerance operates
and in your ability to manage your emotions.

Emotional overload, regardless of its cause, interferes with effective emotional, cognitive, and behavioral functioning. In fact, it can traumatize the mind and body. When this occurs, you can develop a sensitivity to the bodily sensations associated with emotions, which narrows your window of tolerance.

This sensitivity can make it difficult for you to regulate how intensely you feel the emotional stimulation. You may overreact to emotional sensations, have trouble staying connected to your feelings, or become reactive in situations unrelated to what you are feeling. Your emotions may shut down to the point that it is hard even to know what you feel.

You may also feel powerless to restabilize yourself into your window of tolerance because it may be difficult for you to regulate how long your feelings last. When you are over-stimulated, your feelings may linger far beyond their usefulness for providing you information, even to the point where your feelings start to interfere with your functioning abilities. When you are under-stimulated, you may have difficulty mobilizing the emotional energy, motivation, and effort needed to function fully.

In addition, when you are overwhelmed you may unconsciously distort your perceptions of your experience, because emotional overload interferes with emotional processing. For example, you may perceive experiences that are not inherently dangerous as threatening. You may experience others as being critical or neglectful of you even when, in reality, they are trying to be sensitive and responsive or are only busy with their life tasks. If you are frequently overwhelmed, you may even begin to experience emotions themselves as threatening in some way, even as traumatic.

Although emotional overload or trauma can negatively affect your ability to manage all of your feelings, you may have particular difficulty handling your fear and aggression. You may become fearful of and hypersensitive to many things. You also may find yourself snapping at others and losing control of your aggression over seemingly small events.

Conversely, you may disconnect from your emotions and feel very little fear at all, even fear that could help protect you. You may not be able to muster up enough anger or positive aggression (energy) to help protect yourself in hurtful or dangerous situations.

The cognitive processing parts of the brain function less effectively when you are operating outside your window of tolerance. These interruptions in cognitive functioning interfere with the interworking of the attitude components and other parts of your internal operating system. This makes it difficult to think in ways that are adaptable, flexible, symbolic, and conceptual.

If the emotional overload becomes overwhelming, your cognitive system may also shut down, just like the circuit breaker in your home's electrical system shuts off during system overload. When this shutdown occurs, it usually creates a disconnection between your mind and body.

These cognitive limitations during emotional overload impair your ability to function in several ways. They disrupt your ability to observe your experience and to think clearly and rationally—and abstractly—which makes it difficult to reflect on and process your experience. For example, when you are outside your window of tolerance, you are more apt to distort the cognitive meanings of your experience, creating meanings that leave you feeling more emotionally vulnerable.

In particular, you may you may end up attributing negative motivations to what others do, and the meanings you place on their actions may cause you to feel hurt. When you are calmer and better able to reflect, you may realize you misread their motivation.

Because these cognitive impairments interfere with your ability to make connections between experiences, principles, and ideas, they also make decision making and problem solving more difficult. Both of these abilities are necessary to deal with the stresses and challenges of daily living. It is hard to regulate your emotions when you cannot determine what you are feeling and how to stabilize yourself.

It is especially difficult to navigate relationships when your analytic and conceptual abilities are limited. Thinking through how you will relate to others, manage conflicts, and enhance your relationships depends on your cognitive abilities.

Behaviorally, it may be very difficult to manage and control what you say or do when your emotions are disrupting your thought and impulse control processes. When you operate outside of your window of tolerance, it is more difficult to control your impulses. This limitation can result in your reacting impulsively or compulsively, with more frequent and intense emotional outbursts.

Emotional overload can leave you feeling, thinking, and acting in distorted and dysregulated ways.

As Sofia and I continued working together over the next six months, Sofia began seeing and understanding other ways her difficulty regulating her emotions was negatively affecting her thought processes and ability to manage her behaviors.

One day Sofia described her current observations.

"I've been noticing that it's easier to manage my emotions and think more clearly when I'm not too stressed-out. This week, though, was terrible. I've been sick and not sleeping well … But that's not the worst! My boss re-assigned me to a new position at work (with *no* training) *and* my parents showed up this week to visit, even though I told them it wasn't a good week to come." Sofia shuddered and frowned.

Then Sofia continued, "I've really had to watch out because my old attitude patterns have been working overtime! I've noticed that I've been feeling sorry for myself and thinking crazy thoughts all week, like, 'No one cares about me.' Not only that, but I've also caught myself shutting down inside and rushing around trying to take care of everything—the whole time trying not to think about how irritated I am that everyone is so selfish. I find myself snapping at *whoever* crosses my path, and a few times I've even been abrupt and sarcastic with co-workers." A look of pleasure passed fleetingly across Sofia's face.

I reflected, "I noticed just now that you seemed to smile with satisfaction. Did you notice that?"

"No, I didn't, but it's interesting that you caught it. I've been noticing for the first time this week that sometimes I feel a twinge of pleasure and power when I let out my frustration and anger, even though it is very short lived. I've even found myself thinking, 'That's what other people get for not caring about me.' Clearly, some part of me likes punishing others for disregarding or mistreating me. (Those are two of my triggers, you know!)

"The trouble is, I also hate it when I act that way because it's not helping me, or others, and I end up feeling crappy ... *and crazy*. Not only that, but then I also start worrying about others retaliating and making me pay for how I acted. Talk about internal conflict!" Sofia sighed deeply, and then muttered, "Sometimes I feel trapped by the old patterns."

I observed, "Part of you feels quite delighted and powerful when you verbally whack someone for not showing you the caring you need. But another part of you knows that all the old painful feelings of guilt and shame will eventually rush in and annihilate your sense of victory, leaving you feeling helpless and stuck." I paused and then commented, "You *are* paying a big price when you use the outdated ways of trying to protect yourself."

Sofia responded with chagrin and determination, "I can see how when I lose control, I'm doing the same damn thing that my parents used to do, and I hate it. I'm sick and tired of the cycle. I really don't want to hurt anyone ... including myself! It's not worth it! And that's not the person I want to be or how I want to live my life.

"I'm going to keep working on paying attention to my body and emotional signals and doing something to keep my stress levels down *before* I get overloaded! If I stay on an even keel, I know I can handle my triggers and respond better instead of just reacting."

Clearly, Sofia was struggling to regulate her emotions, especially when she felt emotionally overloaded. Her parents' lack of emotional attunement and regulation had provided too much challenge and very little support for her developing mind.

Although her parents' limitations had negatively affected her ability to care for her feelings, to Sofia's credit, she persisted making the effort to learn to manage her emotions and establish healthy relationships.

As Sofia and I continued to work together, we were also mindful of the ways Sofia would re-enact her internalized scripts with me. We were alert to how Sofia unknowingly (and sometimes knowingly) tried to engage me in re-enacting her familiar scenarios.

When she was playing out the parent role, Sofia would angrily complain about me and try to provoke me into getting angry with her. When she would act in these ways, I found myself wanting to disconnect from Sofia emotionally and flee from her intense anger, just as she had once fled to her room as a child when her parents were angry.

When she was enacting the child role, Sofia would experience me as her emotionally distant, uncaring, or angry parents. In those moments,

Sofia described feeling anxious and uncertain. She was afraid that I was upset with her (like her parents had been), although I was feeling none of those emotions.

As we processed the re-enactments that occurred in our relationship, Sofia became even more aware of her deep-seated anger, resentment, and disappointment about how her parents' limitations were negatively affecting her life. She also began to see more clearly how her feelings of vulnerability would readily activate her childhood survival system, which undermined her ability to develop the emotional closeness she longed for with others (including me).

Sofia was getting more in touch with her pain and sorrow about how her emotional, cognitive, and behavioral patterns—originally developed to protect her—were actually causing her more pain.

As Sofia bravely struggled with her unhelpful ways of relating to her emotions and continued grieving her losses and disappointments, her attitudes were changing. Fortunately, even though she still had very difficult days, Sofia was clearly developing her ability to regulate her emotions more effectively and was moving forward in her life.

Let us look now at some of the principles of emotional regulation that were proving helpful to Sofia in her efforts to change her attitudes and save her life from self-defeating attitudes and relationship patterns.

Updating How You Regulate Your Emotions

Updating how you regulate your emotions involves all three components of your attitude system. Although this chapter primarily focuses on making changes in the emotional component of your attitudes, the cognitive and behavioral components are an integral part of this process. (We will look in more depth at the cognitive and behavioral aspects of attitude change in the following two chapters.)

So let us explore three key aspects of the process of regulating your emotions: developing a secure relationship, becoming mindful of your emotions, and modulating your emotions.

As we continue, remember that attitude change, including emotional regulation, does not occur in a linear fashion. Attitude change is a process in which all of the dimensions involved in change continually and dynamically affect each other.

Developing a Secure Relationship

Part of changing your attitudes so you can save your life from the deleterious effects of your childhood survival system involves developing a secure relationship. This requires letting go of problematic emotional patterns and creating new, more effective ones.

Struggling to let go of old emotional patterns. It is often an epic struggle of old versus new to let go of unhealthy emotional patterns so you can develop emotionally healthy relationships and an internal sense of security. In this conflict you, the hero in your real life story, must fight to save your life from the entrenched and intractable attitudes and relationship patterns that undermine you. You must also do the work required to create a new life-enhancing attitude system.

This transformational process is challenging. You cannot deactivate the attitudes and relationship patterns that developed as you bonded with an emotionally enmeshed, domineering, unavailable, or inconsistent parent easily. Rather, your childhood coping system resists efforts aimed at remodeling the psychological and physical structures that developed during your formative years.

However, as you do the work needed to let go of entrenched, undermining emotional patterns, you *can* create new ways of feeling, thinking, and behaving.

Striving to create new emotional patterns. As you strive to develop new and healthier ways of relating to the emotional part of yourself and others, it is important to have the external resources that will make change possible.

Because attitudes and relationship patterns initially develop in the context of relationship, one essential resource is a relationship with an emotionally safe person.

Although you cannot go back and become a child again, it is critical that you establish a relationship with a mature and supportive person in the present. This person needs to be able and willing to work with you in the process of developing healthy attitudes and relationship patterns.

Healing and growth as an adult are only possible
if you have a safe and secure relationship in which to evolve.

Unfortunately, if your earliest attachment was to a parent who provided Too Much or Too Little, it is hard to develop healthy relationships. The tendency will be to re-enact the early dysfunctional attitudes and relationship patterns with others. For example, if your parent was not emotionally available, you may unconsciously gravitate to people who are not emotionally available, leaving you without the emotional support you need. A part of you may even pull back when you attempt to connect because your unconscious mind signals, "Don't go there; it's not safe."

Although Sofia longed to be emotionally close to others, whenever she began to share her feelings with anyone, she would move away in fear. So Sofia and I worked on her fear of closeness in our relationship as well as in her relationships with others.

Even though this type of internal conflict is likely to occur as you are changing your attitudes, your healing and growth depend on having a real experience with someone who is respectful of you and your emotions. In this relationship, you become more aware of yourself.

You also observe and experience the other person's healthier (though not perfect) emotional, cognitive, and behavioral patterns. In the process, you modify your attitudes, and you develop your ability to relate in healthier ways.

As you learn to regulate yourself internally—while in relationship—you begin to

- become more observant of and better able to reflect on yourself and your emotional (and cognitive-behavioral) processes;
- increase your ability to regulate your emotions more effectively;
- develop a broader and more flexible range of emotional tolerance, so you can care for yourself in healthier ways.

As you grow in these ways, you will develop greater resilience, which enables you to deal with the distressing experiences of life. A healthy relationship creates the space and experience that enable you to change ineffective, outdated attitudes and emotional relationships patterns and to create new ones.

Although emotionally safe, consistent, reliable, knowledgeable, and capable people can be hard to find, they do exist. Many people will search until they find a professional, such as a psychotherapist, with whom they can develop a good *therapeutic relationship.*

In a good therapeutic relationship, the therapist has the knowledge, skills, and emotional capacity to guide and support you on your journey to change your attitudes and save your life. The therapist will facilitate change by focusing less on giving advice and more on relating in healthy ways. In such a relationship, you will be able to process your past and present experiences *with* the therapist, while keeping your emotions in a manageable range. This type of support will help you develop a healthy tolerance for emotional distress.

Because not everyone has access to this type of therapeutic relationship, some people search until they find someone with whom they can develop a *helping relationship.* You can establish a helping relationship with someone such as a mentor, teacher, relative, counselor, or spiritual leader who has some of these capabilities. In a helping relationship, the focus is on the helper supporting you in your process of changing unhelpful attitudes and relationship patterns.

Natural relationships, such as those with a spouse, friend, or sibling, can also be supportive. In these relationships, however, you share the focus of attention between both people rather focusing on you alone. It is also difficult for natural partners to be as observant and reflective as you might need because of their emotional involvement and perhaps even limited abilities to provide the resources you need. Moreover, in all likelihood, they will tend to replay their old internalized attitude and relationship patterns with you.

The more understanding, knowledge, expertise, and healthy emotional capacity the person who is helping you has, the greater the likelihood that you will be able to make the changes you need. Even though it may seem like a daunting, and even impossible, task to find and develop an emotionally safe relationship, do not give up.

To save your life from self-defeating re-enactments and to create new emotional patterns, it is critical to have a safe and secure relationship with an emotionally available and capable person. These relationships help open the door to a new future for yourself.

Becoming Mindful of Your Emotions

In order to work with and regulate your emotions more effectively, it is crucial that you learn to be mindful of your emotions. Being *mindful* (as I will be using the term) involves being aware of and keeping in mind your attitudes.

As you learn to be mindful of your emotions, it can be helpful to view emotions as mind-body signals that communicate how you are processing your experience. These signals provide you with valuable information about your experience and the meanings you are making of it. If you are unaware of or disregard your bodily sensations and emotional signals, it will be difficult to care for yourself in healthy ways.

Learning to become more mindful of your emotions
is central to developing the capacity and ability
to regulate your emotions more effectively.

There are two main aspects of becoming mindful of your emotions: developing awareness of your emotions and identifying your emotions. It is important to develop both capacities. If these abilities are lacking or underdeveloped, instead of being able to care for your emotions effectively, your mind will tend to defend against your emotions. Unfortunately, the various protective maneuvers the mind uses to deal with actual or anticipated distress can interfere with your ability to function effectively. Therefore, it is critical that you develop healthy ways of relating to your emotions.

Let us explore these aspects of mindfulness.

Developing awareness of your emotions. It is normal to be conscious of some of your emotions and bodily sensations but unconscious of the ones that are less accessible. In order to use your feelings as signals or sources of information, it is important to become more aware and observant of all aspects of your emotions. When you are aware of your feelings, you can use the information from your observations to care for yourself.

As you emotionally and cognitively perceive your emotions and bodily sensations, you can pay attention to and reflect on them. This focus provides you with a wealth of useful information. For example, your physical sensations let you know if your body is preparing for a perceived threat with a fight, flight, freeze, or fold reaction.

Your emotions let you know what you are and are not comfortable with, what you like and dislike, and what you need or do not need. All of this information helps you identify what is important to you and to develop a better sense of yourself.

As you become aware of your emotions, it is also important that you carefully observe and differentiate between your emotional states (what you feel) and external reality. Being mindful of your body and emotions can be even more challenging if you confuse your feelings with what is real and true externally. Consider these examples:

- You may *feel* that your family does not love you when, *in fact*, they love you very much.
- You may *feel* that your emotions are unbearable when, *in fact*, you can endure them. In reality, you may not want to, and you may fear you cannot survive them.
- You may *feel* that you cannot accomplish a task when, *in fact*, you can. In reality, you may need time or support from others or more information about the task.

It is important to remember that people's emotions,
often expressed as thoughts or beliefs,
are often not a statement of external reality.

In addition, as you observe your affects, it is important that you learn to distinguish your emotions from other people's emotions. Seeing yourself as separate from others makes it possible for you to own your emotional responses and not take on others' emotions. You will be able to identify the source and cause of the emotions, as well.

For example, imagine a friend feels hurt and angry about something you said. If you stop to consider the situation carefully, you may realize that the source of your friend's distress is the *meaning* she is attaching to what you said—not what you actually said.

Your emotions can also signal when you need to be on the alert. For example, your feelings and intuition can signal when someone is trying to manipulate you so you can set boundaries and disengage from the situation. When you are aware of your feelings and use your awareness to act on your own behalf, your emotions serve to protect you.

Although focusing on your emotions may increase your awareness of your emotional experience, paying attention to bodily sensations often provides the first awareness of emotional experience. A wide variety of bodily sensations can indicate that something is going on emotionally.

Typical signals of emotional distress are muscle tension, stomach upset, and headaches. A sense of being hyper-alert, on-guard, or even that a dark cloud is hanging over you may also signal that something needs to be addressed.

When you take notice of these signals, you can use the information you gain to act in ways that help you manage your emotions, as Sofia was learning to do.

One session, Sofia excitedly announced, "You know how we've been working on me becoming aware of the feeling sensations in my body as well as my emotions? You'll never guess what I noticed this week! It's the oddest thing, but I just realized that the first sign that I'm feeling anxious or frustrated is that the muscles in my scalp start to contract. If I don't do anything about my feelings, they get worse.

"So now, whenever I first notice the contractions starting, I've been taking a few minutes to do my deep breathing and relaxation exercises and reassuring myself like we talked about. I keep that up until I feel the muscles relax, and I calm down. Since I've been practicing this, I've noticed that I am less irritable and anxious. It's great! But the *best* thing is I'm able to ward off a lot of my anger and anxiety attacks!"

Sofia was learning to break the cycle of emotional dysregulation. She was noticing her body's signals that her body was getting ready to react, and she was stopping the reaction before it got out of control. In essence, she was "putting out the spark before it ignited the fire."

Identifying your emotions. Just as it is important to be aware of your emotions, it is also important to be able to identify your feelings. Identifying your emotions includes naming them, understanding them, and, whenever possible, making the connection between your emotional responses and their internal or external triggers.

Many people have difficulty making the connection between their feelings and internal and external triggers. This difficulty is a common limitation. If no one helped you observe and understand your feelings when you were young, or if you experienced emotional overload (trauma) when these parts of the mind were developing, you may not have developed these abilities.

Your parents may have taught you to call the barking creature behind the fence a "dog." However, they may not have adequately helped you learn to identify your emotions (e.g., fear, sadness, worry, and loneliness) or talk about your emotional experience. They may not have helped you observe your physical and emotional responses, stay present with them, or care for them adequately.

Instead, your parents may have over-reacted to your feelings. Or, like Sofia's parents, they may have ignored your emotions, treating them as if they did not exist, were immaterial, or were something you should just "stop."

Although you may not have learned to identify your physical and emotional signals well as a child, it is important to develop your ability to do so as an adult. Being able to use words to name (label) your emotions is an important part of emotional regulation, although scientists are not sure yet exactly how this works.

The ability to describe the different parts of your emotional processes, to explain what your emotions mean, and to express your emotions effectively has a significant impact on how you take care of your feelings.

These abilities also affect how you manage your and others' emotions in relationships. It is difficult to ask for what you need or to resolve conflicts in relationships if you can't articulate how you feel. In addition, your emotions provide useful information about your motivations and cognitions that can help guide you. Learn to read and understand the signals well.

It is also crucial that you learn to identify your emotions as accurately as possible. Erroneous labeling and interpretations of emotions and motivations can interfere with your relationships with yourself, others, and the world.

When you or others mislabel or attach inaccurate meanings to feelings, you are likely to experience more emotional pain and conflict in your relationships. For example, sometimes when people are feeling anxious, uncertain, or angry they may say they are "bored."

The strategies to care for boredom, however, are very different from those that care for anxiety, uncertainty, and anger. When you identify your emotions inaccurately, it is hard for you and others to respond effectively to them and to the needs that they express.

How you experience yourself, others, and the world
and how you manage your life depend on your ability to identify
your emotions and motivations accurately.

As you pay attention to and observe your emotions, you learn to identify the connections between various emotions and between your feelings, thoughts, and actions. For example, you may become aware that you feel guilty about your anger or anxious about your feelings of helplessness. You may become aware that when you are afraid you become more controlling or that when you are feeling powerless you snipe at others.

You also begin to recognize that your thoughts and beliefs can intensify your emotions. You begin to notice that when you are sad and you allow yourself to think your life is hopeless, you become more melancholy or even depressed.

Another important aspect of identifying and understanding your emotions is determining what activates them. Biochemical changes in the brain or psychological and relational processes can trigger an emotional reaction.

When you can identify what triggers you emotionally, you are better able to anticipate your reactions and develop a proactive plan to manage your responses. When you are not aware of your emotional triggers, however, you are more apt to be reactive (which usually is not helpful) rather than mindful.

Lack of mindfulness promotes problems in emotional and cognitive management (e.g., rigid thought processes, lack of thinking, distorted and overly emotional thoughts, or under- and over-reactions to stimuli).

To help you identify, understand, and describe your emotions and internal processes more accurately, you can practice asking yourself questions to clarify your experience:

- Is the uncomfortable feeling in my chest an ache? A knot?
- Which emotions is the sensation signaling? Delight? Sadness? Anger? Fear?
- Am I experiencing several emotions at once?
- Where is my emotional level in my window of tolerance?
- On a continuum, how strong is the emotion? Mild? Moderate? Severe?

- What triggers the emotion? Something external? My thoughts? Other emotions?
- What happens to the feelings when I respond to them in different ways?

As you improve your ability to be aware of and identify your emotions and the body sensations associated with them, you will understand what you are experiencing more fully. These abilities will help you stay connected to yourself and help you make and maintain better emotional connections with others. You will be better able to communicate what is going on inside you to yourself and others. You also will be better able to solve problems, resolve conflicts, and access support systems.

Modulating Your Emotions

Just as developing a secure relationship and becoming mindful of your emotions are important to your ability to regulate your emotions, so too is modulating your emotions. These processes operate in concert. So let us consider two key aspects of modulating your emotions: learning to stay present with your feelings and keeping your feelings within your window of tolerance.

Learning to stay present with what you are experiencing. In order to regulate your emotions effectively, it is important to develop your ability to stay present with your distressing emotions and the physical sensations associated with them. A curious, open, investigative approach to your emotions will help you increase your capacity to tolerate and stay present with them.

Martha Stark comments that "[t]hose ... who do not have the capacity to sit with internal conflicts will be in the position of forever giving important parts of themselves away, leaving themselves feeling internally impoverished and excessively dependent upon others" (Stark, 1999, p. 269).

Learning to stay present with what you are experiencing makes it possible for you to observe, understand, and care for your emotions. These abilities will help your confidence, identity, security, and self-worth to grow. Your sense of self-efficacy increases as you learn to experience and manage your various emotional states without becoming emotionally overwhelmed. You can be more accepting of your distressing emotions when you recognize that they are signals rather than threats to your sense of self or well-being. As you become more familiar with your emotions, you learn to value the emotional parts of yourself.

It can be especially helpful during this process to experience holding on to your emotions with a therapeutic, helping, or natural partner who can accept, tolerate, and help you work through your feelings.

In Sofia's and my work together, as we experienced and processed her anxiety, depression, and frustration together, she began to feel safe enough to stay present with her feelings more often. Over time, she became less afraid and more tolerant of her emotions. As Sofia's emotional distress lessened and her newly emerging capacity to tolerate her feelings continued to develop, Sofia was better able to work with her emotions instead of against them. She was then able to act in ways that further decreased her emotional distress.

Allowing yourself to experience and sit with your emotions can be particularly difficult, especially when your emotions and the body sensations associated with them are unpleasant or painful.

Withdrawing from your emotions by judging them harshly is a typical psychological protective maneuver that makes it difficult to be aware of and stay present with distressing emotions.

Although you may tend to judge your emotions harshly, especially the more distressing ones, it is important to be aware of, pay attention to, and stay present with your emotions— without condemnation.

Criticizing or negatively judging yourself and your emotions (consciously or unconsciously) does not help you modulate your emotions. Instead, it can make staying present with your emotions difficult. Judging your feelings usually results in a tendency to avoid, deny, minimize, disconnect from, or reject them. All of these responses undermine your ability to obtain the information that you could glean from staying present with your emotions. A lack of information, in turn, makes it difficult for you to regulate your emotions.

When you work to accept your feelings as information or signals, you become aware of aspects of your experience that may not be apparent initially. For example, in a conflict you may be able to identify and express that you feel angry. You may have difficulty, however, noticing and observing the underlying feelings of vulnerability that are evoking your angry reaction, such as feeling discounted, ignored, abandoned, or rejected. When you can stay present with and tolerate your distressing emotions, you can begin to recognize and modulate them.

If you judge your emotions, criticize yourself for your feelings, or disconnect from your vulnerable emotions, your distress is likely to increase because you are not caring for your emotions. As you gain awareness of, observe, and accept what is happening to you internally, you are in a better position to address your underlying vulnerabilities that are giving rise to your reactions. As you do, you can then take action to work through and resolve your internal conflicts.

Maintaining emotions within your window of tolerance. In order to stay present with your emotions so that you can regulate them, it is important to keep your feelings within your window of tolerance. It is also important to develop your ability to tolerate a broader range of emotions and higher degrees of emotional intensity. As you regulate your emotions and develop the ability to keep yourself emotionally safe, you will increase the capacity to tolerate your feelings and become more secure internally.

Maintaining your emotions within your window of tolerance involves monitoring and managing your emotions. As you become aware of, observe, and identify your feelings, you can then modify them in ways that increase or decrease their intensity or duration or change them all together. As you learn to maintain your feelings within your window of tolerance, you may need to practice staying with your feelings; first in little, brief doses, then in progressively higher doses, for longer periods.

While you are learning to sit with your body's feedback signals, you need to be careful to do this at a pace you can handle so you do not overwhelm yourself. It is important not to re-traumatize yourself by allowing your emotions to exceed your window of tolerance.

If you grew up with a parent who was emotionally enmeshed, domineering, unavailable, or inconsistent, you probably did not receive the help you needed to maintain your emotions within your window of tolerance. Instead, in all likelihood, you (and your parent) were emotionally overwhelmed on many occasions. This emotional overload, often experienced as traumatic, makes it difficult for you to stay present with and tolerate your feelings.

In addition, traumatic experiences later in life, as well as genetic tendencies, can result in a hypersensitivity to the body sensations that go with your feelings. For example, just as there are people who have a lower pain threshold, there are people who have a lower emotional sensation threshold. When you have a narrow window of tolerance, what may seem like a minor frustration or disappointment to others manifests as a significant event to you. This hypersensitivity can make it very difficult to stay present with, tolerate, and regulate your emotions.

Instead, when your body starts to register an emotional response—good or bad—you may find yourself shifting into a fight, flight, freeze, or fold mode. These reflexive reactions are especially common when you are in a highly aroused emotional state. It is important to develop the ability to experience your body's feeling sensations and emotions without acting on them, which can include disconnecting from your emotions in some way.

Everyone experiences disconnection, which psychologists often refer to as *dissociation*, at times. Mild forms of dissociation, such as daydreaming, are not generally problematic. More severe forms, such as loss of memory, or feeling like you or the world are unreal, however, can be very disruptive to your ability to function.

Dissociation can occur for brief periods, or it can affect more aspects of your attitudes for longer periods. Your emotions may disconnect from your thoughts and behaviors, or your thoughts can detach from your behaviors.

When you dissociate, you can have difficulty telling the difference between what you are experiencing internally and the reality of what is happening around you. Regardless of the form dissociation takes, however, it involves a detachment from reality.

For example, when people are flooded with rage their emotions may dissociate from their thoughts and behaviors. When this occurs, they may reactively strike out in anger without any awareness of their fury, what they are thinking, or the effect it is having on others. It is only after the anger subsides that they can take in the reality of what they said or did. "I can't believe I said (or did) that!" is a common refrain of those who dissociate when angry.

In addition, many people acknowledge that when they become overly anxious or fearful, their minds, like Sofia's, shut down. When they dissociate, they cannot speak up for themselves. "I can't think of what to say when something is happening; my mind goes blank. I always think of what to say afterwards," is their refrain.

It is clear that when you dissociate from your emotions, it will be hard to process your emotional experience adequately. It also will be difficult, or at times nearly impossible, to use the thinking part of your mind to help regulate your emotions or use them effectively.

Being aware of your emotional responses,
so you can slow down or stop your reactions
while still staying present with your emotions,
is critical to regulating your emotions.

Although you may not be sensitive to emotions and body sensations to the point of frequently dissociating, you still may have difficulty tolerating and staying present with your emotions. This limitation may show up in different forms.

You may not handle stress very well, even normal levels of stress from everyday events. You may find yourself nervous, worried, and fearful in situations that others seem to handle with ease. You may find yourself sad or depressed for long periods and have difficulty motivating yourself. You may become frustrated quickly and strike out in anger at others when something seems to threaten your emotional well-being.

In addition to learning to stay present with and tolerate what people commonly consider negative emotions, it is also important to learn to stay present with positive feelings. Although this may not be difficult for most people, others may find it very difficult to tolerate feelings and sensations that most would experience as positive. For example, consider these situations:

- Someone touches you or gives you a hug, and you draw away or freeze up.
- You start getting closer in a loving relationship, and you run away or do something else to disrupt the relationship.
- Someone compliments you, and you push the compliment away by denying or minimizing what the person has said.
- Someone says or does something kind, and you do not let it register in your mind.
- You start relaxing and then jump up to do something that keeps you busy.
- You notice yourself starting to let loose and have fun with others, and you promptly put yourself down in some way and pull back.

To be able to stay present with your emotions, *it is important to accept your emotions, not reject them.* Discounting your emotions, dissociating from them, or acting as if they do not exist does not magically erase them. Trying to use just your cognitions alone does not change the fact that feelings do exist and that they work in tandem with your thought processes. Your emotions affect you, whether or not you are aware of them, acknowledge them, or stay present with them.

Remember, your feelings are not the enemy.
They do not make you inadequate or a terrible person.
They are just mind-body processes.

In order to accept your emotions, it is important to grieve the losses and wounds that caused your pain and your difficulty regulating your emotion. As you work through your grief, you increase your awareness of your underlying feelings and develop the capacity to stay present with them. These abilities will allow you to get to know yourself as an emotional person and to accept the value emotions add to your life.

And, as you become familiar with the emotional aspects of yourself, you can also learn to manage your emotions. You will not have to deny or avoid your feelings or let your emotions run wild; these ways of coping only reinforce your feelings of vulnerability and your beliefs that emotions are dangerous.

Instead, as you let yourself experience them in doses you can handle, you can learn to care for and regulate your emotions.

Summary: Creating New Emotional Patterns

Learning to regulate your emotions is a developmental process that is critical to your ability to function effectively. Unfortunately, if you grew up with a parent who provided Too Much or Too Little emotionally, you probably did not receive the challenge and support you needed to learn to care for your emotions in healthy ways.

Instead, you may have learned to disregard or discount the emotional part of yourself in the same ways that your parent treated your emotional self. These unhealthy ways of relating to emotions can make it difficult to manage your life as an adult.

Fortunately, your early experience is not the end of your story. Just as your childhood experiences created structural changes in your developing brain, in the same way, the experiences you have in your adult relationships create structural changes in your adult brain.

Therefore, it is important to establish an emotionally safe relationship with someone who is empathetic and skilled in emotional regulation as you work to change your attitudes and develop internal security. *Internal security evolves, in part, as you learn to regulate your emotions in a secure relationship.*

When you are mindful of your emotions and the bodily sensations associated with them, you will be better able to create new and healthier emotional patterns. As you become more aware of your feelings, observing how they function, you will gain insight into how they are affecting you. You can use that information to discern when your emotions are distorting your experience.

As you identify, name, and understand your emotions and the triggers that can activate them, you will be better able to deal with both your feelings and the triggers. Being mindful of your emotions in these ways will help you respond to your emotions more effectively, adapt to present realities, and enjoy your life.

However, developing a secure relationship and being mindful of your emotions are not sufficient in and of themselves to transform your wounds into wisdom.

It is also important to learn to modulate your emotions. This requires that you learn to stay present with what you are experiencing, maintaining an open, curious, nonjudgmental approach to your emotions. It also requires that you monitor and manage your emotions, keeping them within your window of tolerance. When you modulate your emotions, you prevent yourself from becoming emotionally overwhelmed and re-traumatized.

Learning to regulate your emotions is an important part of your journey to transform your wounds into wisdom. As you work to let go of the undermining emotional patterns that are part of your childhood survival system and develop new ways of relating to emotions, you will begin creating attitudes that save your life.

CHAPTER 10

Developing New Ways of Thinking

The world as we have created it is a product of our thinking; it cannot be changed without changing our thinking. —Albert Einstein

Human beings are meaning makers. While you were growing up, your mind (even though it had not fully formed yet) was busy making some kind of meaning out of what you experienced internally and through your senses.

Although your earliest meanings developed from your brain's emotional processes, as the cognitive part of your mind developed, your cognitive perceptions and interpretations also became part of your attitude system.

Because of this, your cognitions affect how you experience and make sense of life, as well as how you relate to yourself and others. In this sense, your thought processes help create the world you live in.

Although the outside world also affects you, your cognitive processes have a major impact on the quality of your life—for better and for worse.

When you think about your thoughts, you may discover that the meanings attached to your experience when you were a child may or may not be helping in your adult life. You may even find that some of what you have come to believe about yourself, others, and life is not accurate.

In fact, some of the ways of thinking you internalized as an understudy to your primary caregiver may be impairing your ability to operate effectively in the present. These difficulties can arise whether your parent provided Too Much, Too Little, or even Just Right.

The ability to create the life you want depends on how you think and the meanings you make out of your experience.

In order to change the attitudes that impinge on your life, it is critical to change the ways you think and believe that interfere with your ability to function in healthy ways. Fortunately, as an adult you are in a better

217

position to make these changes than you were as a child. As an adult, you have a broader and deeper understanding of yourself, people, and life. You also have a greater capacity to integrate the complex elements that affect your thought processes, emotions, and tendencies to act in certain ways.

Because your cognitions have such a profound and far-reaching impact on your life, it is important that you utilize these more mature capacities to develop your understanding of how your cognitions affect you. Therefore, in this chapter, we will consider the impact of outdated attitudes on your perceptions, thought processes, and the meanings you have attached to (and are attaching to) your experience.

We will also investigate the process of updating how you think and what you believe in more depth. In particular, we will discuss how to develop your ability to reflect on and manage your thoughts and beliefs. These enhanced abilities will help you create a new and more coherent narrative (meaning) for your experience, which in turn will help you enhance your life.

As we begin, let me share a bit of Michael's struggle coping with his life. In particular, we will see how the beliefs Michael developed growing up with a father who provided Too Much and a mother who provided Too Little were negatively affecting him.

Michael's Story

Michael was a precocious 12-year-old boy (an only child) who came to therapy because of his parents' concerns about his decreasing functioning at home and school during the previous several months. The progressive deterioration had intensified after an upsetting conflict between Michael and his father in late summer about Michael getting a job.

I had my first glimpse of Michael when he was sitting alone in the waiting room, engrossed in playing a video game on his phone. After introducing myself to Michael, I led him into my office and we settled in.

As we began, I commented, "Your parents met with me last week and asked me to see you because there's lots of stress at home, and they're worried about you having trouble getting motivated. But I'm wondering what *your* take is on what's going on in the family."

Michael looked up at me briefly and then announced in a defeated tone of voice, "I don't know what's wrong." Then, after a brief silence, he continued, "My parents are mad at me all the time, and my dad is constantly telling me that I'm lazy and irresponsible because I don't do my homework or chores anymore. I'd rather be listening to music and playing video games. So I guess it's my fault they're upset."

Michael heaved a deep sigh and then said, "My dad also says that I'm a 'lost cause.' He's probably right because I don't really care about anything anymore, not even my saxophone lessons."

I responded, "It's hard to care about anything right now—especially when almost everything seems really hopeless."

"Yeah," Michael replied, as he shrugged his shoulders. Suddenly there was a flash of anger in his eyes, as he spit out, "But my *dad's* the one who is a lost cause! He's always yelling at me. And no matter what I do, it's not good enough. Like this past summer …

"My dad told me I had to grow up, get a job, and make some money, even though I'm only twelve. So I came up with the idea of making candy and selling it to the neighbors and the kids at school once school started. I figured I could take the money I made, buy more supplies, and sell more candy. I would make a profit eventually.

"I tried to talk my ideas over with my mom, but she just said, 'Whatever your father says.' She's *so* irritating! She never sticks up for me. When I asked my dad, he said that making candy wasn't an okay way to make money because it isn't 'manly' enough.

"So I came up with some more ideas, like walking people's dogs for them. But my dad shot all my ideas down, even though they would have worked out really good. He expects me to make money the way *he* thinks I should— like mowing grass and things like that—even though I'm not a grass-mowing kind of kid."

I commented to Michael, "It's *very* frustrating not to get support from either of your parents for your very creative ideas."

"I'll say!" Michael responded. Then his anger subsided briefly, as he said with a tear in his eye, "But at least my *grandma* thinks that I'm a good kid." He hesitated, and then he said, "But what really sucks is that my dad won't stop pressuring me about getting a job.

"I *tried* to get the neighbors to let me mow their lawns *and* wash their cars, like he told me to do, but, of course, those ideas didn't work. What did he *think* would happen? Everyone in our neighborhood has gardeners and goes to the car wash! I even tried a few of his other dumb ideas, which didn't work either. I finally got fed up and gave up trying to do anything. What's the point? He won't listen to anything I say, anyway." Michael sighed and said again, "I guess they're right. I'm lazy … I'm a lost cause."

"*So* painful when your parents say hurtful things," I murmured. "It makes you think, 'Why bother?' And, it's even more discouraging when you find yourself thinking, 'Maybe they are right.'" We sat quietly for a moment, both of us feeling the pain of his sadness.

So began my work with Michael. It had become clear during our first meeting that Michael had internalized his parents' attitudes toward him. Taking in his domineering, demanding, and critical father's view that he was lazy, irresponsible, and hopeless, Michael had now become self-critical, believing that he—and anything he might do—was doomed to fail. And from his more passive, disempowered, and emotionally unavailable mother, Michael had internalized a sense that he was powerless. He had developed a sense of futility about whatever efforts he might make to get his life back on track.

Although her sympathy was with her son, Michael's mother had not effectively stood up for him or for herself. By acquiescing to her husband's demeaning and authoritarian style of relating, she had failed to provide Michael with a model of caring for oneself with a healthy sense of power.

These internalizations of his parents' ways of feeling, thinking, and treating each other, as well as him, were profoundly affecting Michael's own attitudes. Those attitudes were now undermining his sense of identity (the sense of who he was) and self-worth.

In addition, without emotional support to buffer the barrage of demands and criticism from his father, Michael had become overloaded emotionally. He was now operating outside his emotional window of tolerance and had shut down, to the extent that he was having difficulty functioning at home and school.

Fortunately, through nurturing experiences with his maternal grandmother (and other key people in his life) Michael had developed some ability to be in touch with and reflect upon his thoughts and feelings. Those positive experiences were undoubtedly part of why Michael was able, in fairly short order, to engage with me emotionally so he and I could do the work necessary to develop his new ways of thinking.

Despite his parents' limited involvement in his therapy, Michael and I continued to move forward in our work together. We explored how his upsetting experiences on the home front were negatively affecting his thoughts and feelings about himself and his ability to function.

We also discussed positive ways he might deal with his parents. Gradually, Michael returned to spending more time on his homework and doing his chores more consistently. And although his parents continued to make negative remarks from time to time, Michael was responding to their hostility much better.

One day, about eight months into treatment, Michael entered the room with a big grin and shared the following incident with me.

"Last week when my dad came home from work, he looked into my room from the hall and saw that my room hadn't been cleaned yet and that I was sitting at my desk. Without even asking how I was or what I was doing, he yelled at me, 'There you go again, being lazy!' I could feel my body tense up. I wanted so bad to yell back at him, 'To hell with you!' But I thought to myself, 'I'm not falling into *that* trap! That will just give him an excuse to yell at me even more. *I* know that I'm not being lazy and that he's just being mean.'

"So, instead of getting upset and yelling back at him or clamming up like I used to do, I said, 'I'm sorry my room is not clean yet, Dad. I've been busy working on a big school project that's due tomorrow. I'm planning to clean my room after my homework is done.'" Michael chuckled impishly, "That sure took him off guard! My dad looked around like he didn't know what to say or do. Then he mumbled under his breath, 'You'd better,' and walked away.

"I just shook my head and told myself, 'He's upset, but it's not because of me. I'm doing what I need to be doing.' Then I went back to working on my project. It was awesome!" Michael reached forward saying, "Give me a high five!" And I did, with delight.

Michael paused before continuing, "You know, sometimes when I think about how my dad acts, I get sad. But it feels good to know that I can think things through for myself and don't have to believe that *everything* my parents say is true, just because they say it. And it feels *really* great to know that I don't have to be so afraid of him and can stand up for myself."

"I bet it does!" I responded. Then I said softly, "When you keep clear what is real and true about you *and* what is real and true about others, you don't have to be afraid of what others might think or say."

Because of what Michael was learning in therapy, his beliefs that he was powerless and that something was wrong with him were beginning to change. These changes were making it possible for him to deal with his parents and the other aspects of his life in more adaptive ways.

Just as Michael had become aware of how his ways of thinking (and feeling and behaving) had been affecting him and his life, it is important to consider how your cognitions have been affecting your life.

As you become aware of the thought processes and beliefs that are not serving you well, you can begin to develop healthier ways of thinking that will enhance your life and relationships. Let us explore both of these concepts in more depth.

We will begin by looking at the impact of outdated attitudes on thoughts and beliefs. Then we will examine various ways to update how you think and what you believe.

The Impact of Outdated Attitudes on Your Beliefs

Although the attitudes you developed as a child may be understandable and perhaps were useful in some way, given what was happening at the time, they may be outdated.

When you operate as an adult with attitudes that are part of your childhood survival system, which is still part of your internal repertoire, it can be difficult to process your life experiences cognitively in helpful ways.

Outdated attitudes usually have a negative effect on both the meanings you make of your experience and what you have come to believe about yourself, others, and the world.

The Meaning You Make of Your Experience

Attitudes are constantly evolving. As you grow and develop as an infant and child, several factors affect the meaning you make of your experience. We will consider the impact of three of these factors: your level of cognitive functioning, your family and social environment, and traumatic experiences.

The impact of your level of cognitive functioning. Your level of cognitive and emotional functioning at the time of an experience will affect the meanings you attach to it. For example, imagine that a mother of two boys is involved in a car accident and hospitalized for several weeks. Her eight-month-old infant will experience the absence of his mother very differently than her six-year-old.

The baby (who does not have the ability to put words to experience yet) cannot cognitively "make sense out of" the mother's absence or his emotions. Instead, the infant will retain the memory of his physical experience of his emotions (e.g., anxiety, fear, sadness, or emptiness) associated with his mother's absence on the level of body sensations.

Later, as an adult, he might find himself feeling a deep anxiety or emptiness when others are not present that is out of proportion to the current situation and not understand why he is so distressed.

In contrast, although the six-year-old will also process the experience on an emotional and body level, his more evolved cognitive abilities will enable him to process the experience differently than his baby brother.

He will be able to understand that his mother has not disappeared forever but is in a place (the hospital) and will come home, which can help him feel less anxious. If he has received adequate support in learning to care for his feelings, he will be able to identify and articulate his sadness about missing his mother and his concerns about her well-being.

He also will be able to reach out for comfort. He will be able to use both his thoughts and the comforting, reassuring words and presence of others to manage any fear or anxiety he may have.

Since children from two years old to about seven years old are generally egocentric, they tend to think they are the cause of things that occur. So the six-year-old may believe that he caused the car accident because he had been angry at, and wanted to punish, his mother that morning.

If she were to die, he might believe her death was his fault because he could not comprehend that her severe injuries caused her death, not his anger. Later, as an adult, he might notice himself feeling a vague sense of guilt when he thinks of his mother's death, even though by that time he knows intellectually that her death was not his fault.

Young children also think in primarily concrete, dualistic ways. So if you grew up with a parent who provided Too Much, as an adult you might tend to think that people are either dominant or submissive, intrusive or intruded upon. You may believe that people are bad if they exercise control in any way and good if they "cooperate" with others, letting others have dominance over them.

If you grew up with a parent who provided Too Little, as an adult you might think that you only have two options in getting your emotional needs met. You can either not care about getting close to others or try to connect with others and be hurt because they will not be there for you.

Unfortunately, many adults still struggle with these outdated egocentric and dualistic ways of thinking because some of their cognitive abilities have failed to develop sufficiently. This difficulty is particularly evident in situations that evoke memories of their parent-child experiences.

For example, when you are thinking egocentrically as an adult, you might believe that if someone fails to show you attention, it is because something is wrong with you. Or you may be flooded with guilt if others are angry because you believe your actions *caused* their angry feelings.

You might also find yourself thinking that you must have done something wrong *because* they are directing their anger at you or blaming you for their distress.

If you developed the dualistic belief as a child that you are only loveable if everyone likes you at all times, you may still operate with that belief as an adult Or you find yourself believing that others are bad if they do not want to spend time with you and good if they are friendly.

In all of these scenarios, the meanings generated from these early stages of cognitive development are illusions or distortions, and they interfere with your life and relationships. Fortunately, your cognitive capabilities can continue to mature throughout your lifespan.

The impact of your family and social environment. The specific family culture and the broader social environment you grow up in influence the meanings you make of your experience. They also affect how you process information, as well as how your value and belief systems evolve, because cognitive processes develop as you interact with others.

> ***As you grow, you tend to internalize the ways those around you think and believe; these thoughts and beliefs become part of your internal reality—whether or not they are real and true.***

The impact of the family environment. It is clear that your family environment plays a major role in the development of your cognitive processes. Although the focus so far has been on the effect of your primary caregiver, the entire family system influences how your thought processes and beliefs develop.

Imagine you are growing up with a mother whose has an enmeshed parenting style. Because of her internalized scripts, your mother tells you, overtly or covertly, that it is your "job" to take care of her and make her happy. She gives you the clear message, directly or indirectly, that you are selfish (i.e., "bad") if you do not do your job. Since children usually internalize their experience of the parent's cognitive meanings, in this scenario you may develop the belief that it *is* your job to provide whatever your mother wants.

In contrast, imagine that while your mother is operating with attitudes based in enmeshment, your father (or another significant family member) is relating to you with healthier attitudes. Instead of being critical and demanding, your father reassures and validates you—whether or not you are meeting his expectations. He helps you understand the difference between "helping" and "being responsible for" others. He supports you in being kind and thoughtful but also guides you in developing the ability to set effective boundaries with others.

In this scenario, your father's different ways of thinking and relating serve to challenge your mother's attitude system and provide you with more helpful alternative relationship experiences to internalize. As a result, you may not take in your mother's attitudes to the same degree that you otherwise might.

In addition, these interactions with your father make it possible for you to become aware of the reality that you are worthwhile and loveable as a person, in your own right. You also can learn that it is acceptable to have your own thoughts and beliefs. And you can begin to understand that although your actions may *affect* others, you are not *responsible* for how others feel.

More importantly, you can begin to accept the reality that, even though your parents' attitudes have affected how your attitudes developed, in the end, you are accountable for your attitudes and can change them.

The impact of the socio-cultural environment. In addition to the family environment, the socio-cultural environment you grow up in shapes your beliefs and thought processes, both indirectly and directly.

Indirectly, because the socio-cultural environment has influenced your family members' ways of thinking and beliefs, it in turn affects what you experience and record internally. More directly, your own encounters with the diverse ways of thinking others outside your family (e.g., neighbors, schoolmates, spiritual leaders, or the media) have affects how you think and what you believe.

For example, as you are growing up you will begin to see that in one family or socio-cultural context

- honesty and integrity are considered virtues—in another, they may not be valued at all, or they may be actively devalued;
- "doing your best" means you must be perfect—in another, it means doing the best you can at any given point in time while striving for quality;
- being responsible for yourself means you are mature—in another, finding a way for others to be responsible for you is considered clever and your just due;
- making a mistake is considered a learning opportunity—in another, mistakes are despised and mean you are a failure;
- if you make a decision that does not work out well, it means you must try to solve your problems a different way—in another, it means you are inadequate or that others are the cause of your ongoing problems.
- sharing your feelings and thoughts with others is a welcomed delight—in another, opening up to others is considered a sign of weakness and is to be avoided at all costs.

It is important to become aware of and reflect on how your relationships within both your family system and the socio-cultural environment you grew up in had, and continue to have, an impact on your thoughts and beliefs.

Only then can you determine which beliefs and values you have experienced have enhanced your attitudes and which ones have negatively influenced you. With this increased clarity, you can begin changing your cognitions that do not serve you in healthy ways.

The impact of traumatic experiences. Traumatic experiences negatively affect how you think and what you believe. These cognitive changes can occur when a singular "major" occurrence (e.g., a natural disaster, an accident, severe abuse, or the death of a close family member) overwhelms you emotionally. They also can also occur with "minor" distressing incidents (e.g., shaming, being criticized, being left alone for long periods, or being over-controlled).

Even though the apparently inconsequential experiences of minor painful experiences may *seem* less significant, their effects tend to accumulate over time. This cumulative effect can lead to your internal operating system becoming overloaded, causing a deleterious effect on your emotional and cognitive functioning as great as that of a major trauma. Trauma experts refer to these repetitive psychological minor injuries that occur over time as *cumulative strain trauma.*

Although you may or many not experience any major traumas as a child, if you grow up with a parent who provides Too Much or Too Little, you are likely to experience cumulative strain trauma. Because emotional enmeshment, over-control, unavailability, and inconsistency can leave you flooded with painful emotions, these parenting styles tend to distort your thoughts and beliefs about yourself, others, and the world.

The beliefs that develop from both types of trauma (often referred to respectively as big "T" Trauma and little "t" trauma) commonly become part of core attitudes grounded in excessive vulnerability, insecurity, and a lack of a sense of self-efficacy.

If you are not adequately able to process the thoughts, feelings, and behaviors that occur at the time of a trauma, these attitudes interfere with your perceptions of your experience and thus your ability to function effectively. These impairments put you at greater risk for future difficulties.

For example, when your mind computes an experience in your present life as similar to a childhood trauma, it triggers the attitudes associated with the earlier overwhelming experience. When this occurs, you are likely to re-experience different aspects of the *past* traumatic experience in the *present.* So if you felt helpless during a childhood traumatic incident and experienced a freeze response, you are likely to feel helpless in the present and not take action to help yourself.

At the risk of being repetitious, let us take a more in-depth look at some common ways family, socio-cultural, and traumatic experience affect the cognitive component of attitudes.

What You Have Come to Believe

Attitudes you have developed about yourself. Recall that your core thoughts and beliefs about yourself develop in childhood as you interact with your primary caregiver.

Unfortunately, a parent who provides Too Much or Too Little usually has negative or distorted attitudes about herself and you, which you are likely to internalize. When this occurs, you can develop a variety of problematic beliefs about yourself based on an impaired sense of your identity, self-worth, competence, and self-reliance.

Consider these examples of common core beliefs that can develop early in life, along with the emotions that are frequently associated with them.

- **Core belief: "I don't know who I really am."**
  (Lack of a Sense of Identity)
  Thoughts/beliefs: "I don't know what I think or feel. I don't know what I like, or dislike."
  Common associated feelings: "I feel confused, uncertain, lost, or fragmented."

- **Core belief: "I am worthless or bad."**
  (*Lack of a Sense of Value*)
  Thoughts/beliefs: "I am unlovable, despicable, worthless, totally damaged, or unimportant. I might as well not exist."
  Common associated feelings: "I feel guilt, shame, despair, or self-hate."

- **Core belief: "I am helpless and powerless."**
  (*Lack of a Sense of Self-Efficacy*)
  Thoughts/beliefs: "I am weak and cannot care for myself. I need someone else to tell me what to think, feel, and do."
  Common associated feelings: "I feel fearful, anxious, or inadequate."

- **Core belief: "I am undependable."**
  (*Lack of a Sense of Self-Reliance*)
  Thoughts/beliefs: "I cannot count on myself to know what is true or real. I don't know what I am responsible for and what others are responsible for. I can't count on myself to take care of things."
  Common associated feelings: "I feel uncertain, fearful, or anxious."

Attitudes you have developed about others and the world. When you grow up with a parent who provides Too Much or Too Little, you also may develop distorted ways of thinking and believing involving others and the world. The distorted conclusions (meanings) about others and life can be overly negative, fearful, and hostile.

You can also develop illusions that assign truth or reality to things that are not true and prevent you from seeing truth for what it is.

Consider these common distortions and illusions.

- **Core belief: "Others and the world are dangerous."**
  (*Lack of a Sense of Internal Safety*)
  Thoughts/beliefs: "People are against me, or they will hurt me in some way. Others will try to take advantage of or use me for their ends."
  Associated feelings: "I feel vulnerable, at risk, fearful, anxious, in danger, and defensive."

- **Core belief: "Others and the world are not trustworthy."**
  (*Lack of a Sense of External Reliability*)
  Thoughts/beliefs: "I cannot count on other people to be there for me. If anything can go wrong, it will happen to me."
  Associated feelings: "I feel insecure, uncertain, suspicious, or distrustful."

- **Core belief: *"Others and the world are bad."***
  (*Lack of a Sense of Goodness*)
  Thoughts/beliefs: "Other people are the cause of my problems. The world is a bad place."
  Associated feelings: "I feel angry, resentful, fearful, or unsafe."

As you can see, your beliefs and thoughts about yourself, others, and the world (and the other attitude components associated with them) clearly affect how you experience your life. When your mind uses protective maneuvers such as over-generalization, all-or-nothing thinking, denial, and minimization, your thoughts and beliefs may *seem* accurate and reliable. However, they are not.

Upon further consideration, you will discover that these dualistic ways of thinking are full of illusions or distortions. Because of that, the meanings you create from illusions and distorted ways of thinking about your experience usually cause you great distress or difficulty functioning in your relationships and your life as a whole.

But there is hope!

You *can* clear up these distortions and illusions. You can develop new ways of thinking, feeling, and acting that are more reality-based and helpful. Let us look at some ways to update how you think and what you believe.

Updating How You Think and What You Believe

In order to save yourself from re-enacting unhealthy, internalized parent-child experiences (and other past traumatic experiences), it is critical to update how you think and what you believe.

If you live your life based on meanings you attached to your experience during childhood, adolescence, or earlier adulthood, it is important to consider that those meanings could be outdated.

Two key thinking processes and capacities that are important to develop in order to update the cognitive component of your attitudes are developing your ability to reflect and managing your thoughts and beliefs. These abilities are critical to enhancing your life and relationships.

Developing Your Ability to Reflect

Have you ever said to yourself, "What in the world was I thinking? I should never have said or done that!" It is common to experience your feelings, think automatic thoughts, and act reflexively without reflecting on these attitude components. In order to change your attitudes and save your life it is important to develop the ability to reflect on your attitudes.

Reflection involves noticing and paying attention to what and how you are thinking. It also involves observing and thinking about—considering—how your and others' thought and belief patterns work.

Peter Fonagy and Mary Target, clinical psychologists, researchers, and faculty members at Yale University, write extensively about the importance of reflecting on emotional and cognitive processes. Reflecting on your emotions and thoughts is crucial, they say, to finding your experience meaningful. It may also significantly influence how you regulate your emotions, control your impulses, monitor yourself, and act on your own behalf (Fonagy and Target, 1997, pp. 679-680).

Before we examine different aspects of self-reflection more closely, let us first consider the following discussion Michael and I had during one of our sessions about a year into therapy. At this point, we had been working together for some time on developing his ability to be mindful of and reflect upon his emotions, thoughts, and actions.

Michael walked comfortably into my office, sat down on the couch, and pronounced matter-of-factly, "I was lazy yesterday. I didn't do all of my homework." Despite his apparent nonchalance, Michael gave me a sly look that was a bit provocative. It seemed to me that he wanted to see how I would respond to his calling himself "lazy." (Since Michael's parents had labeled him with this word, it had come up frequently during our discussions.)

"There's the 'L' word again," I teasingly noted.

Michael responded with a grin and said, "Well—I really wasn't being lazy. I *did* want to get my homework done and was trying really hard, but I was frustrated because I couldn't figure out the math problems. It didn't help that those old 'I'm so stupid'—'I'll never figure this out'—'There's no point in trying' thoughts kept coming into my mind the whole time I was trying to study. I felt like throwing the book on the floor and going outside and riding my bike, but I knew I'd get in trouble if I did that because my homework wasn't done yet."

I commented, "It's hard enough to run into roadblocks when you're trying to figure something out, but to have put-down thoughts popping into your mind and pestering you makes it even worse. The thought of escaping probably sounded like a *great* idea."

"No kidding! I finally left the dining room table, even though my homework wasn't really done, and went to my room and played video games," Michael replied. Then he fell silent, his mood dropping.

Quietly I noted, "Your mood just changed. What are you feeling and thinking right now?"

Michael's brow puckered into furrowed concentration as he responded, "You know, most of the time I do okay at math. But I think the real problem was that I was worried about Duke (Michael's dog). He was so sick that my mom had to take him to the vet. I was upset because I wanted to go with them, but she wouldn't let me. She told me I had to do my homework instead." Michael looked up at me and, with angst in his voice, asked, "But, what if something bad had been wrong with Duke? He would have wanted me with him."

I responded to Michael's distress, "It was scary to think that Duke might have had something seriously wrong with him and that you wouldn't be able to be there with him." I paused for a moment and then shared how I was experiencing his situation. "I feel sad that you were all alone with your worried thoughts and scared feelings and that you couldn't be with your mom and Duke."

Michael sat quietly for a while before saying, "Me, too." Then he commented, "You know, I'm really not dumb or lazy. I was just having trouble concentrating because I was feeling sad and worrying about Duke."

"I think you're onto something there," I replied. "It's really hard to concentrate when you're imagining scary things. But I'm glad that you are coming to realize that those old critical thoughts about yourself aren't necessarily the truth. They just popped into your mind yesterday because you were really frustrated, worried, and maybe a little mad."

Paying attention to your thoughts and beliefs. Just as Michael was developing his ability to reflect on his experience, it is important that you develop your ability to reflect on your experience. However, in order to do this you must learn to pay attention to your thoughts and beliefs and the attitude and relationship patterns associated with them.

Paying attention to your cognitive processes enables you to become aware of your strengths as well as the areas creating difficulty for you. It is necessary to be aware of your cognitions if you are to take the steps needed to update how you think and what you believe so you can move forward.

One aspect of paying attention to your cognitive processes is noticing the thoughts that pass through your mind. In essence, this ability to focus on your thoughts and beliefs is *thinking about thinking.*

It is also important to develop the ability to notice and think about what you are thinking *while you are thinking* the thoughts. Developing these cognitive abilities takes time and practice because new neural pathways must develop in your brain.

In addition, just as it is important to notice your body signals and emotions without reacting to or judging them, it is important to be attentive to your thought processes without judging them. As you notice how you think and what you believe without reacting to, judging, or even believing your thoughts, your capacity to reflect will increase.

When you attend to your thoughts and beliefs without prematurely stopping your thought processes, giving yourself time to assess them, you will be in a better position to manage them more effectively. You will gain useful information from this awareness, just as Michael did when he realized how his worry and self-critical thoughts were making it difficult for him to get his homework done. This awareness puts you in the position to make informed decisions about your attitudes and plans.

Observing recurrent thought and belief patterns. When you experience something, whether the experience originates from an external or internal source, it activates your internal operating system, including the cognitive component of your attitudes.

It is important to consider this activation process—the what, when, and how you think. As you observe your thought processes, you will begin to notice patterns in the ways you think and what you believe. You will also become more aware of how your beliefs and thoughts affect your perceptions and vice versa.

In addition, you will be better able to understand how your cognitive processes and patterns affect your emotional and behavioral responses. As you do, you will become more aware of how the three components of your attitudes affect each other.

Over the course of the next several years following his initial work with me, Michael would periodically come in to see me for short-term work when he needed help sorting out a situational problem. One day, Michael (now 29-years-old) called me to set up an appointment.

> "It's time for another 'booster shot,'" Michael jokingly said over the phone. I could picture him grinning when he used the term that meant he needed some extra help. Then he became serious as he said, "I've been handling things pretty good for the most part. But lately I've been falling back into old habits. I've been having trouble sleeping and I don't feel like doing anything, not even hanging out with friends. And I've been having trouble getting things done at work. I've even called in sick several times. I know the problem has to do with my boss, but I'm struggling here and need some help getting back on track."

Even though Michael was doing his best to keep himself stable, the call made it clear he was overwhelmed. But it was also clear that his ability to observe his thoughts and emotions, as well as his behavioral responses (which he had developed during our earlier work), was still intact. Later, at his appointment, Michael described the following painful experience, which he believed had started his downward spiral.

> "My boss is nuts. He walked up to me six weeks ago and started yelling at me in front of everyone. He told me that I wasn't taking care of the customers' accounts properly. I was confused. I tried to explain to him that I was managing the accounts according to the policies that the trainers had given to me, and that the clients had expressed satisfaction about how I was handling their accounts.

> "But my boss didn't want to hear any of it. He just kept at me, telling me that he didn't care what the trainers had said or what the policies were. I was

supposed to do things the way he wanted them done. The only trouble is, he had never told me to do anything different!

"I asked him how he wanted the accounts handled. I couldn't believe it—he just got madder. He told me—you won't believe this—but he said that I was just being lazy or I would have figured that out by now. Whoa! That did it. I backed off and shut down." Michael sat back in the chair with frustration.

"Unbelievable is right!" I spontaneously concurred. "I'm *so* sorry that you have to deal with someone who's being that irrational and aggressive, Michael. It was definitely *not* okay for him to say those things … *especially* our old familiar 'L' word."

Michael looked startled for a moment, then let out a deep breath and said, "I figured you'd catch that." Then he gave me a wry grin as he continued, "My boss is a lot like my dad. For a while, I did pretty good handling his bad attitudes, but this last episode put me over the top.

"I've been realizing that I'm feeling afraid of my boss and resenting him. I've also been noticing that all sorts of angry thoughts about my boss keep coming into my mind, just like they used to do when my dad was being unreasonable and demeaning.

"What's really bad, though, is that even though I know better, I've caught myself worrying about not being good enough and putting myself down—just like I used to do when I was a kid. It's frustrating because I can't seem to get myself back. This situation has really thrown me for a loop, and my confidence has taken a big hit."

I responded quietly, "Hit, but not knocked down or out."

Fortunately, because of the work Michael had done in his previous therapy, Michael had been able to realize that his job situation had reactivated his old childhood attitudes and that he was re-enacting his self-sabotaging parent-child scripts with his boss. And, although he had been *feeling* helpless and hopeless in this situation with his boss, Michael knew he was not stuck, nor did he have to handle the situation alone. This awareness helped him reach out for help so he could find someone who could help him process his current experience and who would support him in staying reality-based in the present.

As Michael and I continued our work together, we initially focused on Michael's regulating himself in his emotional window of tolerance. Part of the self-regulation involved feeling his distress about his boss's behaviors without allowing himself to become overly distressed.

Over time, as Michael began to restabilize emotionally, he was better able to reflect on his experience with his boss. We worked together to reinforce his ability to pay attention to, observe, and think about his thoughts without reacting to them or becoming overwhelmed.

One exercise Michael found helpful in this regard was observing his thoughts as if he were watching the words scrolling across the screen on an electronic reader board. He would practice thinking ("reading") his thoughts without reacting to or absorbing them.

Because of his past and present work in therapy, Michael also had developed his capacity to be resilient. His increased ability to recover from and adjust to his experiences helped him restabilize in a shorter amount of time.

As he worked to calm his physical responses to the stress he was feeling and to regulate his emotions, Michael's fears of his boss and of failure began to dissipate. He was able to bring his thoughts and beliefs about himself back in line with the truth—that he was a competent, creative, and reliable man who sometimes, but only sometimes, made mistakes. In addition, Michael's feelings of being out of control and helpless lifted, and he was able to resume functioning effectively at work.

At times you, like Michael, will probably find yourself filtering your experience according to unhelpful attitudes and relationship patterns developed early in life. As you pay attention to and observe your cognitive processes, however, a few common undermining thought patterns may become apparent.

You may realize you are second-guessing yourself, obsessing, judging and criticizing yourself or others, catastrophizing, believing what others say without evaluation, or predicting that the worst will happen. As you observe the ways you think, you will begin to see which thought and belief patterns are most common for you.

Although it can be easier to recognize these patterns *after* a situation has occurred, it is extremely helpful to learn to identify the patterns *as they are occurring*. When you are aware of your experience *in the moment*, you are in a better position to make conscious decisions about how you will manage your thoughts and how you will respond to the situation. You will able to exercise self-control rather than reacting in out of control ways that escalate the problem situation or your distress.

In addition, as you observe your thought and belief patterns, you will also become more aware of how familiar types of situations can trigger your core beliefs.

For example, imagine that a family in the process of moving out of your neighborhood asks you for help. If the people have been kind and helpful to you, and you have a core belief that you should be (or are) a kind and considerate person, you probably will help them move. If they have mistreated you and been obnoxious, however, their request might activate a different belief.

Although you believe you should be helpful, you might also believe it is important not to put yourself in a position where you are likely to be mistreated. The belief motivated by self-protection (and its associated emotions), in all likelihood, will override your belief about the value of being helpful. You might choose not to help the neighbors because your earlier experience with them had been hurtful.

As you observe your thought and belief patterns, you will begin to notice that the meanings you assign to your experience are not only due to your past. They are also highly dependent on the context of your experience.

Being alert to how different contexts affect your thoughts and beliefs can help you evaluate your experience and develop more cognitive flexibility. Having an aware and observant mindset can alert you to the multiple dimensions of the meanings you can put on your experience.

As you continue to develop your ability to be aware of and observe the ways you think and what you believe, you will develop a more flexible mindset. This mindset enhances your ability to choose what you will do with your cognitive patterns.

Over time, you will begin to develop a more flexible understanding of yourself as you see that different situations, perceptions, motivations, and the meanings you put on things affect how you experience your life.

Reflecting on what and how you think is helpful to you in many other ways. As you attend to your cognitive processes, you increase your capacity for self-observation. When you reflect on your thought processes, you also become more aware of your intentions and motivations.

For example, in Michael's situation, he was able to discern that his motivation for failing to do his math homework was not laziness as his parents had declared. Rather, it was an unconscious effort to decrease his internal distress by getting rid of one factor that was stimulating his frustration.

Paying attention to your thought processes also can expand your intuitive capabilities that help you perceive and understand things without conscious thought. In addition, as you think about what you are thinking, you will be better able to engage actively in the process of taking ownership of your life.

Managing Your Thoughts and Beliefs

Just as developing your ability to reflect is important to attitude change, so is developing your ability to manage your thoughts and beliefs. Let us examine some key aspects of managing your cognitions.

Evaluating how you interpret your experience. Because what you think and how you feel represent reality to you, it is important to evaluate how you are interpreting your experience. Although they may be connected, what you experience internally may be very different from what is real from an external point of view.

Just because you think or feel something internally,
does not mean it is real externally.

Many thoughts enter your mind every day. Some of your thoughts develop from perceptions that are reality-based, and these can be quite helpful. Other thoughts and beliefs emerge from your imagination, mental associations, re-enactments, or internalized beliefs.

These ways of thinking may or may not be congruent with external reality, even though they may *feel* very real because your internal attitude system can distort what is occurring externally.

Because of these potential discrepancies, it is important to be aware of your thought processes and to develop the ability to think about and question your observations, perceptions, and conclusions. *It is essential to try to stay as reality-based as possible.*

Staying reality-based involves not only distinguishing your internal and external experience but also evaluating others' attitudes toward you. It is crucial to remember that just as your attitudes influence your experience, so too other people's attitudes affect how they process their experience. Therefore, what others feel, think, and believe about you and what they say to you may or may not be true in external reality.

Because others' attitudes can distort their experience in the same way that your attitudes can misconstrue your experience, it is critical to take the time to consider what is real and true in any given situation. It is important to remember that you are not the *cause* of others' experience, just as others are not the cause of your experience.

For example, imagine a neighbor saying something to you, which you experience as a criticism. In this situation, you will tend to react automatically based on how you have processed your previous experiences with criticism. To help you evaluate how you are interpreting your experience, you might want to consider the following questions.

- What is *really* going on here?
- Could the attitudes I developed early in life be distorting my experience (internal reality)?
- Is what the person saying or doing *truly* a statement about me— my person, issues, or problems or does it just appear to be?

- What is real and true about me? What is real and true about the other person?
- What does the comment reveal about the neighbor's attitudes (e.g., defenses, emotional difficulties, past traumas, expectations, thought processes)?
- Is it possible that the person is projecting his or her own feelings and thoughts onto me?
- Am I projecting my thoughts or motives onto the other person?

Just like Michael, at times you will undoubtedly think, believe, and even feel things about yourself (and others) that are simply not true. *Instead of believing and reacting to every thought or feeling that passes through your mind and body as if they were true and reliable, it is important to evaluate them thoughtfully and carefully.* Then you will be in a better position to manage your thoughts effectively.

Distinguishing the present from the past. One of the crucial aspects of managing your thoughts and beliefs is to distinguish, actively and intentionally, your present experience from your past experience.

Remember, the mind is ever busy making connections between the bits of information your senses take in, helping you understand and organize your experience. Although this is a very useful function, it is easy for the mind to associate your present and past experiences in ways that may not truly fit what is real and true in the present.

When this happens, the mind's connections may distort how you experience the present. These distortions can cause you to attach erroneous meanings to the present. In turn, the resulting distorted thoughts and beliefs can lead you to act and react based on attitude patterns that developed around these old systems.

To help differentiate the present from the past, you can ask yourself some questions:

- Is what I am experiencing truly based on what is occurring now, or are my old attitudes distorting the present moment?
- Are current my thoughts, feelings, and behavioral reactions similar to those I had as a child in response to my parent(s)?
- Am I experiencing the other person as emotionally enmeshed, domineering, unavailable, or inconsistent like my parent was?
- Are my thoughts, feelings, or actions in the present similar to those of my parent in the past?
- Are there other ways to make sense of this situation other than my automatic thoughts?

- Am I really at risk, *right now*, or do my feelings of vulnerability belong to previous experiences?
- If there are real risks (e.g., emotional, physical, or financial) in this situation, what are they?

In order to distinguish the present from the past, it is important to consider questions such as these since your internal operating system affects how you experience the present. The cognitive patterns you developed from earlier experience may be distorting how you are experiencing the present.

As you learn to reflect on your thoughts, evaluate how you interpret your experience, and distinguish the present from the past, you will be able to create a life that is both healthy and rewarding.

It is also important to develop your ability to think about your thoughts *without responding to them in fear*. Remember that regardless of how uncomfortable your thoughts may be, *they are only thoughts*.

What and how you think provides you with useful information if you stop to consider your thoughts and beliefs. Although your thoughts may have been overwhelming or harmful to you in the past, you can develop the ability to relate to and handle them differently.

As you train yourself to notice your cognitive processes and observe how they operate, you can evaluate how you are experiencing them and distinguish your present experience from your childhood experience. You can adjust them so that they are more accurate and more helpful. Remember, the quality of your relationships and other aspects of your life relies on these healthy, mature abilities.

Framing your experience in new ways. Because your attitudes have a major impact on how you make sense of your experience, it is critical to pay attention to how you frame (make sense of) your experience. The following common thoughts and beliefs reveal unhealthy core beliefs that often develop as a child interacts with a parent who is emotionally enmeshed, domineering, unavailable, or inconsistent.

- I am only acceptable and worthwhile if I am perfect.
- Others will probably abandon me.
- Others are not trustworthy; they usually have bad motives.
- Close relationships are not enjoyable.
- Others are always saying things against me.
- I cannot handle being on my own nor take care of myself.

- I am afraid others will criticize, judge, or ridicule me.
- I am only important and valuable if I am the center of attention.
- Others' rules or boundaries do not apply to me.
- I am more important than others are and am entitled to get whatever I want.

These and similar core beliefs and the thoughts associated with them usually have a significant negative impact on how you frame your experience. They also interfere with healthy functioning in your relationships. When you believe things that are not true or real, you consciously or unconsciously sabotage yourself and your relationships.

It is important to replace any outdated, distorted, or illusionary meanings you may have about others, the world, and yourself with beliefs and meanings based on what is real and true in the present.

To do this, you must take time to examine how you are making sense out of a situation.

Consider the following possible replacements for unhelpful beliefs you may have developed as a young understudy to your parent.

- **Possible Meanings about You.**
  Old Beliefs: "I'm not loveable. I have no worth or value."
  New Beliefs: "I'm valuable and worthwhile regardless of others' actions or beliefs. I am loveable and worthwhile because of who I am."

  Old Beliefs: "I'm helpless. I am powerless."
  New Beliefs: "I do not have the power to *make* others act like I want them to act (turn zebras into giraffes), but I *can* take action to take care of my needs."

  Old Beliefs: "I can't trust myself. I'm not able to handle life."
  New Beliefs: "I can think through situations and evaluate them. I can and will handle my life, even if I feel I can't at times."

- **Possible Meanings about Others and the World.**
  Old Beliefs: "No one is trustworthy. I can only trust myself."
  New Beliefs: "Others and I behave in fairly consistent ways—even if what is consistent is their inconsistency. I can trust that they will usually act according to who they are. I can consider the question: What does this person say or do (positive and negative) that can I count on?"

Old Beliefs: "It's not safe to be vulnerable. People are not safe."
New Beliefs: "I will never be totally safe with others or in the world, but I can take action to protect myself in healthy ways. I can learn to identify safe people and choose to develop relationships with them at a pace I can handle. I can consider the questions: In what ways is this person safe? In what ways is this person unsafe?"

Old Beliefs: "Others are bad if they do not do what I want."
New Beliefs: "Others may not act like I want them to, but that does not mean they are bad or I am bad. I am accountable for what I think, feel, and do. I can learn to handle my frustration and disappointment without making others 'bad' in my mind."

Notice the meanings you are attaching to your experience. This awareness will be helpful to your relationships and to your ability to solve problems and make decisions.

As you think about your thoughts, you will be in a better position to determine how true your thoughts, beliefs, and feelings are. You will then be able to formulate beliefs and meanings that serve you well.

During this four-month period of working with me, Michael was delighted that he was beginning to manage his thoughts better. One day he told me of an episode during the previous week in which his boss had been yelling at him once again.

"When my boss came up to me at work this week, it was easy to see that he was upset and was going to yell at me again. Sure enough, he started berating me and blaming me for things that weren't even my responsibility." Michael paused for a moment, and then reflected, "In the past, I would have taken what he said personally and felt embarrassed in front of my co-workers."

"Not only that, but ordinarily I also would have felt guilty because my old belief that I'm responsible for how others feel and act would kick in. But you know what else hit me this week?

"I realized that deep down I also believed that I couldn't tolerate people being angry with me or wrong about me. So I would argue with them and try to convince them that the problem wasn't my fault, just like I used to do with my dad. If that didn't work, I'd shut down inside.

"That happened a *lot* when I was a kid. Sometimes I think that was the only way I knew how to be safe with my parents. When my boss started attacking me this week, I caught myself starting to go down all the old paths again, but I stopped myself."

I noted, "This time you were able to observe what was happening and were able to recognize how your old attitudes and relationship patterns that you had developed with your dad were being reactivated."

"Yes, and it was *great!*" Michael responded. "This time I was able to do something different! While my boss was yelling at me, I made sure I focused on relaxing my body and being calm. I also reminded myself, I can handle his bad behavior. Just because he is out of control doesn't mean I have to be. Just because he's angry and attacking me does not mean I'm a bad person or a bad worker.

"I am a good person and a good worker, even though I'm not perfect. *His* mad attacks are not my fault. They have to do with how *he* is making sense out of whatever happened. His reactions are not about who *I* am or about *my* worth, even though he may be aiming his frustration and anger at me. I can try to listen to him and see if we can figure out what is really going on here. Maybe I'll come up with something helpful to solve his problem; maybe I won't. Either way, I'm okay. And, for sure, I don't have to be afraid of him!'"

Michael let out a big sigh of relief and then said, "Boy, did *that* ever feel good!"

Just like Michael, you can learn to reflect on and manage how you think and what you believe. You can develop the ability to be mindfully present, becoming aware of and attending to what you are feeling and thinking in the moment, while at the same time observing how your recurrent thought and belief patterns are operating.

As you develop the ability to step back from and reflect upon your feelings and thoughts, *without reacting to them or letting them take you over*, you will become more present and grounded in the reality of the moment. This will allow you to assess how you are interpreting the present and to separate it from the past. Then you can begin to frame your current experience in new ways that will be more congruent with what *is* real and true in the here and now.

Summary: Thinking about Thinking

In order to change your attitudes and save your life from re-enacting the outdated scripts that you have played out throughout your life, it is necessary to think about what you are thinking.

As you focus and reflect on your thoughts, you will become more aware of the aspects of your parent that you internalized and the emotional and relational scripts you developed in childhood as an understudy to your parent.

You will also begin to recognize the beliefs that have developed in the aftermath of experiences, both as a child and as an adult, that overwhelmed your emotional window of tolerance, perhaps even to the point of traumatizing you.

Reflection is the skill that lifts the curtain on the stage of self-awareness and self-knowing. It makes it possible for you to be aware of, empathize with, and understand others and the scripts they are re-enacting.

Paying attention to the thoughts that pass through your mind and the beliefs they reveal, however, is only one part of the process of developing new ways of thinking. Observing the recurrent thought and belief patterns that form the themes of the scripts of your life and becoming mindful of when and how they operate is also necessary to change your attitudes. As you observe and think about your thoughts, you will gather the information you need to change the cognitions that interfere with living your life fully.

Managing how you think and what you believe is another crucial aspect of changing your life scripts. As you evaluate how you are interpreting your experiences and the meanings you are attaching to them, you become aware of the cost of your outdated scripts.

You also begin to realize that you now have choices about your beliefs and values. You can continue tightly holding on to the problematic scripts inscribed in your mind-body system in the past, re-enacting them in the present. Or you can update your cognitive patterns with new scripts that enable you to function more effectively in the here and now.

As you learn to distinguish the present from the past and challenge the distorted, illusionary, dualistic, and egocentric ways of thinking formed by the limited cognitive abilities of a child, you develop more mature, adaptive cognitive capacities.

It is these more fully developed abilities that enable you to frame your experience in healthier ways that transform your life.

CHAPTER 11

Taking Charge of Your Actions

Behavior is a mirror in which every one displays his own image.
—Johann Wolfgang von Goethe

What you say and do reflects what lies deep in your mind and brain—your emotions and thought processes. Because of this, being able to take charge of your actions depends on changing your internal scripts that interfere with your ability to live a healthy and fulfilling life. The scripts that derive from early experience with a primary caregiver, however, are very powerful and tend to pull you back into the behavioral patterns you used to cope with that experience.

As a result, you may find yourself re-enacting behavioral patterns (e.g., compliant, defiant, controlling, competitive, ambivalent, or confused) that are not grounded in a core sense of internal security and self. You may also notice that behavioral elements of your parent's attitudes have become part of your action tendencies.

It is common for people to focus on behavior change as a way to make their lives and relationships better. However, attitudes are comprised of complex, interrelating components.

If you focus *only* on changing your behavior, you are likely to find yourself falling back on the familiar attitude scripts comprised of aspects of your parent's attitudes and your early parent-child relationship patterns. Simply "trying to act different" will not achieve long-term changes in your attitudes.

Changing your behavior depends on how you deal with the intricate interplay between the emotional, cognitive, and behavioral components of your attitudes.

It is important to pay attention to your emotional and cognitive processes (including your body sensations) while you are working on changing your behaviors. As you strengthen your ability to regulate your emotions and develop new, reality-based ways of thinking, your efforts to change your behaviors will be much more successful.

Your behaviors will reveal the internal changes you are making because you will be acting in accord with the new emotional and cognitive systems. In the same way, changing your behavior will affect how you manage your emotional and cognitive processes.

Because the three attitude components are inter-related, a change in one component affects the other two.

As we begin exploring the process of taking charge of your actions, let us consider Emma's efforts to take charge of her actions by changing her problematic behavior and relationship patterns.

Emma's Story

Emma, a 42-year-old woman, came to see me several years ago because of difficulties with relationships at home and work. During the initial meeting, Emma reported having problems managing her anxiety and anger. She was aware that her "habit" of yelling at family members and others when she felt pressure to have things done "right" was preventing the good relationships she desperately yearned to have.

Emma and I had been working together for about six months when she shared an incident that revealed how her attempts to control others (so she could feel emotionally safe) were undermining her relationships.

"I'm so fed up with people caring only about themselves!" Emma lamented to me one day. They don't even bother to think about how what *they're* doing might be affecting *me* ... and, heaven help us if they were to do anything that would actually help me. But they sure have the audacity to expect *me* to take care of *them*. It's just not right! *I* try very hard to do what I'm supposed to do and to be thoughtful of others. But most people don't seem to have any consideration for anyone but themselves! I just don't understand. ... You know, life would be a *whole* lot easier if people would just be responsible, help others, and do things right."

I observed, "You work so hard to care for others and to make everyone happy. Even though, on some level, you *know* in your head that others don't generally operate as you do, still, each time they disappoint you—yet again—you end up feeling frustrated and angry. And you wonder why they can't live up to expectations that seem perfectly reasonable and justifiable."

"Right. Why can't they just get it? It's *so* aggravating!" Emma said adamantly. After a moment of stillness, she continued in a less agitated tone, "Sometimes, I can't take it anymore, and I lose it ... like I did this past weekend.

"You know how we've talked before about how frustrated I am that Myron, my "responsible" child, has started thinking that he should be able to do whatever he wants now that he's 18 years old. Well, he and I have been arguing for the past two months about him staying out until the early hours of the morning with his friends. I know that he's technically an adult now, but he's not very street smart, and it's still my job to protect him and his sister, who is 22 years old. I've warned them both more times than I can think of that nothing good can come of them staying out at night later than their two o'clock curfew.

"But no matter how many times we've gone round and round on this, Myron still comes home late. He's being *so* disobedient! Sometimes he's just a few minutes late, but this past weekend he didn't come home until seven o'clock in the morning! I'd been up all night worrying about where he was and if he was safe. I tried to call him several times on his cell phone, but he never answered.

"By the time he got home, I was so mad that we ended up in a screaming match. I know that Myron's not a child, but still ... I'm his *mother*! How can he *do* this to me? He lives under my roof, and I do everything I can to make him happy. The *least* he could do is honor his curfew and me and come home on time, or, at the *very* least, call me if he'll be late. He knows how frantic I get when I don't know that he's safe, but he doesn't even seem to care. I was a nervous wreck!"

"It was terrifying to think that something bad might happen to your son," I responded. After pausing, I asked, "Have you noticed how your old fears about safety are kicking in as Myron is becoming more and more independent? And that you're falling back into using your old default control strategy as a way to feel safe? It's *really* hard to let go of the illusion that controlling Myron's comings and goings will protect him ... and you."

"I've been thinking about that a *lot* since Myron's and my blowup," Emma replied. "I know I haven't been handling my fears very well lately, but it's been *so* hard. I remember you and me talking about what to do when I feel anxious and start worrying. So I've been trying to remind myself to step back and observe what I'm feeling and thinking when I'm feeling anxious ... and to use the relaxation strategies we've talked about to get my emotions down to a level I can handle.

"But on Wednesday, it was the middle of the night, and when Myron wasn't home on time, the panicky feelings just took over. Nothing I did was helping me calm down. By the time Myron got home, I couldn't even think straight. I was so mad that I started doing what I've always done—I tried controlling him even more.

"When we were arguing, I told him, 'If you want to be an adult, go for it! But don't expect to live with me or have me pay your bills unless you plan to respect my feelings and come home by your curfew.' Myron just glared at me. I know what I said was out of line, and I feel guilty about saying it, but I couldn't stop myself." Emma let out a helpless sigh.

"Sometimes the fear can be *so* overwhelming!" I gently responded. After a brief pause, I continued, "It's *so* frustrating to know that no matter how hard you try to keep everyone safe, the reality is that you don't have that kind of power. It would just be so much easier if people could understand that they should be more thoughtful and considerate. And when they aren't, you want to *make* them understand that what they are doing is not only inconsiderate, but it's also just plain *wrong!*"

Tears started pooling in Emma's eyes as she said, "I wish I *could!* I wish I could get *someone* to understand how important it is to consider other people's feelings and to be responsible enough to do the right thing."

Like Emma, you may find yourself reacting in habitual, predictable, and defensive ways that are outdated and no longer serving you well. In order to save your life from these self-sabotaging ways of behaving, it is important to be aware of the impact of your outdated attitudes on your behavior. This awareness will help you determine how to bring about the behavioral changes that will enhance your ability to reach your goals.

To help in this process, let us consider for a moment your investment in your defensive reactions and the price you pay for holding on to the childhood behavioral scripts. (Later we will discuss the behavioral component of your attitudes, exploring what is involved in rewriting your internal scripts so you can behave differently.)

The Impact of Outdated Attitudes on Your Behaviors

Your Investment in Defensive Reactions

Defensive emotional, cognitive, and behavioral reactions are the result of both biological and psychological processes. Biologically, researchers in emotional attachment and neuroscience have found that as infants interact emotionally with their primary caregiver, these emotional experiences become "hard-wired" into the emotional processing circuits of the infant's brain. Because this imprinting occurs before you are able to talk, the emotional and behavior patterns that develop as part of these neural pathways are reflexive and automatic; they are not based on conscious thought.

When these systems are operating, you do not consciously think before you act. You do not consider the meaning of your behaviors nor assess the effect of your actions on yourself or others. In fact, you may not even be aware of what you are saying or doing in the moment. Without some awareness of your reactions, your behaviors may seem beyond your control.

This reflexive functioning of the brain can be helpful. It takes much less effort to behave reflexively. Imagine how time consuming it would be to think about every movement *before* you take any action! This reflexive ability can also protect you, such as when the fight-flight-freeze reactions occur in dangerous situations. Managing life without the hard-wired neurological pathways would be extremely challenging.

Even so, when you develop unhealthy behavioral, emotional, and cognitive patterns, this reflexive functioning of the nervous system often interferes with your ability to function effectively and flexibly. It is extremely difficult to control and manage your behaviors when you are not aware of the body sensations that begin to signal you before you act. When you do not mindfully process your emotions and thoughts before you act, your defensive reactions can create problems, including conflict with others.

Changing your outdated, dysfunctional behaviors (and other attitude components) when they are hard-wired into your neurological system can seem impossible. But even if certain behavioral tendencies are part of your neurological system, it does *not* mean you cannot change the patterns.

Making changes to outdated ways of behaving, feeling, and thinking involves intentionally providing your mind-body system with experiences that create new neurological connections and patterns.

From a psychological perspective, you have an investment in your defensive reactions because they seem to benefit you. This may sound contradictory, since reactive behaviors usually create difficulties. But because they are part of the primary mode of behaving you developed early in life, they can seem necessary on an unconscious level. After all, they are familiar, and they provide an emotional and neurological tie to your childhood survival system.

Let us consider for a moment these two *apparent* psychological benefits of maintaining your current core modes of behaving.

The lure of the familiar. As distressing as the status quo may be, because the undermining scripts are familiar, they do not usually evoke any obvious warning signals to indicate that they may actually be putting you in danger. Instead, the familiar exerts a certain "siren call" that can lure you into behaving according to attitude scripts you developed in early childhood.

In the famous Greek epic poem, *Odyssey,* the Greek hero Odysseus was embarking on his sea voyage home after 10 years battling in the Trojan War. A fellow soldier warned Odysseus that he would encounter Sirens (sea nymphs) on his journey that lured sailors away from the sea and onto their island with beautiful voices and songs.

The Sirens' song held out the promise of pleasure and gratification, but in reality, it rendered the sailors incapable of rational thought. Once seduced onto the Sirens' island, the sailors were condemned to stay on the island forever and die there.

It promises to provide your needs. Like the Sirens, your internalized attitude scripts try to beguile you into staying on the "island" of familiar childhood ways of relating to yourself, others, and life. They promise things such as, "If you just continue doing what you are used to doing, somehow you will eventually get what you need." Or, "We will keep you safe so you will not get hurt again."

Emotionally, this is very seductive. But when you succumb to the power of the enticing, unhealthy scripts, you end up experiencing a greater sense of need and more injury, like the sailors in the Greek poem. The wounds you incur can be severe enough to threaten the survival of a part of your self.

It promises to keep you comfortable. The siren call also promises to keep your uncomfortable emotions (e.g., anxiety, fear, and sadness) at bay. Remember, a key aim of the attitudes you developed early in life was to keep your distressing emotions at a level you could tolerate. Therefore, confronting your familiar and comfortable ways of behaving will probably be stressful.

It promises to make life easier. The siren call can also entice you with the illusionary promise that life will be easier if you hold on to the outdated childhood scripts. The belief that "it takes less effort to live with what is familiar than to develop new scripts" can lure you into staying with the status quo. Even though this promise is illusionary in many ways, there is a kernel of truth in it. A self-organizing system, such as your internal operating system, resists disruption. Because of that, it takes less work to re-enact your familiar patterns from childhood than to establish new behavioral patterns.

It takes time, thoughtful effort, and courage to reroute the current neurological pathways and create new ones. The change process also requires a great deal of energy, as you learn to manage yourself and respond more effectively to others who are used to your current behaviors. Learning something new is always a challenge.

Nevertheless, what is easier in the short term is not really easier from a broader perspective. Just as sitting and watching TV is easier than engaging in physical activity, in the end, you pay the price of losing the energy, strength, flexibility, and health that come with being active.

In the same way, when you continue using the old dysfunctional scripts instead of developing new ones, you lose the rewards that come with being able to function more effectively. Choosing to resist the siren's false promises involves reinvesting your time and energy into efforts that can change your old behavioral patterns and save you from potentially debilitating emotional pain.

Emma was clearly struggling with the lure of the familiar as she worked on changing her outdated attitudes. She had spent her life taking care of others, striving for perfection, and being controlling, under the siren's illusionary promises that those behaviors would keep her emotionally safe and provide for her emotional needs.

Although these familiar, reflexive efforts had provided Emma with moments of feeling safe, at ease, and comfortable, those moments had been temporary. Eventually, the ineffective childhood survival behaviors had left Emma feeling more emotionally vulnerable, frightened, frustrated, and angry—just the way she had felt as a child.

The attachment to early ties. Recall that the scripts you develop as you internalize aspects of your parent's attitudes and record your parent-child relationship patterns serve as ties that attach you psychologically to your early significant caregivers, particularly your primary caregiver. These attachment bonds are critical to your survival as an infant.

When your parent's style of parenting provides Just Right, you develop healthy, secure emotional ties. In contrast, when your parent's style of parenting provides Too Much or Too Little, you form attachments to unhealthy attitudes and parent-child relational patterns. Your behaviors will reflect the insecurity that results from these harmful early ties.

Regardless of whether the primary relationship pattern you develop as a child is primarily secure or insecure, you develop a loyalty to the early ties of your infantile attitude scripts—even the unhealthy scripts. These early scripts resist change, in part, because your early psychological attachment is not simply to an individual (i.e., your primary caregiver).

Your attachment is to *your entire early attitude and relational system.* This system provides you with a sense of yourself and others. It also organizes your experience of life and provides you with a way to operate in the world.

Even as an adult, you may believe that your well-being depends on maintaining these early scripts. Therefore, when you think about making a change in this system in order to develop healthier attitudes, you may find that various fears emerge about how the changes will affect you and others. Most of these fears evolve from the distortions and illusions associated with childhood experience.

Let us consider how your investment in defensive reactions can be an attempt to avoid dealing with these fears.

It avoids fears related to your parent. Several common fears related to parents often emerge during the process of developing new behavioral scripts. For example, you may fear that if you fail to conform to the patterns you learned early in life, you will destroy your current relationship with your actual parent.

This fear arises because your emotions, thought processes, and behavioral tendencies are part of your internal early attachment system. The anticipated destruction of these emotional ties can leave you envisioning both you and your parent as angry or perhaps emotionally alone and bereft.

Your mind also may call up images (historically real or not) of your parent putting frightening and unbearable pressure on you to conform to the old familiar ways of behaving and thinking.

Through the years, many of my clients have reported their mother saying things that have left them feeling guilty: "You'll be the death of me if you do that"; "I thought that you cared about me"; "You're being selfish"; or, "You don't love me anymore."

Although you may feel guilty when your parent pressures you or even become fearful that changing your old ways of operating will destroy your parent, your parent *will* survive. When your parent reacts in ways like these, she is experiencing your efforts to change and grow as a threat to her internal attitude system.

She *will* develop ways of handling the changes you are making over time. It is important not to let your or your parent's fears or disastrous thoughts and images undermine your efforts to change your attitudes.

It avoids fears related to your self. You may fear not only that changes in your outdated behavioral patterns will negatively affect your parent and your relationship with her, but also that they will jeopardize your relationship to yourself.

For example, recall for a moment the physical sensations and emotions (e.g., tension, heart pounding, fear, anxiety, and guilt) that you felt as a child when you did not conform to your parents' expectations and demands. Thoughts undoubtedly emerged in tandem with these sensations and emotions that threatened some dire consequence if you failed to follow your parents' rules or if your thoughts and opinions were different from hers.

You may have thought, "She won't love me anymore"; "She'll hate me"; "She won't talk to me anymore"; or, "She's going to kill me!" Whether or not these thoughts and beliefs were reality-based, they would have been very, very scary—particularly to a child whose life depends on the emotional connection and other provisions of the parent.

Recognizing and facing your *internal parent and the parent-child relational system in your mind* can be just as anxiety provoking, frightening, and even terrifying as confronting your actual parent!

Imagine yourself now—as an adult—behaving with a set of values and beliefs that are different from what your parent expected or even demanded when you were a child and perhaps still does in the present.

Even more challenging, imagine yourself confronting your parents about the ways they (wittingly or unwittingly) have failed and injured you emotionally! You *still* may feel guilty and may be afraid that there will be negative consequences if you separate psychologically from your internal parent and parent-child relational system and become an autonomous, fully functioning adult.

After all, developing a sense of self that is separate from the parent's self will loosen the internal parental control, which you may have learned is "against the rules."

When you feel guilty because you are changing your old, unhealthy ways of relating to others, remember that the guilt comes from breaking the "rules" that are inherent in the old patterns. It is not because you are doing something wrong.

Another negative consequence you may fear is that any changes in your behavior (or other components of your attitude system) will dismantle or destroy your sense of self. When you have not experienced yourself functioning as a mature, healthy, adaptive adult, you do not know what the changes will look like. It can be extremely frightening to think that you might become someone you do not know.

Through the years, different clients of mine have described their fears of being wiped out, destroyed, or even annihilated in images. They have reported fears of falling apart, evaporating, flying into pieces, disappearing, not existing, or fading away.

One client described his terror of letting go of what was familiar before he knew what would take its place. He said, "It is more terrifying than letting go of a trapeze bar before you have securely grasped the bar swinging toward you. The bar is barely visible, far beyond your reach. You don't know if you are capable of grasping it. There is no net, so if you fall, you will die."

Although you may not experience this degree of fear as you strive to change your attitudes, you are likely to experience feelings of tension and vulnerability.

In addition, different aspects of the change process can evoke more or less emotional and physical distress than will others. Core attitudes will undoubtedly be more difficult to change than the behaviors, emotions, and beliefs that are less central to how you function.

The distressing emotions and related body sensations that commonly arise when you to begin to dismantle unhealthy behavioral scripts can feel extremely powerful and tenacious. It is understandable that you might resist confronting your internal childhood survival system.

Remember, however, that regardless of the intensity or duration of any distressing defensive reactions that you may experience, *they are temporary; you will survive.*

When these frightening emotions and related body sensations arise, face them. Learn to separate the sensations you are experiencing in your body from the images and thoughts in your mind and observe them. Go into them. Sit with them. Then, gradually begin to release the tension you are experiencing, and your emotional distress will subside and become more manageable.

Peter Levine describes this process and its importance in this way.

> *The uncoupling of sensation from image and thought is what diffuses the highly charged emotions and allows them to transform fluidly into sensation-based gradations of feelings.* This is not at all the same as suppressing or repressing them. For all of us, and particularly for the traumatized individual, the capacity to transform the "negative" emotions of fear and rage is the difference between heaven and hell (2010, p. 322, emphasis in original).

As you face and transform your uncertainty, anxiety, and various fears, it is also important to speak the truth about the changes you are making. Regardless of your fears, the truth is that the change process we are discussing is *not* about severing emotional ties to (i.e., loving or caring about) the person who is your actual parent. It is *not* about dismantling or destroying who you truly are. It is about freeing yourself so you can live your life fully.

To free yourself so you can change your behavior,
you must face your fears and relinquish your attachment to
the internal childhood coping system that undermines
your ability to act and relate in healthier ways.

Freeing yourself from your early unhealthy behaviors and relational patterns is part of an ongoing, evolving, transforming, internal process aimed at developing the undeveloped parts of your self. It involves forming healthy ties to who you truly are underneath the defensive survival system that developed early in childhood and that subsequent painful life experiences reinforced.

It is about transforming your wounds into wisdom so you can use the lessons you learn as your past injuries heal to enhance your life and the lives of those you touch in the present.

In order for a new, healthier, and more adaptive self-care system to develop, you must begin to take charge of your actions. To do this, you must begin facing the truth about the price you are paying to hold on to the dysfunctional aspects of your internal system.

To be free of the power of your internal siren, you must let go of your psychological ties to the unhealthy aspects of your childhood attitude system. Facing the reality of these long-term costs and changing your action tendencies that undermine your life make this possible.

The Price You Pay for Reflex Action

Because the lure of familiar, early attachment ties and ways of behaving is so strong, you may not be aware of the price you are paying at any given moment for following the siren's call.

The price you always pay, however, is continuing to experience the distress that comes with feeling—and even being—stuck repeating dysfunctional relationship scripts and inadvertently reinforcing self-sabotaging behavior and thought patterns. When this happens, you fail to act in ways that make your life more meaningful and fulfilling. You also sacrifice the emotional security that develops when you relate to others, the world, and yourself in healthy ways.

Let us consider in more depth these two major costs of operating with behaviors that undermine healthy core attitudes.

Costs of repeating dysfunctional relationship scripts. When you play out in your current relationships behaviors associated with early dysfunctional scripts, you are operating from unconscious defensive reactions.

These automatic reactions are external expressions of the feelings and beliefs associated with your internalized childhood attitude scripts. When this happens, you repeat undermining relationship scripts in at least two significant and problematic ways that cost you dearly.

They recreate the past in the present. Failing to recognize when you are re-enacting your dysfunctional relationship scripts and to modify those behaviors in healthy ways, recreates the pain from the past in the present.

Unfortunately, even though the childhood behavioral coping strategies may have been protective in some way in the past, in the end they undermine your internal security.

When you operate with the unhealthy behavioral scripts from childhood, you usually experience the same lack of emotional security that you experienced as a child.

Moreover, since the three attitude components (emotional, cognitive, and behavioral) are interdependent, you also experience the painful emotions (e.g., fear, loneliness, helplessness, and frustration) and hurtful thought patterns associated with these scripts.

You cannot keep re-enacting dysfunctional relationship scripts and realistically expect to have healthy relationships.

They confuse the past with the present. In addition, when you repeat dysfunctional behavioral scripts in the present, you are not operating in the present *as the present* but as if it were the past.

When you base your actions in the present on problematic attitudes developed in the past, you are likely to misperceive your experiences with others—just as you did as a child. These distortions are not only confusing, but they also keep you from seeing and understanding what is real and true about yourself, others, and the world.

Just as you can find yourself repeating dysfunctional childhood relationship scripts on your current life's stage, other "actors" are likely to be replaying their early scripts as well. This is often the cause of many relationship conflicts, because your and their problematic attitudes and relationship scripts are triggering each other.

It is important to keep this in mind as you observe and think about what is being re-enacted so you can disengage from repeating the patterns and respond in healthier ways.

In Emma's case, as she continued working in therapy, she began to realize how her perfectionism and other anxious efforts to keep her and others safe, secure, and happy ultimately had the opposite effect.

The more Emma had tried to protect herself and others from anticipated dangers, the more discouraged, helpless, and vulnerable she had felt. All her frantic and agitated behaviors had been interfering with the healthy relationships she wanted so desperately.

Since her perfectionism and anxious over-control had been defensive, they had not promoted the healthy internal psychological structures necessary for healthy adaptations. Instead, these behaviors had perpetuated Emma's dysfunctional relationship scripts.

Costs of reinforcing self-sabotaging behavior patterns. Each time you repeat your self-sabotaging behavioral scripts, you reinforce all the components of your undermining attitudes. These behaviors can cost you a great deal because they can create problems, distract you from the real issues in your life, and keep you from acting in healthy, self-caring ways.

They also can prevent you from taking the steps necessary to reach your goals. Reinforcing self-sabotaging behavior patterns can trap you in destructive behavioral patterns and can even jeopardize your safely.

They trap you in destructive patterns. The more you engage in self-sabotaging behaviors, the stronger they become because repetition strengthens the biochemical and psychological connections in your brain and mind associated with the patterns.

The bolstering of this neural network makes it difficult to dismantle the neural connections that keep your ineffective and even harmful behavioral patterns operating. It can also interfere with the development of new neural pathways.

The price for maintaining these connections is being trapped in destructive behavior patterns, just as the Sirens imprisoned the sailors on the island.

Chronic behaviors such as procrastination, eating disorders, disorganization, over-committing, trouble completing tasks, substance abuse, giving up on your dreams, destroying relationships with anger, and avoidance are common examples of self-sabotaging behavior patterns. They are part of the cost of holding on to your attachment to the internal siren and its false promises of security and well-being.

As Emma continued her work in therapy, she began to see how her rigid beliefs and expectations had trapped her in a *negative feedback loop*—a system that reinforced itself. She began to observe how her unrealistic expectations and demands for perfection and her frequent anxious and angry reactions would evoke other people's feelings of being emotionally unsafe. In response, they would not only resist her efforts to control them, but they would also avoid her.

Emma became more aware that when she was faced with her family and friends' reactions, she would become more anxious and, at times, even panicky. In addition, her fear that others might abandon her and her belief that she was in danger if she felt anxious became even more entrenched.

These convictions, coupled with her difficulties regulating her anxiety, had intensified her frantic efforts to be perfect. They had also reinforced Emma's trapped feelings and her belief that she had no way out of her self-sabotaging childhood attitude system.

You are only trapped if you continue to believe what is not real or true and act or fail to act based on those false beliefs.

If you fail to take charge of your actions, your self-sabotaging behavior patterns can interfere with your ability to function effectively in additional ways. For example, it may be hard for you to regulate your emotions or express them in relational ways.

You may have difficulty with cognitive processes such as reasoning, responding flexibly, problem solving, planning, and executing tasks. Making mature decisions may seem formidable because you lack a healthy sense of self, autonomy, self-esteem, and moral values.

In addition, difficulty perceiving others' emotional states and motives accurately will make it difficult to form healthy relationships.

They jeopardize your safety. Although the familiar childhood filters and self-sabotaging patterns hold out the promise of protecting you, they actually jeopardize your safety. They increase your risk of being wounded once again because the old system involves many illusions and distortions that cloud what is real and true.

These misrepresentations make it difficult for you to see and understand the signs of dysfunction and danger in yourself, others, and the world around you. When you fail to perceive harmful re-enactments or unsafe people, you are unable to disengage from them and act in healthy ways that truly protect you. This can be a terrible price to pay for holding on to the old attitude system.

These and other emotional and cognitive limitations that arise from your internal operating system can compromise your ability to behave in mature, healthy, adaptive ways. Fortunately, because of the brain's neuroplasticity, you are not doomed to live out your life under the control of your powerful internal siren's song. Because of the brain's ability to change its structure and reorganize the way it functions, it *is* possible to change the outdated behavior scripts that undermine your life.

About eighteen months into therapy, Emma and I discussed her progress in developing new attitudes that would free her from the power of her childhood survival scripts.

"I'm going to give you the good news first," Emma said as the session began. "I think the big fight with Myron last year was a turning point for me. It made me aware of what a strong grip my fear and anxiety have had on my life for as long as I can remember.

"As I've watched myself doing things over the past months, I've realized how quickly I react to things I perceive as dangerous—even if they really aren't—but I'll start worrying or being mad in a nanosecond. At those times, I don't just drive my kids and my husband crazy, I drive *myself* crazy! It reminds me of when my mom used to yell at my brother and me when we were kids, and I would feel so awful.

"It's hard to face the fact that when I feel that I am in danger, then I start doing the very same thing my mom used to do to *me* ... and I *hate* it! Sometimes I even hate *myself* when I can't control my temper."

I commented, "The early ways of feeling, thinking, and acting can have a very tight hold that can be as disturbing as it is powerful."

"I'll say!" Emma rejoined. "So I came up with a plan to loosen their grip. I've been reminding myself every morning of the things that we've been working on. I tell myself, 'Don't let the sirens trick you today. Remember, when you start feeling upset, step back, and observe what you're feeling and thinking and calm yourself down. When your emotions are more manageable, figure out what meanings you are making of what's happening and take the time to reflect on what's really going on so you can use your thoughts in ways that will help you. *Then* choose the thing to say and do in that particular situation that is most helpful.'"

For a split second, a mischievous looked flitted across Emma's face as she jokingly said, "Sometimes I even *remember* those strategies when I start feeling upset, and I actually *do* them." We both chuckled.

Emma continued, "On a more serious note ... obviously, I'm not very good at doing all that yet, and for sure not very fast, but I'm hoping that I'll get better at it. What I *have* noticed is that when I start getting upset and I *am* able to calm myself down, the thinking part of my brain comes back on-line. Then the self-talk and reality-checking strategies we've talked about *definitely* help my anxiety go down even more. That makes it much easier to figure out what would be beneficial to say and do instead of just reacting. It's great! I'm developing a real tool kit—and it feels good."

I responded, "You've been working really hard to create the changes you want, and all your efforts are beginning to pay off."

For a brief moment, Emma's face lit up. Then the light in her face dimmed as she let out a big sigh and continued, "It feels so good when I'm able to handle situations well. But the trouble is, sometimes something will happen that triggers a reaction inside me that's *so* strong that my ability to take care of my feelings, thoughts, and actions flies out the window. When that happens, it feels like I haven't made any progress at all, and that I'm back to square one."

I responded, "It's very distressing when you want so desperately to respond in a healthy way to situations that stir up your old wounds but instead find yourself doing the very things that you don't really want to be doing— despite all your hard work. And it's really easy for that all-or-nothing thinking to sneak in again!"

"Isn't *that* the truth!" Emma sadly replied. "But I'm *not* giving up the fight to silence my sirens." Emma shifted her focus. "I know that I've told you about my dad dying in a car accident when I was seven years old, but I've been thinking more about that the past several months. I've realized that I've spent my whole life feeling like I had to be responsible for other people."

Emma paused briefly and then continued with a touch of sarcasm, "That's my job, you know—to take care of everyone so they can be okay and happy. After my dad died, my mom got so depressed that she had a hard time doing anything, so I had to take care of her.

"Things got even worse, though, after she started drinking heavily, and then when my brother got older, he was hardly ever at home because he was out with his friends all of the time. No one seemed to realize just how lonely and scary it was for me to have to take care of everything all by myself. It was horrible! I was the *only* one who seemed to care enough to try to hold the family together."

I responded, "How incredibly painful and lonely to have lost first your dad, then your mom, through alcohol and her depression, and then even your brother when he started hanging out with his friends."

Emma sat quietly for a moment and then said with pain in her voice, "It was harder than you can imagine." After a pause Emma's thoughts shifted. "You know, I still keep thinking about that horrendous fight that Myron and I had over a year ago now. I think that's probably why I overreacted with him. He was just off doing his thing, like my mother and brother used to do. I knew he was just trying to be independent, but I couldn't stand it that he didn't seem to care about how I might feel. He treated me like I didn't matter, and worse still, like I didn't even exist! I felt totally out of control and like everything was falling apart."

I commented quietly, "So terribly frightening—and enraging."

"For sure." Emma sobered, then thoughtfully responded. "But you know what just came to me? I don't remember feeling scared about things when I was *really* little. But after my dad died—that's when I started worrying all the time about things that *could* go wrong and working *really* hard to make sure things were done right so nothing *would* go wrong. I've *tried* not to worry, but sometimes it seems like no matter what I do, the fears that something bad might happen keep hounding me.

"That's probably another reason why I got so upset with Myron—and mad at him—for not coming home, or at least calling to let me know where he was. The dangers of what could happen loomed so large, and I felt so helpless. All I could think of was he was being inconsiderate by putting himself—and me—in harm's way. And I couldn't do a thing about it."

Emma paused, and her body shuddered slightly. Then she noted, "Now that I'm calmer, I realize that's not *really* what he was doing, but it sure felt like it in the moment. When things get out of control and I feel like I, or someone I love, am in danger, I get *absolutely* frantic. …

"Hmm—I just thought of something. Maybe *that*'s why I get so mad. It's probably my body's fight response kicking in, like you explained to me once, because I definitely feel like I'm in danger when things seem out of control. It's not until after the fact that I realize my reactions are overkill. But I can't seem to get my reactions under control when it feels like everything is coming down around me—at least not yet."

I reflected, "When you're experiencing the present as if it were the very frightening and out of control past, it's very hard *not* to keep operating according to your childhood survival patterns. They are *so* familiar—*so* automatic—and their power *so* compelling. But how amazingly wonderful it is that you're getting better and better able to catch what is happening, even if it's sometimes after the fact!

"You're also understanding more about how your efforts to take control when you were feeling so out of control as a child were your way of surviving in the aftermath of some very overwhelming experiences.

"And you're understanding that trying to feel safe by worrying, by trying to control things, and by getting angry can't actually prevent bad things from happening."

Emma was nodding and looking at me intently as I continued. "I know that the process of changing attitudes can be very frustrating and difficult at times. It can often feel like progress is on the one-step-forward- two-steps-back plan. But you're doing it—you're moving forward! So keep doing exactly what you're doing.

"As you keep doing the work, you'll shift from realizing that you have repeated your old attitudes scripts *after the fact* to catching yourself while you are *in the middle* of using the old coping strategies. Then, gradually, the time will shorten, and eventually you will become aware of them *before* you fall into the trap of operating with the old patterns. You'll be able to disengage from them and do something healthier."

Emma sat quietly for several moments. Then, as tears began to trickle down her cheeks, Emma commented, "The old ways all seem so good and right at the moment—but hurt so bad in the end. Thank you for helping me see that there is a light at the end of the tunnel."

Just as Emma was discovering and beginning to deal with the impact of her outdated attitudes on her behavior, so too it is critical that you become aware of how your undermining emotional and cognitive patterns are affecting your behaviors. For only then can you truly begin to change the ingrained behavioral patterns that are interfering with your efforts to act in the present in life-enhancing ways.

To help you on your journey, let us explore ways to take charge of your actions and begin to free yourself from the power and deception of the internal siren call.

Updating How You Behave

Although the focus here is primarily on changing attitudes that create problems in your life, it is also important to remember that some of your behaviors, emotions, and cognitions have healthy elements. You can tap into these healthy elements and use them to help change your actions (and your entire attitude system).

As you challenge the internal siren, you can draw on the strengths you have developed during adversity (e.g., a certain amount of resilience, endurance, and adaptability). These internal resources, combined with available external resources, are important allies as you dismantle the power of the destructive forces in your life. Even if you are not aware of them, these internal and external resources are there to help you rewrite your internal scripts.

Rewriting Your Internal Scripts

In order to function in healthier ways, you must become actively involved in rewriting your internal scripts. This process involves updating not only the way you manage your emotions and cognitions but also the ways of behaving that you developed in childhood that are not helping you in the present.

Recall that as you manage your behaviors and regulate your emotions more effectively, and as you develop more reality-based ways of thinking, the brain reorganizes itself by forming new neural pathways and connections (synapses).

Over time, unused synapses weaken and eventually they are eliminated in a process known as *synaptic pruning*. This reorganizational process transforms your brain and mind—literally. Therefore, to be able to create the life you want, it is important to update your hardware (neural pathways) and your software (psychological structures) by rewriting your internal scripts.

So, let us consider two aspects of rewriting your internal scripts: designing healthier goals and redirecting your energy toward pursuit of your goals.

Designing healthier goals. In order to design goals that can help you change your attitudes and save your life, it is important to begin clarifying and deciding which attitudes you want to direct and operate your life. Although you will ask yourself many questions during the process of designing healthier goals, there is one central issue to consider.

The most critical question to ask yourself as you move forward is, "Who do I want to become?"

Since your goals organize your life, they affect what you choose to do and what you choose not to do. If you want to become an emotionally secure person who can relate to yourself, others, and the world in healthy ways, it is important to create goals that support that developmental process. As guideposts, your goals will help provide the structure that directs you as you stop operating with behaviors that interfere with attaining your goals and take action to create the life you want.

As you seek to move forward, it is important to consider three essential qualities of useful goals.

Goals that are self-motivated. Self-motivated goals are more effective. In order to become a more secure, autonomous person, it is important that you initiate and set your own goals. Although support systems that encourage and motivate you are important, developing your ability to self-motivate and self-initiate is critical.

When your goals and motivation derive solely from someone else, you compromise your sense of self, competency, and self-agency (the ability to act on your own behalf). Discussion with others about your goals can be helpful, but in the end, the goals you set must be your own.

Goals that are attainable. Goals that are realistic, specific, and attainable in this lifetime are more satisfying and motivating than goals that are vague or idealistic. For example, at the beginning of therapy, Emma had said that her goals were to "not get angry with others" and "not worry." The motivation for both of these goals was a sense of unhealthy shame and false guilt.

In addition, these goals were not realistic, attainable, or specific. Emma had based them on the irrational belief that "A truly good person never worries or gets angry."

The following possible goals for Emma involve self-initiated motivation and. are be more realistic, attainable, and specific.

- I am learning to take the time to identify and attend to the feelings of vulnerability and the beliefs that underlie my anger and worry when I am upset *before* I act on them.
- I am practicing thinking about my feelings and thoughts while I am feeling and thinking them.

Notice that part of what makes these goals attainable is that they are *process oriented.* Process oriented goals involve repeated choices to do what is necessary to achieve your goals. They are not based on one-time decisions.

Goals that are grounded in the present. It is also important to design goals grounded in what is real and true in the present, rather than goals based on the past. For example, early in Emma's therapy she made the goal-related comment, "Because I trusted my mother and she broke my trust, I'm never going to count on anyone again."

Even though Emma did not recognize this as a goal statement, it was an unhealthy goal based on scripts developed in her past. Furthermore, it was undermining her ability to form healthy relationships in the present.

In contrast, goals such as, "I'm learning to relax my body and calm my emotions"; "I'm learning to assess what I am thinking"; I'm learning to observe what I can and can't rely on in others"; and "I'm learning to stop my efforts to control others" are clear, attainable goals grounded in the present.

Redirecting your energy toward pursuit of your goals. If you want to reach your goals, it is important to allocate your resources in a way that helps you achieve them.

Peter F. Drucker, an influential corporate consultant and leader in the development of management education, says, "Objectives [goals] are not fate; they are direction. They are not commands; they are commitments. They do not determine the future; they are means to mobilize the resources and energies of the business [you] for the making of the future" (Drucker, 1993, p. 102).

Keeping this insight in mind, let us consider two aspects of redirecting your energy toward pursuit of your goals. Both will help you mobilize your resources so you can change your unhealthy attitudes and make a new future for yourself.

Committing yourself to your goals. You will only reach the goals that empower you to transform your wounds into wisdom—to change your attitudes and save your life—if you commit yourself to those goals.

At its core, the motivation for commitment arises from a *strong* need or desire to do something. It is not based on an intellectual acknowledgment that doing x, y, or z is the "right" thing to do or on a belief that you "should" do it.

Commitment is an *active choice*—a *firm resolve*—to devote yourself to your goals—*because reaching your goals is what you want.*

In the case of attitude change, commitment arises from realizing (and deciding) that the cost of continuing to operate with old scripts is not worth the benefits you receive from the outdated system.

It also results from the conviction that the benefits of functioning with healthy attitudes are worth the price you must pay to develop those new ways of feeling, thinking, and behaving. It is worth the time, energy, and effort involved in establishing the new neural networks that enable you to achieve your goals.

Directing your energy toward pursuit of your goals. Consider how you are currently using your energy and other resources (e.g., time, passion, support systems, and finances). Instead of choosing to use your resources in ways that maintain and reinforce old attitudes and relationship scripts, you can intentionally choose to allocate your resources in ways that help you reach your new goals. For example, you can choose to use your energy to visualize, think about, spend time with, and develop new attitudes.

You can expose yourself to new experiences that will help you reach your goals. And you can search out and bring into your life healthier people who will support you as you work to change your attitudes.

As you redirect your energy, focusing it on efforts that can create the attitudes and relationship scripts you want, you will create what you desire.

In the end, the outcome of your life depends on directing your energy toward the pursuit of goals that fulfill the meaning of your life.

Behaving Differently in the World

In order to behave differently, it is imperative that you take ownership of your power, hold yourself accountable for your choices, and establish life-enhancing relationships. These three foundational behaviors will help make it possible for you to make the changes necessary to enhance your life. Let us explore these behaviors in more depth.

Taking ownership of your power. In order to behave differently, it is imperative that you take ownership of your power. For example, imagine for a moment that you inherit a house from a relative. You wish the house had a new central air and heat system because you know that a house with effective temperature regulation would be much more comfortable than one with an old, broken system.

But unless you accept that you are the new owner—exercise your power of ownership—believe that you can figure out how to get the job done, and install the new system, you cannot make the necessary improvements to your house.

In the same way, it is only as you take ownership of your power that you can create the changes in your attitudes that will save your life from self-defeating ways of dealing with your emotions, thoughts, and beliefs.

Taking ownership of your power involves choosing what you will say and what you will do with regard to yourself, others, and life.

A critical factor in taking ownership of your power is a sense of *self-efficacy*, commonly defined as the belief in your capability to achieve your goals. However, several factors can interfere with this. If your sense of personal power is *dormant* because you never developed a sense of self-efficacy, it may not even cross your mind that you could do something to make your life better. If you only developed a *partial* sense of self-efficacy—one that is situational or limited in some other way—your belief in your capability to accomplish your goals may be restricted to certain aspects of your life.

If traumatic experiences injured your sense of self-efficacy, you may develop passive attitudes filled with pervasive feelings of powerlessness and beliefs that you are weak, helpless, and unworthy. These attitudes make it difficult to problem-solve and act on your own behalf. In any of these situations, you can perceive challenges as threatening to your sense of self and self-esteem.

If your sense of self-efficacy is impaired in some way, it is imperative that you engage in the process of reclaiming the parts of your sense of personal power that are dormant, failed to develop adequately, or were injured so you can develop more adaptive capacities.

Fortunately, you *can* choose to take ownership of your power, whether you believe, partially believe, or do not yet believe that you can make the changes you desire. You *can* develop support systems that will challenge and support you as you both establish and accomplish your goals.

As this occurs, you will be better able to take ownership of your power instead of merely reacting with old scripts to the people and events in your life. You can use your power as you rewrite your internal scripts in ways that help you take charge of your behavior and act in ways that serve you better.

Power over what you do with your emotions. Taking ownership of your power over what you will do with your emotions is a critical part of changing your behaviors because laying claim to your power over yourself allows you to act on your own behalf.

One aspect of exercising your rights and responsibilities of ownership involves *using your power to develop your ability to be mindful of your emotions.*

As discussed previously, being mindful of your emotions is an on-going process that includes being aware of your emotions, identifying (naming) them, and modulating them in order keep them within your window of tolerance. When you are mindful of your emotions, you are better able to use your power to attend to your feelings and regulate them as they shift.

The following are just a few examples of the many behaviors you can practice that will help you exercise power over what you do with your emotions.

- You can minimize your exposure to stressors that are (or could be) emotionally harmful.
- You can calm, soothe, and comfort yourself when you are feeling vulnerable or distressed, or you can take steps to energize yourself emotionally, as needed.
- You can choose *when and how you express your feelings* rather than expressing them impulsively.

- You can allow yourself to experience your distressing emotions while observing your responses and relaxing yourself, which will help you learn to tolerate your emotions.
- You can slowly expose yourself to thoughts, images, or situations that distress you (in small amounts so as not to overwhelm yourself), which will increase your resilience.
- You can practice visualize yourself responding to emotional triggers calmly and assertively.

Power over what you do with your thoughts. In order to take ownership of your power over what you do with your thoughts, it is important to pay attention actively to your own and others' mental states.

Peter Fonagy (an expert in child development and attachment research) and Jon Allen (an expert in trauma) refer to this process as *mentalizing* (Allen, 2006, p. 3).

They describe mentalizing as "the ability to understand behavior in relation to mental states such as thoughts and feelings" (Allen, Fonagy, & Bateman, 2008, p. xvii).

The extent to which you have developed the capacity and ability to mentalize impacts your ability to be aware of, understand, and act in caring ways toward yourself and others.

It enables you to be imaginative and to tolerate the ambiguities in life. It also helps you determine what is real and true in the present so you can act on current reality rather than reacting with behaviors based on your interpretations and inferences arising from the past.

One important aspect of mentalizing is the ability to *be aware of, think about, and put your thoughts and emotions into words.* This ability assists your brain and mind in processing (*metabolizing*) your internal experience, which in turn makes it possible to regulate your behaviors and emotions. It also enables you to determine what action you want (or need) to take so you can care for yourself.

Taking ownership of your power over what you do with your thoughts also affects *your ability to be empathetic.* Empathy is the ability to be aware of, tune in to, vicariously experience, understand, and respond to the feelings and thoughts of others.

Even though empathy involves both perceiving someone else's emotions and imagining what the other person might be feeling or thinking, when you are empathetic, you still maintain a sense of yourself as a separate person. You are able to think your own thoughts and regulate your emotions; you do not allow yourself to take on the other person's thoughts and feelings as your own.

In essence, empathy is "putting yourself in someone else's shoes" without losing a sense of yourself.

Empathy involves being aware of and appropriately responsive to others' thoughts and emotional states—while still maintaining a sense of yourself as a separate person, with your own feelings and thoughts.

Developing the ability to be empathetic is like learning to drive a car. When you drive a car, you use different skills simultaneously. You have to pay attention to other drivers and their vehicles *while* you are steering the wheel, using the gas pedal and brakes, judging distances and speed, and dealing with distractions.

At first doing all this at once can seem impossible. As you practice driving, however, the necessary neural pathways in the brain develop, and your ability to do several things at once becomes more fluid and automatic.

In the same way, the ability to empathize develops as you practice simultaneously tuning in to, observing, and understanding your own and others' emotions, thoughts, and behaviors. As you develop these abilities, you will become more emotionally accessible to yourself and others. When you operate with empathy, you can choose to use your power to act in ways that enhance your relationships by taking yourself and others into consideration.

As you take ownership of your power over what you do with your thoughts, you will learn to act in ways that save your life from ineffective ways of relating to yourself, others, and the world.

Power over what you do with your behaviors. When a parent's style of parenting is Just Right, she challenges and supports you in your growth and development. She makes decisions for you, speaks up for you, helps you control your behaviors, and directs them in socially acceptable ways according to your age and capabilities.

As your parent and you interact, you begin to internalize these positive maternal functions. Gradually you take over these functions yourself as you develop the ability to act on your own behalf, with a healthy sense of personal power.

If your parent's primary style of parenting provides Too Much or Too Little, however, you are likely to have some difficulty using your power in helpful ways. You may find yourself behaving in ways that recreate the painful parent-child relationship patterns you experienced as a child. For example, you may act in ways that are:

- passive, unmotivated, indecisive, detached.
- impulsive, overly aggressive, reactive.
- self-centered, overly confident, thoughtless of others.
- stubborn, controlling, overly competitive.

In order to take ownership of your power over these or other behaviors, it is important to develop three foundational abilities: the ability *to exercise good impulse control, to delay gratification,* and *to think before you act.*

Having good impulse control means you can stop harmful or destructive impulses and make choices based on sound judgment (good decision making). Being able to delay gratification means you have the ability to wait for what you want instead of impulsively demanding or grabbing whatever you want. Good impulse control and the ability to delay gratification work hand in hand.

Good impulse control and the ability to delay gratification also depend on your ability to think before you act. Between the impulse to do something and an action, there is a space—a brief moment—in which to process your impulse and choose how you will respond to the impulse.

Learning to be aware of and expand this time is vital to developing your ability to respond flexibly and exercise healthy power over what you say and do. As you learn to control your impulses and delay gratification, you can use this space to experience and think about your emotions and thought processes (mentalize). You can use it to exercise empathy, taking yourself and others into consideration before you act.

Most importantly, as these processes occur, you can remind yourself of your goals and mission, considering the impact immediate or short-term gratification will have on your ability to meet your goals and fulfill your purpose in life. Ultimately, as you exercise your power over your behavior, you support your growth and your freedom to be in charge of yourself.

It is important to remember that even if your healthy adult capacities are underdeveloped or damaged, you *can* develop and repair them. For example, instead of being compliant, defiant, over-controlling, overly competitive, avoidant, detached, ambivalent, or confused, you can *learn to be assertive in caring for your needs.* Being assertive means speaking up for yourself and taking charge of your actions. It is not about controlling others or trying to make them act the way you want or think they should behave.

> ***Being assertive is about using your power to act in ways that accomplish your goals without disregarding others.***

You can also *develop your ability to handle conflict.* Managing conflict effectively relies on the ability to mentalize and empathize. These abilities help you maintain a clear sense of what is real and true about you and the other person. They also help you stay engaged emotionally and handle your power with integrity.

As you think about your thoughts and feelings, while you are thinking and feeling them, reflexive feelings (e.g., fear, false guilt, inadequacy, helplessness, frustration, and anger) will have less power over you. In turn, you will become more comfortable with, and confident in, who you are and what you can do. This confidence enables you to care for yourself while still being mindful of others in conflict situations.

As you take ownership of your personal power over your emotions, thoughts, and behaviors, you develop the internal psychological structures that will help you care for yourself and function effectively.

Your identity (who you are) and self-esteem (your sense of worth) will evolve and flourish. Your sense of yourself as a separate, unique individual with your own mind and source of motivation will grow and mature.

You also will develop a sense of competency and mastery as you learn that you can do for yourself what previously others had to do for you.

Fortunately, because of the process of synaptic pruning, as you manage your emotions and behaviors and take charge of your thought processes in healthy ways, over time your unhealthy scripts will gradually go "off-line."

Attitude scripts that you do not use regularly will eventually become more and more difficult to activate. When your old, ineffective scripts are activated, you will be better able to be aware of, reflect on, and attend to your reactions. You will be able to anticipate what will probably occur (including the price you will pay) if you act based on those old scripts.

The ability to be mindful in these ways puts you in the position to choose to respond based on what is real and true in the present rather than reacting to internal or external triggers. You can use your power effectively to act in ways that care for your thoughts, feelings, and relationships.

Holding yourself accountable for your choices. Accountability involves assuming responsibility for your choices about what you say and do. However, in order to hold yourself accountable, you must let go of the illusion that the external environment (or old neural connections) has total power over you. Letting go of this illusion is part of developing psychological maturity.

As you realize that even though you do not have total power over yourself, you do have power over your choices. And you are accountable for how you exercise that power. Your life depends on it!

For it is in the exercising of your power to choose your responses to life's challenges and joys that you both empower and free yourself to live your life in the present, free from the undermining scripts learned in the past.

In addition, you need to shift from the mindset that you are responsible only to *others* for your behaviors to the awareness that you are ultimately accountable to *yourself for your actions.*

For as important as it is to take ownership of your actions and face the reality that they do impact others (and you may have to answer for that). *in the end, as an adult, you must give an accounting to yourself for your choices and behaviors in life.*

Ultimately, you have to answer to yourself for your choices about your goals and what you have (or have not) done to reach those goals. You are accountable to yourself not only for who you *have become* but also for who you *are choosing to become.*

Setting boundaries is an important aspect of holding yourself accountable. Boundaries establish areas of rights and responsibilities, as you choose what you will and will not do by saying "yes" to some things and "no" to other things.

Boundaries are important in goal setting because they help you establish your goals and the structures you need to put in place so you can fulfill your goals. Boundaries also help you keep out distractions and other things that might interfere with reaching your goals.

When you set boundaries that support your goals, you protect yourself and, ultimately, your purpose in life.

***Your emotional, psychological, physical, and spiritual survival—
and your ability to flourish—require that you hold yourself
accountable for your choices and actively take charge of your life.***

Although Emma expected others to be accountable for their behaviors, she had difficulty seeing how she had failed to take charge of her own actions, particularly in the early and middle phases of her therapy. Emma had difficulty realizing that she could choose to care for her emotions, determine the meanings she placed on her experiences, and act independently in the face of others' attitudes.

Her childhood scripts had made it difficult for her to take in the reality that others' behaviors did not have power over the meanings she made of her experience nor what she chose to do with those experiences.

Establishing life-enhancing relationships. When you were a child, you had limited ability to choose the people who would influence you. You could not choose your parents or your family. You could not determine who lived in your neighborhood or who attended your school, church, or other extracurricular activities. Fortunately, some of the people you interacted with were undoubtedly helpful. Unfortunately, some were not.

As an adult, however, you *are* in the position to choose to establish relationships with emotionally safe people. These relationships are important for your psychological, physical, and spiritual well-being.

Emotionally trustworthy people do not usually provoke or elicit re-enactments of your unhealthy attitude scripts but instead support you in your development. Even so, since no one is perfect, disruptions in your connections can occur, even with emotionally safe people; they are bound to happen from time to time. However, with an emotionally safe person you can work together to repair the breaks in connection and restabilize the relationship.

In contrast, exposure to people and situations that frequently activate your outdated childhood scripts reinforces your unhealthy attitudes and relational patterns. As you work to change your attitudes, it is important to keep in mind that others (e.g., family, friends) are used to your old attitudes and relationship patterns.

Because their patterns of relating are counterparts to your old system of relating, your new system will unconsciously press them to change. In response, they (consciously or unconsciously) will naturally tend to react in ways that put pressure on you to keep the unhealthy system in place.

Nevertheless, you *cannot continue operating with old systems and realistically expect you will end up with new results.* Change is necessary—unless you want to continue playing out dysfunctional understudy scripts on the stage of your life.

Because exposure to unhealthy people can evoke your old childhood patterns, when you encounter these people *it is important to stay as reality-based as possible.* (You were not able to do that as a child, due to your limited cognitive resources.)

In addition, it may be necessary to distance yourself from those who evoke and provoke the old patterns, choosing instead relationships with others who will be a healthier "family" for you. This decision is not about avoiding, being passive-aggressive, or fearful. It is a conscious, considered choice not to spend your energy and other resources on people and situations that interfere with reaching your goals.

Establishing a healthy relationship with at least one other person who can work with you on these changes is critical to your progress. Recall that just as your unhealthy childhood scripts developed in relationship, so too attitude scripts that will enhance your life develop in the context of relationship. It is especially helpful to develop a therapeutic relationship with a knowledgeable, seasoned, and responsive clinician who has expertise in changing attitudes, particularly attitudes related to psychological wounds.

Just as a relationship with a wise coach can help you develop your skills in sports, business, or music, this type of therapeutic relationship guides and supports you as you work to transform your life. Over time, with clear goals, effective effort, and an adequate support system, you can make positive changes in the way you feel, think, and act.

Toward the end of her three-year therapy experience, Emma described the changes she and her family had been noticing in her attitudes.

"Over the past year or so, I've been noticing a lot of changes in how I've been feeling, thinking, and acting—thanks to you," Emma said gratefully. "I haven't been getting anxious or angry as often as I used to. And when I do get upset, I'm managing my feelings much better, and I don't react as often or as intensely.

"Not only that, but I've also noticed that I don't try to control everyone as much. My family told me that they've noticed that I'm more patient, flexible, and not as bossy. In fact, they told me to tell you that they love you for making me a better mother and wife!"

"You're all welcome," I responded, my eyes beginning to mist. We both smiled at each other with a sense of camaraderie as Emma continued.

"So much has been changing in my life. I think that working through my father's death and my mother's problems that kept her from being the mother she should have been has been the cornerstone of my work with you. I know I've had to do a lot of grieving, and it's been a long time in coming, but I think I've finally made my peace with what happened when I was a kid.

"I can tell because I no longer have to run away from thinking about my past. I can think about what happened without feeling hurt, scared, or angry. You've helped me realize that I've already survived all the things I've been fearing. And I've seen that I *can* handle my life, even though it may not be easy. I guess I'm becoming more and more resilient.

"On top of all that, one of the really important things that I've come to realize is that my well-being depends more on me than on others. I'm much better at accepting the reality that other people aren't necessarily going to act according to my expectations. And the truth is, I don't really need them to anymore. I've been thinking about the comment you made one day: 'No one can be totally safe in the world, but I can be generally safe in a somewhat unsafe world.'

"And—you'll love this—I've come up with my own personal motto. 'My well-being is determined by my choices, not by how others behave.' I have it posted in my car and at work because it helps me keep my focus on managing myself instead of wasting my energy on what everyone else is or is not doing.

"I know that I'm still a work in progress, but I'm determined to keep moving forward in my life. I'm going to keep working on being accountable for my choices and exercising my power in healthy ways rather than trying to control others.

"The icing on the cake, though, is that my family and friends aren't avoiding me anymore, and we're having a *lot* more fun together. I'm *very* grateful for the hard work we have done together. It's been *totally* worth it!"

Within the context of the safety Emma had felt in relationship with me and the feeling of being in control of what happened in the session, Emma was able to make the changes she needed to make. She felt that she could talk about whatever she needed to talk about, cry if she needed to cry, and get mad and frustrated when she was upset.

Emma had come to realize and accept the parts of her that had failed to develop and been wounded as a child. And because she was supported and not judged, she had been able to move forward in her development and heal her old wounds.

Over the course of our time together, as I listened with compassion and without judgment, Emma had been able to feel safe and secure with me, enabling her, in turn, to feel a little safer and more secure in the world.

Summary: You Have Choices

When you are pondering who you are, your life, and what you want to become, it is important to keep in mind that you have both opportunities and choices.

Every day you have the opportunity to choose the meaning you will make of your life experiences, past and present. You have the option of taking ownership of the impact your early experience has on your current ways of behaving.

You also have the power to choose to stay stuck in behavior patterns that undermine your life and relationships. You are free to decide what you will do with your early childhood survival system. You can choose to do the work required to transform the internal scripts that lure you into acting in ways that damage, or perhaps even destroy, your authentic self.

You have options and you have choices—
even though it may not feel like it.

In fact, every day, whether you realize it or not, you make decisions about what you will do. You choose whether or not to work toward the goal of becoming healthier and stronger emotionally. If you decide to develop your emotional capacities and abilities, you will find that taking the time to observe your attitudes and relationship patterns and to consider how you will manage them is invaluable.

If you choose to forego re-enacting, and thereby reinforcing, your outdated behaviors, you can move forward, doing the work necessary to transform your attitudes and your life, creating the person you want to become.

You can take charge of your behaviors by designing healthier emotional and relational goals, redirecting your energy toward the pursuit of these goals, and rewriting your internal scripts.

You can begin owning your power and asserting yourself in ways that create a life that is meaningful and rewarding and that can have a positive impact on others.

In order to have the outcome you want, it is important not only that you accept accountability for your choices but also that you set the boundaries necessary to protect you and your goals.

Most significantly, it is important to choose relationships with emotionally safe people, especially with those who have the ability to travel with you on your epic journey to change your attitudes and save your life.

Epilogue

Transforming Your Life

As my sufferings mounted I soon realized that there were two ways in which I could respond to my situation—either to react with bitterness or seek to transform the suffering into a creative force. —Martin Luther King, Jr.

Transforming your wounds into wisdom is a journey—an heroic journey—that requires you to leave the only home you have ever known in order to create a new one. Leaving the old, familiar ways of being in the world evokes uncertainty; you have not yet experienced living differently. Remember, however, that like all heroes, you are taking action for a cause—the goal of creating healthier attitudes and relationship scripts that will enable you to actualize your potential and realize your dreams.

It is in the process of transforming your wounds into wisdom that you will become the hero of your life. As the well-known saying goes, "Heroes are not born; they are made."

Your commitment and persistent efforts create the space for you to develop the psychological structures that will enable you to survive life's adversities with courage, strength, and resilience.

These structures and heroic qualities will make it possible for you not only to survive but also to thrive in the face of life's myriad challenges. They will help you continue moving forward on your journey to save your life from ineffective childhood survival strategies and to create a new home filled with life-enriching experiences.

You may fear that it is too late to start the journey to change your attitudes and save your life—but it is never too late! Remember, the brain's neuroplasticity makes change possible *throughout* your lifespan. Nevertheless, only *you* can choose to make this journey. You are the *only* one who can choose what you will do with the dysfunctional attitudes that have become part of your internal operating system.

Obviously, you could continue playing out your undermining childhood scripts by mindlessly feeling what you have always felt, thinking what you have always thought, and doing what you have always done.

You could persist in re-enacting your parent scripts by being, for example, emotionally enmeshed, domineering, unavailable, or inconsistent, whereby you would do to others what your parents once did to you as a child.

Or you could replay your child scripts, by being, for example, avoidant, detached, confused, or ambivalent, in which case you would experience with others (or yourself) what you experienced as a child in relation to your parents.

Regardless of which role you replay, however, you are compromising your life. If you continue to re-enact the self-sabotaging parent-child scripts resulting from the cumulative impact of dysfunctional interactions with your parent who provided Too Much or Too Little, you will ultimately pay a price.

The problematic attitudes and relationship patterns you developed as a child will become more entrenched over time. Whether or not you are aware of it, these attitudes will continue to affect you, your relationships, and your life, impinging on your ability to achieve your goals.

Remember, in re-enactments you operate under the influence of childhood misperceptions (including distortions and illusions) that interfere with your ability to process your experience with more mature strategies. During re-enactments, you may not notice that you are replaying your parent and your child scripts.

If you do become aware that you are repeating the harmful patterns, it may seem to you—and you may actually believe—that others are *making* you feel, think, and act in those ways. You may also find yourself feeling as if you cannot do anything to change those scripts, even though you may desperately wish you could.

When caught in this vortex of feelings of powerlessness during a re-enactment, you may hold on to the distorted belief that you cannot do anything to alter what you are experiencing. You may continue clinging to the illusion that others *can* provide you with the emotional supplies your primary caregiver failed to give you.

You may also hold tenaciously to the belief that others *should* make up for what you missed as a child. This sense of entitlement, coupled with the distorted belief that you have the power to make others be the Just Right parents you never had creates an untenable situation. It can result in your going through life relentlessly demanding that you and others measure up to unrealizable expectations.

Unfortunately, because your unrealistic demands derive from the illusions and distortions that result from your attitudes, those demands will, for the most part, be futile. When you realize you will not get what you believe you are entitled to, you may find yourself becoming outraged. You may direct your anger at others for failing to meet your expectations—failing to feel how you want them to feel, to think what you want them to think, and to do what you want them to do.

You may also rage at yourself for failing to measure up to the idealistic standards you have set for yourself. When all your insistent, unproductive raging leaves you worn out and feeling defeated, you may give up in despair—and then retreat.

But because you have not yet fully grieved and made peace with the losses and wounds you have experienced along the way, you will inevitably continue to search for and demand what you should have received—but failed to—as a child; namely, emotional safety and security.

Instead, you can courageously decide to embrace the process of transforming your outdated emotional, cognitive, and behavioral patterns so you can save your life. You can also choose to reframe the meanings of your experiences in ways that enable you to become healthier, more empowered, and wiser.

You can consider your past and present experiences opportunities for on-going growth and development, allowing you to use them to become, in essence, a Just Right parent for yourself.

Regardless of any fears or apprehensions you might have, you can choose to accept ownership of your life, so you can begin to establish more mature and effective ways of adapting to the present realities of your life. As an owner, you can begin remodeling your home—making necessary repairs, dismantling outdated features, and building useful additions—so that it enriches your life and the lives of others.

Even as an owner, however, you cannot construct your new home single-handedly. As you engage in the process of transforming your life, it is important to marshal both the external and internal resources available to you.

Although you may fear that others will re-injure you if you look to them to help you move forward in your life, it is crucial to strive continuously to establish, maintain, and access an ongoing external support system. It may take time, and you may need to persevere as you seek out these external resources, but these relationships are critical to your ability to transform your attitudes. And they will make your journey so much easier!

Admittedly, developing support systems can be a daunting project. In fact, sometimes it can seem impossible. Even so, there *are* emotionally safe people around you (e.g., psychotherapists, friends, spiritual leaders, family, and teachers) who have the knowledge, skills, and willingness to guide and travel alongside you on your journey. But you will need to invest time, energy, and effort to find them.

Remember that you can also use the internal emotional, cognitive, neurological, and spiritual capacities you now have by virtue of being an adult—resources that were not available to you as a child.

You can also call upon the internalized and evolved healthy aspects of your primary caregivers and others you have encountered along the way. Access the determination, tenacity, resilience, and spiritual resources that have helped you survive the wounds you have incurred through your own limitations and those of others.

Although you may have used your strengths and resources defensively in the past, you can now use them to develop healthier adaptations that are truly protective.

As you leave your old home, remember that you also have this book to guide you as you establish a new home. As you read and study this map, you will begin to see and understand more and more of where you have come from, where you are now, and where you can go. But observing, understanding, and explaining how your emotions, thoughts, behaviors, and relationship patterns came into being and how they are affecting your life today are not enough.

There are things you need to do if you are to create a new home that has a firm foundation grounded in healthy attitudes. This book, in addition to the other resources you might have, will provide you with an opportunity to consider the changes you need to make both to design and build your new home.

Creating new attitudes requires that you gradually relinquish the psychological attachments that have kept you tied to the unhealthy aspects of your old scripts. Facing and grieving the losses you have encountered in the past—and will experience along the way—make this possible.

As you begin to confront and to accept the reality of your losses, allow yourself both to experience the range of your emotions relating to these losses and to stop struggling to change the past.

When you process your grief in these ways, you will gradually begin to make peace with the pain of your disappointments and the heartbreak of your losses. Allowing yourself to work through the mourning process will free you from the harmful effects of the past so you can focus your energies on moving forward in the here and now.

Letting go of the familiar—but deleterious—scripts that have been holding you captive is not easy. As you face and grieve your disappointments, however, you will be establishing stronger, more effective mindsets. These mindsets will enable you to progress in your life. As you do so, your psychological capacities will continue to grow and mature, enhancing your ability to *tolerate the tension that is inherent in the growth process.*

These new, more evolved psychological structures and internal capacities will provide the strength and courage you need to face and mourn your losses. You will no longer need to avoid your losses, rage against them, or pretend they do not exist.

And these enhanced abilities will also enable you to stop searching relentlessly—and futilely—for the perfect parental nurturing you did not receive as a child—and can never have now. They will empower you to disengage from your unyielding expectations and demands that have kept you stuck in a whirlpool of rage when others have not provided for you in the ways you think they should.

The resilience that you will acquire from these healthier structures will keep you from giving up and becoming immobilized by or collapsing under the weight of old methods of managing your feelings, thoughts, and actions. Instead, they will make it possible for you to continue confronting and correcting the myriad of fears, distortions, and illusions that are part of your outdated attitude system.

Because you will now have a greater sense of your self, your worth, and your self-efficacy, you will no longer need to transfer ownership of your life to others. The knowledge that you can care for yourself will reinforce your courage and your efforts both to take ownership of your life and to do the work necessary to build the home you desire.

As you persist in your endeavors to take charge of your life, the old, familiar, self-sabotaging scripts will gradually lose their stranglehold on you. And as they release their grip, you will gain more freedom to work on enhancing your ability to modulate your emotions, keeping your thoughts and beliefs reality-based, and managing your behaviors effectively.

Using your emerging freedom to become mindfully aware of what you are feeling, thinking, and doing is crucial to the process of changing your attitudes. As you learn to pay attention to and stay connected with your feelings and thoughts moment by moment with a sense of openness and curiosity—without judging them—you will be enhancing both your physical well-being and your mental capacities.

From this place of awareness, you will be better able to reflect upon (i.e., mentalize) your feelings, thoughts, and actions while you are experiencing them. This ability will make it possible for you to identify, process, and respond more flexibly to your feelings and thoughts in the present moment. It will also help you to assess how your attitudes have operated in the past and to plan for how you will deal with them in the future.

As you practice tuning in to, staying present with, and thinking about your internal dynamics, you will be in a position to develop healthier adaptations to the ongoing stressors in your life. Rather than creating problems for yourself by reacting to emotional triggers, you will be able to modulate your feelings, keeping them within a range that you can tolerate.

Instead of reacting impulsively according to self-sabotaging childhood scripts, you will be able both to think about your experiences and choose to respond to yourself and others in ways that will benefit your life and relationships.

You will be able to respond empathetically because of your increased ability to be aware of your own and others' internal processes. And as you practice reflecting on your experience and managing your thoughts, you will able to interpret your experiences more accurately.

These new meanings will make it possible for you to establish a more coherent narrative of your life, which, in turn, will help you feel more secure.

Ultimately, these more effective adaptations will provide you with a greater ability to relate in healthier, more mutually fulfilling ways to yourself, others, and the world.

As you gain more mastery over what you are feeling, thinking, and doing, you will be transforming the experiences that once were deeply injurious. As this evolution occurs, you will be not only healing from your wounds but also growing because of them.

In the process, you will discover that you have indeed chosen the hero's path—a path that, although less traveled, leaves you far wiser than if you had never incurred the losses or suffered the wounds.

You will come to know on a profound level that if you had never experienced your disappointments and your pain, you would never have had the opportunity to accrue the wisdom you now have. And at some point along your heroic journey, you will come to realize that you are who you have become by virtue of having liberated yourself from the stranglehold of the seductive, ravenous sirens.

In your experience of woundedness lies the opportunity for your growth and development.

Again, like many heroes throughout the ages, you may feel and even believe that you are not capable of making the heroic journey of changing your attitudes and saving your life—*nevertheless, you are.* Continue steadfastly moving forward on your journey toward your goals.

Even though you will undoubtedly stumble and fall many times along the way, when you do, refocus your attention on staying present in the moment and on taking one step at a time. And when you find yourself despairing that all the hard work you are investing in the process of establishing a new home will ever bring about the changes you desire—know that it will.

Finally, as you do the work necessary to change your attitudes and to save your life from the powerful lure of your internal sirens' songs, I share with you the following wisdom that I have garnered on my journey.

Wisdom

Wisdom emerges out of the crucible of our suffering
as we lovingly embrace the undeveloped and wounded parts
of ourselves with truth, acceptance, and mercy
and engage in the process of transforming our lives.

Wisdom evolves as we let go of our attachment to
our childhood survival system—a system permeated by
scripts and relationship patterns that are self-sabotaging.

Wisdom enriches us as we develop life-enhancing ways
of dealing with our emotions, thoughts, and behaviors
that will enable us to establish mutually rewarding relationships.

Wisdom empowers us to save our lives
from the tyranny of our wounds. It transforms us
so we can live freely and fully in the present moment.

As you close the pages of this book, I leave you, dear reader, with my heartfelt hope and prayer for you:

May you, through the knowledge and insights you have gained from reflecting on my words and from immersing yourself in the lives of the people whose stories I have told, have the deep awareness and faith that change *is* indeed possible.

May you recognize there truly is a way to create the changes you desire and you do have the power to choose how you will live.

May this road map serve as an on-going resource that will challenge, support, and guide you as you move forward on your journey of transforming your wounds into wisdom and saving your life.

References

Akhtar, S. (2001). From mental pain through manic defense to mourning. In S. Akhtar (Ed.), *Three faces of mourning: Melancholia, manic defense, and moving on* (pp. 97-113). Northvale, NJ: Jason Aronson.

Allen, J. G. (2006). Mentalizing in practice. In J. G. Allen & P. Fonagy (Eds.), *Handbook of mentalization-based treatment* (pp. 3-30). Chichester, UK: John Wiley & Sons.

Allen, J. G., Fonagy, P., & Bateman, A. (Eds.). (2008). Mentalizing in clinical practice. Washington, DC: American Psychiatric Publishing.

Beebe, B., & Lachmann, F. M. (2002). Infant research and adult treatment: Co-constructing interactions. Hillsdale, NJ: The Analytic Press.

Boorstin, D. J. (1992). The image: A guide to pseudo-events in America. New York: Vintage Books.

Drucker, P. F. (1993). Management: Tasks, responsibilities, practices. New York: HarperBusiness Book.

Emerson, R. W. (1926). Essays by Ralph Waldo Emerson: First and second series complete in one volume. New York: Thomas Y. Crowell.

Fonagy, P., & Target, M. (1997). Attachment and reflective function: Their role in self-organization. *Development and Psychopathology, 9*(4), 679–700.

Frankl, V. (1963). Man's search for meaning. New York: Pocket Books.

Hedges, L. E. (1994). Working the organizing experience. Northvale, NJ: Jason Aronson.

Levine, P. A. (2010). In an unspoken voice: How the body releases trauma and restores goodness. Berkeley, CA: North Atlantic Books.

Remen, N. (2000). My grandfather's blessings: Stories of strength, refuge, and belonging. New York: Riverhead.

Siegel, D. J. (1999). The developing mind: Toward a neurobiology of interpersonal experience. New York: The Guilford Press.

Stark, M. (1994). Working with resistance. Northvale, NJ: Jason Aronson.

Stark, M. (1999). Modes of therapeutic action: Enhancement of knowledge provision of experience, and engagement in relationship. Northvale, NJ: Jason Aronson.

Winnicott, D. W. (1953). Transitional objects and transitional phenomena: A study of the first not-me possession. *The International Journal of Psychoanalysis, 34*(2), 89–97.

About the Author

JOLYN DAVIDSON, a graduate of the University of Washington (Seattle), is a licensed psychotherapist who has been in private practice for over thirty years in the Greater Los Angeles area. She holds a BSN in nursing, an MSW in clinical social work, and an MA in social science. In addition, she holds diplomates from the National Association of Social Workers and the American Board of Examiners in Clinical Social Work. She has also served as a faculty member at both Biola University and Azusa Pacific University, where she (as Associate Director) was instrumental in developing an international Human Resource Leadership MA Program.

Jolyn provides clinical consultation to healthcare practitioners from a variety of disciplines and is a contributing author to psychotherapy books focusing on advancing the treatment of emotional traumas incurred during early childhood. In addition, she has been a trainer for, and consultant to, leaders in profit and non-profit organizations—both here and abroad.

In *Transforming Wounds into Wisdom*, Jolyn draws upon her broad-based and comprehensive experience as a clinician who has spent decades deeply immersed in her clinical work and study of the human psyche. Through in-depth, relationally oriented therapy, she has helped children, adolescents, and adults change the dysfunctional attitudes and relationship patterns that have resulted from the early emotional injuries they have sustained. Her focus is on promoting psychological healing and integration—mind, body, and spirit. Jolyn is passionately committed to supporting others on their courageous journeys from woundedness to wisdom.

For further information on Jolyn Davidson's private practice and availability for consultation, training, and workshops, please contact her at: woundsintowisdom.jdavidson@gmail.com or P.O. Box 4817, San Dimas, CA 91773.

Made in the USA
Las Vegas, NV
06 August 2022

52831579R00167